A Season of Madness: Fools, Monsters, and Marvels of the Old-World Carnival
by Al Ridenour

ISBN 9781627311564

Feral House
1240 W. Sims Way Suite 124
Port Townsend, WA 98368
www.FeralHouse.com

Design by Sean Tejaratchi

Printed in China.

10 9 8 7 6 5 4 3 2

A SEASON OF MADNESS

FOOLS, MONSTERS, AND MARVELS OF THE OLD-WORLD CARNIVAL

A True Accounting of Its
FEARSOME RITES
& MERRY FROLICS,
from
ANCIENT TIMES
to the PRESENT DAY
with
Descriptions & Details,
Many so Peculiar
as to Be
Scarcely Believed

BY

AL RIDENOUR

Author of *The Krampus and the Old, Dark Christmas*

Host of *Bone & Sickle*

2024
NEVER BEFORE PRINTED

FERAL HOUSE
(est.1989)
PORT TOWNSEND, WASHINGTON

FOR LAUREN

A Carnival unto herself

MER DU NORD
LA MANCHE
MER D'IRLANDE
Canal de Bristol
Golfe de Gascogne
ANGLETERRE
IRLANDE
ECOSSE
EMPIRE
CONFÉDÉRATION DU RHIN
ROYme DE DANEMARK
ROYme DE SARDAIGNE
ESPAGNE
SUISSE
CORSE
ILES BALÉARES
MER
Edimbourg
Glasgow
Perth
Berwick
Dumfries
Carlisle
Newcastle
Dublin
Galway
Limerick
Cork
Wexford
York
Leeds
Liverpool
Lancaster
Kingston
Birmingham
Nottingham
Oxford
Cambridge
Yarmouth
Londres
Windsor
Bristol
Portsmouth
Plymouth
Douvres
Pembroke
Amsterdam
Hambourg
Brême
Hanovre
Magdebourg
Munster
Cassel
Gottingen
Coblentz
Francfort
Darmstadt
Cobourg
Nuremberg
Stuttgard
Wurtemberg
Ulm
Munich
Augsbourg
Ratisbonne
Inspruck
Salsbourg
Anvers
Bruges
Liége
Calais
Boulogne
Dieppe
Cherbourg
Amiens
Rouen
Caen
Bayeux
Paris
Versailles
Chartres
Evreux
Compiègne
Laon
Soissons
Reims
Luxembourg
Trèves
Metz
Nancy
Strasbourg
Landau
Mayence
Rennes
Brest
Quimper
Vannes
Nantes
Angers
Le Mans
Tours
Orléans
Blois
Vendôme
Troyes
Dijon
Beaune
Besançon
Vesoul
Châtillon
Chaumont
Sancerre
Nevers
Bourges
Châteauroux
Poitiers
Niort
La Rochelle
Rochefort
Saintes
Angoulême
Limoges
Guéret
Clermont
Périgueux
Bordeaux
Moulins
Mâcon
Lyon
Vienne
Bourg
Genève
Chambéry
Grenoble
Valence
Privas
Le Puy
Tulle
Cahors
Aurillac
Rodez
Mende
Montauban
Agen
Auch
Tarbes
Pau
Toulouse
Albi
Montpellier
Nîmes
Avignon
Arles
Marseille
Toulon
Draguignan
Digne
Gap
Montélimar
Perpignan
Narbonne
Carcassonne
Foix
Napoléonville
(La Roche sur Yon)
Vendée
Berne
Zurich
Turin
Alexandrie
Milan
Bergame
Parme
Modène
Bologne
Florence
Sienne
Pérouse
Rome
Bastia
Ajaccio
Détroit de Bonifacio
Sassari
Cagliari
Oristagne
Burgos
Pampelune
Navarre
Saragosse
Aragon
Catalogne
Barcelone
Madrid
Tortose
Valence
Murcie
Alicante
Cuenca
Jaen
C. Palos
Carthagène
Almeria
C. de Gata
Majorque
Minorque
Ivice
Mahon

MER BALTIQUE
Göthland
Oland
Norkoping
Linkoping
Wisby
Calmar
Ösel
G. de Livonie
LIVONIE
Pernau
Dorpat
Pskov
Valdai
Tver
Dmitrow
Moscou
COURLANDE
Riga
Mittau
Goldingen
Libau
Windau
Polangen
Memel
Konigsberg
Dantzick
Tilsit
Kowno
Wilna
Troki
Grodno
Minsk
Lida
Vitebsk
Polotsk
Dunabourg
Drissa
Nevel
Velikie Louki
Smolensk
Mohilev
Orcha
Briansk
Orel
Kalouga
Toula
Jazdra
EMPIRE DE RUSSIE
PRUSSE
Colberg
Stargard
Culm
Thorn
Bromberg
Posen
Glogau
Kalis
Konin
Plock
Varsovie
Praga
Lowicz
Rawa
Sieradz
Radom
Lublin
Zamosc
Sandomir
DUCHÉ DE VARSOVIE
POLOGNE
Breslau
Brieg
Glatz
Neisse
Kosel
Cracovie
Bialystok
Brzesc
Pinsk
Marais de Pinsk
Kobrin
Kovel
Dubiecka
VOLHYNIE
Zitomir
Kiev
Tchernigov
Novgorod Sieverskoi
Koursk
Kharkov
Poltava
UKRAINE
Mozir
Bobrouisk
Dniepr ou Borysthène
Kremenstchoug
Ekaterinoslav
Bratzlav
PODOLIE
Kamieniec
Tarnopol
Zolkiew
Lemberg
GALLICIE
Sambor
Stanislawow
Monts Carpacks
Olmutz
MORAVIE
Brünn
Znaim
Presburg
Vienne
Comorn
Raab
Ofen
Pesth
Erlau
Kaschau
HONGRIE
EMPIRE D'AUTRICHE
TRANSYLVANIE
Kolosvar
Carlsburg
Hermanstadt
Arad
Temeswar
Seged ou Szegedin
Mohacz
Peterwardein
ESCLAVONIE
Belgrade
Orsova
Tchernowitz
Iassi
MOLDAVIE
Galatz
Bender
BESSARABIE
Ismail
Akerman
Odessa
Otchakof
Kherson
Nikolaïev
Tiraspol
Nogaïs
Perecop
CRIMÉE
Simferopol
Eupatoria
Sebastopol
Bucharest
VALACHIE
Giurgevo
Craiova
Roustchouk
Silistria
Widin
BULGARIE
Choumla
Varna
SERVIE
Semendria
Zvornik
Sophia
Mt Balkan
BOSNIE
Mostar
Scutari
ROUMÉLIE
Philippoli
Andrinople
Bourgas
CONSTANTINOPLE
Canal de Constantinople
M. de Marmara
Gallipoli
Salonique
ALBANIE
Janina
Larissa
Tarente
Otrante
NAPLES
ADRIATIQUE
EMPIRE OTTOMAN
MER NOIRE
Kastamouni
Eregli
Boli
Angora
Brousa
ANATOLIE
Adramitti
Pergame
Smyrne
Scala Nova
Metelin
Negrepont
Zeitoun
Lepante

TABLE OF CONTENTS

· CHAPTER I ·

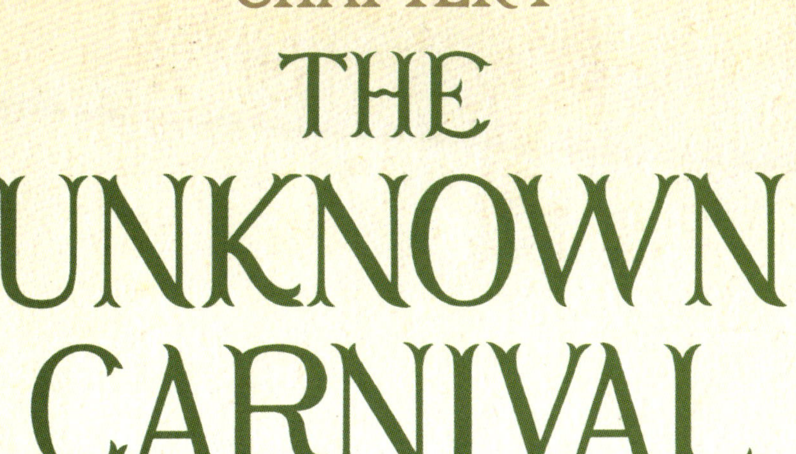

THE PUZZLEMENT AND DISTASTE FOR CARNIVAL
FELT IN PROTESTANT LAND IS BOLDLY LAID BARE
& THE AUTHOR HIMSELF MAKES CONFESSION
OF CERTAIN SURPRISING & SIMILAR AVERSIONS
WITH WHICH HE APPROACHED
THE WRITING OF THIS BOOK

READERS ARE EQUIPPED WITH AN ITINERARY OF

LANDS & ERAS
TO BE EXPLORED

MADE AWARE OF
THE AUTHOR'S SINGULAR FASCINATION WITH THINGS

MONSTROUS & PAGAN.

AN UN-AMERICAN HOLIDAY

Carnival is like a party to which America's not been invited. Yes, we have Mardi Gras, but New Orleans is a world unto itself. Naturally, there's something discomforting about being left out, so we're wrong-footed even in attempting to talk about it. Just to be sure people know we're not discussing Tilt-a-Whirls and cotton candy, Americans may decide the word needs a more "international" spelling ("Carnevale," "Carnaval") or just say it funny: "Carn-e-VAHL." Things got hopelessly muddled in 2003, when HBO came out with a popular show featuring sideshow performers called *Carnivàle,* a uniquely random spelling chosen just to fancify things.

ILLUSTRATION BY MARZOLINO FROM *MAGASIN PITTORESQUE*, PARIS, 1850.

Because America doesn't do Carnival, and since the word was just sitting there unused, we decided to give it a new meaning in the 1890s. *Carnival* began to be applied to traveling shows modeled on the success of the 1893 Chicago World's Fair, specifically the central area's collection of rides, games, and sideshow acts called the Midway Plaisance, giving us another generic term, *midway* (without the *plaisance*/pleasure part, another example of our tendency to arbitrarily internationalize things).

Maybe the transient nature of those midways, set up one day and gone the next, suggested something analogous to Carnival and its fleeting season of pleasures. Like the celebration, the traveling shows arrived in towns annually at roughly the same time but with certain unpredictable variations, just as Carnival shifts slightly year to year, thanks to its date being anchored to Lent (and, by extension, Easter).

The lack of a fixed date also makes Americans uneasy about Carnival. The arcane calculation by which Easter is set is a relic of pre-Reformation Europe, the kind of thing the Plymouth Pilgrims would have decried as "Romish Popery!" It's one thing to submit to the fickleness of moveable feasts when it comes with chocolate eggs and Peeps, but Lent is altogether different, a bridge too far for most Americans. Though Lent's ostensibly part of all Christian traditions, its role is minimal in Protestant churches and among the unaffili-

PREVIOUS: A CARVED LOG SERVES AS A MASK IN WESTERN BULGARIA.

Illustration from *Napoléon: illustrations d'après des peintures, sculptures, gravures, objets, etc., du temps* by Armand Dayot, 1908.

ated, leaving its most powerful legacy in Catholicism. The idea of penitential starvation is un-American enough, but to then precede it with a season of rapacious indulgence does not sit well in a country driven by Yankee pragmatism.

But we are also a broad-minded nation, so we make the effort to squeeze in those foreign words from Catholic cultures: *Carnevale* (Italian) and *Carnaval* (most other Latin languages, as well as Dutch). Americans have assimilated the term Mardi Gras, but it's too tangled up now in beads and breast-flashing to accurately describe what happens outside of New Orleans. Besides, we already have the English equivalent, *Shrove Tuesday* (or *Shrovetide* for the period before Tuesday). But to Americans *Shrove* now sounds just as foreign as French. And being British disqualifies it as our go-to term since Britain doesn't really have Carnival—it's sad, but eating pancakes on a single day doesn't count.

As you will have guessed, this book will be going off the beaten path, beyond festivities designated by Latin-derived names. We'll explore the *Fastnacht* of Germany, the *Zapusty* of Poland, the Czech *Masopust*, the Russian *Maslenitsa*, and the Bulgarian *Sirni Zagovezni*, to name a few.

CARNIVAL ON THE PLACE MASSENA, NICE, FRANCE, C. 1900.

OUR ITINERARY

HISTORY

We'll begin in Italy, looking at Rome's influence, then on to Venice, and finally Germany.

Chapter II, "Sardine versus Sausage," offers a sort of overview, examining how the Church's imposition of Lent shaped Carnival, as well as some artistic responses this engendered.

In Chapter III, "Ancient Roots," we'll look for Carnival's possible origins in traditions of the Roman Empire, both pre-Christian and post-Constantine.

In Chapter IV, "Rome," we'll stay in the Eternal City, but move into the High Middle Ages, when the Latin term *carne levare* is first attached to public games and spectacles, practices often reflecting the brutality of the times.

In Chapter V, "Carnival in Venice," we'll encounter equally barbaric customs worlds away from the familiar images of the iconic European Carnival. Moving into the early modern period, we'll see the birth of the city's masking traditions, and, along the way, somewhat more civilized entertainments (acrobatic shows, regattas, religious processions), though ones not widely embraced now as Carnival traditions.

Chapter VI, "German Fools," describes the introduction in the mid fourteenth century of the Carnival parade and the iconic figure of the Carnival Fool. Traditions and history of this character, as well as contemporary practices of German "Fools' Guilds," are explored.

Carnival in the Country, illustration by Theodor Schmid for *Die Gartenlaube*, 1850. Depicts domestic festivities in the Steinlach Valley, near Tübingen, Germany.

THEMES

After these first, roughly chronological chapters have laid a historical groundwork, subsequent chapters are thematic.

Chapter VII, "Good-Luck Visits," looks at house-visiting customs in Germany, Poland, and the Czech Republic.

Chapter VIII, "Fertility Rites," explores the plow- and log-pulling rites of Germany, Austria, Italy, Slovenia, Croatia, Poland, and Ukraine.

Chapter XIV, "Killing Carnival," provides a wide-ranging look at the mock executions and funerals of figures embodying Carnival and the relation of these customs to German and eastern European traditions of "Driving Out Winter" and "Carrying Out Death."

MONSTERS

Just before the final chapter are chapters devoted to Carnival figures of a monstrous or wild nature:

Chapter IX, the Kurent of Slovenia; Chapter X, the Busó of Hungary; Chapter XI, the Kuker of Bulgaria; Chapter XII, Carnival Bears of the French and Spanish Pyrenees and Basque country; Chapter XIII, Sardinia, describing the diverse menagerie of Carnival characters of the island's Nuorese region.

Carnival figures (Kukeri) from Bulgaria, before 1945.

SKEWING EAST

The preponderance of eastern European cultures surveyed reflects my interest in presenting the forgotten Carnival, not simply for the sake of novelty but because I believe these countries offer the best examples of an earlier form of Carnival's evolution throughout Europe—specifically, house-visiting customs, which over time were supplanted and standardized into single municipal parades.

I have largely neglected these larger parades, some of which nonetheless have important and interesting histories. The Carnivals of Cologne, Germany; Nice, France; and Binche, Belgium, are all very old and significant but, like other omissions, did not serve the book's thematic or historical narrative.

NO LOVE FOR CARNIVAL

At least that partially explains my selectivity. But there are other reasons.

To be honest, I always considered Carnival a bit boring. You may too, and for perfectly understandable reasons. But I've come around and have high hopes of helping like-minded readers beyond this.

Allow me to first lay out some of my own ugly prejudices. Perhaps you share some of them.

- I don't like plastic.
- I don't like fluorescent colors.
- I don't like crowds.

There is something soulless in plastic, but all the most famous Carnivals, barring that of Venice, rely on plastic (fiberglass) for the construction of floats and sometimes masks. Fiberglass is no good at representing texture or detail, so this is approximated through the heavy use of airbrushed colors. I probably should have included airbrushing in my list, but I didn't claim it was exhaustive.

Fluorescent colors perhaps don't dominate the palette of every large Carnival, but they needn't. Even a moderate use of fluorescent colors is enough to arouse in me a crippling distrust of Carnivals across the board.

As for crowds, this *is* universal with any Carnival of note, as well as any unremarkable but large urban Carnival. It necessitates arriving too early and taking too long to get to your ride when it's over. In between, there's lots of standing—at least five deep (usually more)—and straining to see over and around heads as plastic, fluorescent, airbrushed monstrosities creep by—all while enduring a growing numbness in your feet and considering the obstacles faced in negotiating a path to a public restroom, if such a thing exists.

Also: no one likes marching bands. No one.

And finally, an ideological issue: if Carnival represents a seasonal spree of madness, is that best expressed in the form of these large parades with celebrants regimented into identical costumes and marching between fife and drum corps? It is all a bit militant and miserably fails Carnival's promise.

A FOLK AESTHETIC

But underneath all this, there's another Carnival to discover. This book focuses on the celebrations of smaller towns and villages, in part because these have received less attention and in part because they illustrate that earlier stage in Carnival's development—but also as a purely aesthetic choice.

In these folk Carnivals, costumes are made by hand, improvised from hides, horns, and plaited straw; faces are often blackened with soot or hidden under wooden masks with sheepskin hoods. Figures wearing these costumes gather in town squares and central streets, in village inns and halls, but also visit homes and isolated farmhouses, sometimes in groups no larger than a handful. Such celebrations generally exist alongside much larger ones. In these, participants from the hinterlands come together to demonstrate their local customs in regional exhibitions. In recent years, most of these have become quite large, even drawing visitors from overseas. But the style of celebration and the costumes have retained their original look, as the cultures hosting these gatherings are more bound by tradition and heritage.

PAGAN HORRORS!

I'll happily confess that my interest in such things has grown side by side with an interest in a genre which only recently received a name: "folk horror." This probably accounts

Carnival Procession, anonymous,
after Adriaen Pietersz van de Venne, 1599–1662.

for my predisposition to focus on certain darker aspects of Carnival and its history. I notice this is quantitively evidenced in the text, discovering a telling frequency of certain words: "blood" or "bloody" appearing thirty times, "pagan" twenty-nine, and "devil" showing up forty-seven times. In particular, the chapters examining the roots of Carnival in Rome and Venice contain horrific elements, including brutal rites, cruel games, and animals ritually put to death. Please consider this your trigger warning.

These are not, however, sacrifices offered to pagan gods, as imagined in folk-horror tales. The paganism presented in this book consists of rural superstitions and beliefs that largely have coexisted with Christian practice, undifferentiated in the common person's world, but condemned by the more exacting Catholic or Orthodox clerics. The pre-Christian roots of Carnival traditions, which might be expected, are in fact difficult to prove, no matter how often connections to Dionysus might be suggested. In the final chapter on "Killing Carnival," however, I explore some Slavic customs which plausibly could be said to derive from pre-Christian traditions.

KRAMPUS REVISITED

My previous book, *The Krampus and the Old, Dark Christmas* (Feral House, 2016), was inspired, in part, by this enthusiasm for folk horror but also by my interest in German culture, which accounts for any disproportionate treatment of German customs in this book. When I first encountered Krampus customs, I was not aware to what an extent they borrowed from older Carnival traditions (the bells worn being a prime example), nor to what extent the predecessor of the Krampus, the folkloric Percht, itself could be considered a Carnival figure, thanks to its association with Epiphany (January 6). Many aspects of both Krampus and Percht customs that are common in Carnival in German-speaking lands can be found in Carnival celebrations throughout Europe, as far away as Bulgaria and Greece, as we'll see.

In this volume, you'll notice a persistent emphasis on the interplay between Carnival traditions and those of the Christmas season. Epiphany is central to this as it's regarded as the end of the one season and the beginning of the other. At times it may seem I am describing Christmas, as when eastern European Carnival "carols" are mentioned, or in references to snow still being on the ground during many of the celebrations discussed.

A STRANGE AND FEARSOME WORLD

You probably didn't expect Christmas in your Carnival. Nor snow and bloody sacrifices. The book you're holding will push aside the urban fiberglass to show you an unknown Carnival where inflated pig bladders are standard gear carried by clowns and where clubs covered in hedgehog spines are carried by monsters, the blood of costumed bears is drunk as wine, plows are dragged over cobblestone streets and sawdust scattered as seed, where masks are painted in blood and jangling bones worn as costumes, where Basques in underwear take sledgehammers to old cars and Sardinians wail over plastic dolls while making lewd jokes or push bedpans filled with burning hair toward the crotches of onlookers to "induce fertility." Carnival can be a strange and fearsome world.

While I am scrupulous in the reporting of details and in adherence to the historical record, it delights me to showcase all that is peculiar, marvelous, or unsettling in the materials researched. In this way, I feel a certain kinship to writers of late-eighteenth- and nineteenth-century "wonder magazines" later published in book format, that is, publications with absurdly long titles (here truncated) such as:

The Cabinet of Curiosities; or, Wonders of the World Displayed ...
The Wonderful Magazine of All That Is Singular, Curious, and Rare in Nature and Art ...

The chapter summaries I've provided throughout the book reflect my fondness for that genre.

My love for these publications is also reflected in my history podcast, *Bone and Sickle*, which makes generous use of quoted passages from volumes like these. I mention this here, as the topics explored parallel this book's focus on folklore and folk customs, often with a dark overlay of folk horror. Materials presented are drawn from historical sources and dramatized with music and effects, and it may serve readers as an entertaining way to follow my ongoing deep dives into folklore and history.

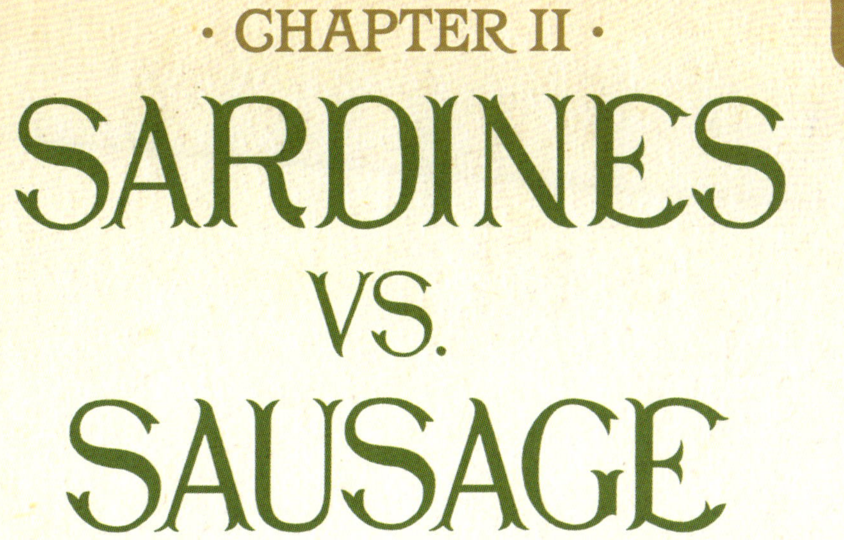

CHAPTER II
SARDINES VS. SAUSAGE

IN WHICH WE LEARN THE DIFFICULTIES OF KNOWING THE DATES OF CARNIVAL; THE MEATY, FATTY SIGNIFICANCE OF ITS NAME; THE ROLE OF THE LENTEN FAST IN DEFINING CARNIVAL;

WHY THIS FAST WAS EMBODIED IN

THE SARDINE

WHILE CARNIVAL BECAME

A SAUSAGE

HOW THESE SWORN ENEMIES ARE MADE TO DO BATTLE IN WORKS OF

ART AND LITERATURE.

CALENDRICAL CONFUSION

It's somehow fitting, for a time of festive madness, that Carnival's date (or dates) can be so maddeningly difficult to fix on the calendar. It might be identified with that single special Tuesday, the French Mardi Gras, when it is celebrated most furiously, but even where Carnival is not part of the culture it's generally recognized that one day does not a Carnival make.

Carnival is an entire season, one with a conditionally fixed end but a maddeningly mobile start date. In Germany, the "fifth season" in some regions is said to begin as early as November 11, St. Martin's Day, the same date formerly regarded as the traditional start of winter—not that celebrations on this day begin in earnest, but the date is marked by the ceremonial appearance of a costumed Carnival fool offering a comic proclamation about the season of madness to come.

However, as it would hardly be possible to begin Carnival without clearing Christmas out of the way, a more common start assigned to Carnival is Epiphany, January 6, the date ending the traditional Twelve Days of Christmas. In Spanish-and French-speaking Europe, King Cakes (Spanish: *roscónes de reyes*, French: *gâteaux des rois*) baked on that day remember the three biblical Kings who visited the infant Christ but can also be associated with the start of Carnival—as they are, most emphatically, across the Atlantic in New Orleans.

In southern Italy, the season begins only a couple weeks later with bonfires on the eve of St. Anthony the Abbot, January 17. While this date lies beyond the Twelve Days of

PREVIOUS: *BATTLE BETWEEN CARNIVAL AND LENT*, JAN MIENSE MOLENAER, C. 1633, INDIANAPOLIS MUSEUM OF ART AT NEWFIELDS.

The Fight Between Carnival and Lent, Follower of Hieronymus Bosch, Museum Mayer van den Bergh, Antwerp.

Christmas, the medieval liturgical Christmastide ran all the way to February 2, or Candlemas, also known as the Feast of the Presentation, as it concludes the biblical narrative of Christ's infancy with his presentation at the temple for ritual purification.

While this is another possible marker between the seasons of Christmas and Carnival, February 2 was also associated with nature's returning vitality, a time hibernating animals would emerge as omens of spring (like the German-American groundhog), a date when the farmer would begin his springtime labors and sheep would begin to bear young and produce milk. Thawing snows and the shift from stale winter reserves and routines would naturally feed the celebratory impulse, expressing itself in Carnival.

As with its ill-defined and regionally variable start date, Carnival's end is only partially fixed. While it absolutely must fall on a Tuesday (always in February or March), the question of *which* Tuesday introduces a further bit of madness.

Fat Tuesday, or Mardi Gras, must immediately precede Ash Wednesday, the start of the Catholic forty-day fast of Lent. As animal products (eggs, meat, butter, and cheese) would be off the fasting menu, Tuesday would be the final day to indulge in these, the final day to use up these ingredients making pancakes, crêpes, doughnuts, and the like. Even Protestant Britain, where Catholic Carnival is all but forgotten, remembers this on Pancake Day, also more somberly known as Shrove Tuesday, that is, the day to be *shriven*, or absolved of sin, in preparation for the hard fast to come.

Choosing which particular Tuesday will be "fat" and when Lent will begin requires a forty-day backward calculation from that most maddeningly slippery date of all, Easter

The Fight Between Carnival and Lent, Pieter Bruegel the Elder, 1559, Kunsthistorisches Museum, Vienna.

Sunday. Complications are rooted in the identification in the Biblical narrative of Christ's Last Supper with the feast of Passover, a celebration fixed by a lunar calendar. Though in its early centuries the Church used the Jewish date to calculate Easter, an inevitable problematic drift occurred as lunar and solar years differ (354 and 365 days, respectively), with both systems employing different arrangements of leap years and leap months to approximate astronomical realities.

By the year 325 C.E., the Church had adopted its date-fixing methodology, which remains today, making Easter the first Sunday after the full moon after the March 21 equinox. While this is confusing enough, it should be noted that the traditional equinox is only an approximation of the astronomical equinox and the full moon referred to is actually what's known as the Paschal (Easter) full moon, not a full moon as observed by astronomers or you or me. It's a full moon on paper only, namely the fourteenth day of a specially devised *ecclesiastic* lunar calendar.

All of which is to say, there's no reason any sane person should be expected to know on which date Carnival falls.

The Fight Between Carnival and Lent (Detail)

ALL IN THE NAME

The Lenten fast that gave shape to the festival is even more prominent in the etymology of the word *Carnival*. A popular interpretation derives the word from the Latin *carne vale*, meaning "farewell to meat," but there's more evidence for *carne levare*, with *levare* meaning either to "remove" or to "lift" something, in this case "meat" or "flesh." *Carne levare*, then may have originally been used to a describe a time to remove (or lift toward the spiritual) man's "carnal" nature (but the not-eating-meat interpretation became the most meaningful to the hungry masses).

Beyond those cultures formed by the Latin Church, a similar Eastern Orthodox influence is reflected in the name for Carnival in Russian, *Масленица/Maslenitsa*), which incorporates the word for butter or oil (*масло/maslo*) and is usually translated in English as "Butter Week."

The peculiar notion that Carnival might begin in Germany as early as November 11 can also be connected to another forty-day fast, the Forty Days of St. Martin, or St. Martin's Lent. Beginning November 12 and ending December 25, the fast is no longer obligatory and scarcely practiced but was once undertaken in northern Europe as discipline in preparing Catholics for Christmas.

November 11 was therefore regarded as a sort of Winter Carnival celebrated as another gustatory last fling. In England, feasting centered upon the Martinmas beef, while in France and Germany a goose was traditional. The prominence of wine in the festivities also promoted jolly St. Martin as patron of wine and winemakers.

Another legacy of the spring Lenten fast in Germany and France was the sale of a type of ecclesiastic indulgence allowing for the consumption during the fast of *lacticinia* (forbidden dairy and animal products). In Germany, the "butter letter" (*Butterbrief*) offered written dispensation allowing this in exchange for the payment of the "butter penny" (*Butterpfennig*). The sale of such indulgences also happened to finance construction of Rouen's cathedral, in particular, its highest tower consequently nicknamed the Butter Tower (*Tour de Beurre*).

FOOD FIGHT

While meat and dairy were forbidden during Lent, fish was not and became a seasonal staple. Even in towns far from any coast, river, or lake, salted or smoked fish became ubiquitous and was regarded as emblematic of the dreary season.

On the other hand, Carnival was represented, particularly in Europe's north, by porcine products, particularly sausage, a food not only particularly rich in greasy fat but visually suggestive of the reveler's gut stuffed by feasting (or even naughtier things) and quite the opposite of the shriveled sardine. Symbols such as these served as attributes identifying embodiments of Carnival and Lent, figures pitched against each other in a variety of allegorical plays and artworks of the late medieval and early modern periods.

A particularly splendid example is the Flemish painter Pieter Bruegel the Elder's 1559 painting *The Fight Between Carnival and Lent*. It offers a panoramic view of a town square populated by roughly two hundred characters grouped behind two battling enemies: a bloated figure of Carnival astride a wine cask jousting with a sallow and haggard representation of Lent. Carnival's weapon is a spit skewering a heavy load of pork and sausage, while Lent is armed with a baker's paddle supporting two meager fish. Carnival's side of the canvas features men guzzling pitchers outside a tavern, gamblers crouched over their games, kids playing tops, musicians, and processing figures in bizarre masks. Here and there on the ground are remains of food prohibited in Lent, namely animal bones and eggshells. Lent's side is populated by a gaggle of hunched nuns, unhappy beggars, and figures carrying baskets of breads, fish, mussels, and greens.

Already two centuries earlier a similar allegorical food fight was described in a French poem parodying chivalric texts, "Bataller de Caresme et Charnage," which translates to something like "The Battle of Lent and Meat," *Carasme* here being a cousin to the modern French for Lent, *Carême*, itself derived from the Latin for "forty." *Charnage* in the title means either "meat" generally or the period during which meat is allowed. In this case, however, that meaty period is not Carnival but Christmas, as embodied by the poem's hero, Noël. That either holiday could easily serve as Lent's adversary and the motif be so easily transferred not only echoes the calendrical overlap earlier noted but also hints at a historical transfer of customs from Christmas to Carnival. Weapons employed in the poem are basically those imagined by Bruegel and others: fish against an indominable armory of sausage and slabs of bacon.

By the sixteenth century, another sausage-oriented embodiment of Carnival had arisen in Germany, Hans Wurst ("Johnnie Sausage"). He appeared in Germany's first secular theater performances, plays written primarily by Hans Sachs as Carnival entertainments reflecting the coarse and irreverent spirit of that season. Part lazy fool and part triumphant trickster, Hans Wurst's clownish antics outlived their theatrical staging to become, in later centuries, a staple of German puppet shows, a role analogous to Italy's Punchinello or Britain's Mister Punch.

BURIAL OF THE SARDINE

Throughout Spain this battle against the emblematic sardine of Lent is embodied in a Carnival-closing ritual called the Burial of the Sardine. There is rarely an actual burial, and instead an effigy of a sardine is usually burned, but the procession making its way to the bonfire is pointedly funereal, usually with a dirge-playing brass band and black-clad "mourners" hammily weeping. Sometimes a satiric last will and testament of the sardine is read before the immolation. Occasionally, masked participants carry real sardines.

Because the privations of Lent once endured in Spain have largely been forgotten, the doomed sardine is now generally understood in the context of the "killing Carnival," a widespread tradition that sees an effigy embodying the season destroyed on the final day (see Chapter XIV).

Unlike the Bacchus-like figures more typically assuming this role, the peculiar choice

of a sardine is explained through various unlikely theories. In Barcelona, for instance, it's suggested the custom began with the actual burial of a shipload of sardines, a gift to the townspeople from King Carlos III which happened to prematurely spoil.

The Burial of the Sardine is also the title of a painting by Francisco Goya. The name was assigned posthumously rather than by the artist, but the annual custom in Madrid, where Goya lived in the 1810s, would have been familiar to the artist. While there is no visible sardine, coffin, or grave in the piece, early sketches feature the word "*Mortus*" on the banner central to the composition. This is replaced in the actual painting by the image of a leering face, but a morbid feel nonetheless hangs over the painting and its portrayal of maddened, grimacing revelers. The work also happened to mark Goya's transition from light, earlier works to the "Black Paintings"—those disturbing scenes painted on the walls of his villa, such as those later dubbed *The Witches' Sabbath* and *Saturn Devouring His Son.* Goya's tormented depiction is hardly the Carnival of Venice postcards but nonetheless evokes the strange and sometimes barbaric spirit infusing the early Carnival, savagery first manifest in ancient Rome.

OPPOSITE: *THE BURIAL OF THE SARDINE*, FRANCISCO GOYA, C. 1812-1819.

· CHAPTER III ·

ANCIENT ROOTS

IN WHICH DIVERSE ANCIENT ROMAN FESTIVALS
ARE CONSIDERED AS THE SOURCE OF CARNIVAL,
LUPERCALIA OFFERING MODEST PARALLELS,
THE SATURNALIA IS FOUND INADEQUATE

&

THE ROMAN NEW YEAR

(KALENDS)

DEEMED MOST CREDIBLE,
OFFERING MULTIPLE POINTS OF COMPARISON,
INCL. COSTUME, PROCESSIONS

&

PUBLIC ACTS OF MISCHIEF

THESE CONTINUING WITHIN THE

MEDIEVAL FEAST OF FOOLS

AND ULTIMATELY CARNIVAL.

LUPERCALIA

While Carnival, as we know it, required Christian Lent to give it form, it necessarily absorbed various pre-Christian elements from the culture of ancient Rome. The festival of Lupercalia, celebrated on February 15, is often suggested as a possible proto-Carnival thanks not only to its position on the calendar but to similar customs described by ancient writers. While this is far more credible than any spurious connections between Lupercalia and Valentine's Day, the comparison also raises some questions.

Carnival's association with licentious behavior offers the most obvious parallel to what is best known about Lupercalia, namely, that it was a rite promoting sexual fertility. During the festival, naked or barely clothed priests, the Luperci, ran through the streets of Rome playfully striking those they passed (especially women) with whip-like strips of goat-hide. Plutarch, in his *Life of Caesar*, written around 75 C.E., describes the already ancient festival and the Luperci running up and down through the city naked, for sport and laughter striking those they meet with shaggy thongs. And many women of rank also purposely get in their way, and like children at school present their hands to be struck, believing that the pregnant will thus be helped in delivery, and the barren to pregnancy.

This activity ranged over the city and was therefore the public face of Lupercalia and as such might draw comparison to the controlled chaos of Carnival as a sort of civic game, but this activity was preceded by a less public ritual bearing little resemblance to any Carnival tradition.

Conducted in the Lupercal Cave high on the Palatine Hill, this rite involved the sacrifice of a goat (or goats) and possibly a dog. Their flayed hides provided the strips made into whips. The sacrificial knife was then used to daub blood upon the foreheads of two young males chosen from prestigious families. The boys were then obliged to clean themselves with a woolen cloth that had been soaked in milk.

The god propitiated is usually described as Faunus, but according to varying sources it may also be Lupercus, Lycaeus, Pan, or Bacchus. What is generally agreed upon is the ritual's aim of purification, whether civic or individual, and later accounts associate the rite with Juno in her aspect *Juno Februtis* (Juno the Purifier) or *Juno Februarius*, a personification of purification and of the month of February, named for the *februum*, an instrument of ritual purification.

Whatever the details of the original religious rite, it seems to have necessarily receded into the background as the festival survived in varying forms into the Christian era. This later version of Lupercalia naturally would be the most relevant to the genesis of Carnival.

What little we know of this comes from a rather scathing letter written in 496 C.E. by Pope Gelasius I titled "Against Andromachus the Senator, and the Rest of the Romans, Who Had Established That Lupercalia Should Be Celebrated According to the Ancient Custom."

PREVIOUS: *A Roman Feast*, Roberto Bompiani, late 19th century.

LUPERCALIA, ANDREA CAMASSEI, c. 1635.

Because it is "the ancient custom" discussed, it is unknown whether certain references describe traditions common in the year 496 C.E. or customs of the distant past which Andromachus wished to see reinstituted. But it is clear that the event existed in some "degraded" form at this time and that its magical efficacy was taken seriously by Andromachus and his colleagues, who believed that a plague ravaging southern Campania at the time might have been averted by conducting these rites in Rome.

We do not know the exact content of Andromachus's original request, but from Gelasius's response it seems the senator believed it was the current degradation of the festival that brought misfortune upon the state. We can presume not only that the Luperci conducting the event no longer functioned as priests but that they were likely not drawn from the noble class as they had been. Those participating in the public rites were regarded by both senator and pope as rabble.

Gelasius scolds Andromachus:

> *the cult that is venerable and salutary for you (you think), you have brought down to cheap and vulgar persons, the worthless, and the lowest.*

While Andromachus may have wished the rites upgraded to a state more worthy of his participation, his personal involvement in the current Lupercalia is doubtful, prompting Gelasius to sarcastically write:

> *If the rite is salutary for you, celebrate it yourselves in the manner of your ancestors, run around naked yourselves with a strap so that you carry out ritually the wanton acts of your salvation.*

Gelasius regarded the rites as genuinely demonic, describing participants as foolish worshippers of a "monster that is a mixture of cattle and man."

To what extent Gelasius describes an actual deity associated with the Lupercalia of 496 is unknown, as some of his references to the tradition source authorities of previous centuries, but the phrase "mixture of cattle and man" does conjure images of some sort of hide-clad version of Pan, or a parading carnivalesque monster similar to those present at the Kalends, another Roman tradition to be discussed shortly.

There is one last detail in the letter worthy of attention. Gelasius writes:

> *Nude runners, not the ancient and honored Luperci, ran to and fro, singing sportive verses in which conspicuous scandals might be aired for the amusement of the people and the humiliation of the offender.*

Humorous mockery of those in authority is a hallmark of Carnival, and invectives are traditionally offered by one in the guise of a fool or social outsider. Like the court jester, the fool, in presenting himself as foolish or mad, is granted unparalleled license to criticize. This figure will become a staple of the later European Carnival and certainly describes whoever might've been running around naked on the streets of fifth-century Rome.

While Gelasius saw to it that Rome's Lupercalia was abolished in the fifth century, a form of the celebration survived in the Eastern Empire into the tenth century. A book of Byzantine ceremonials produced in 950, *De ceremoniis*, includes an entry mentioning special races in Constantinople's hippodrome held in anticipation of the day of "meat leaving," an event various translated as the "Carnival Horse Race" or the "Hippodrome of Meat" and explicitly identified in the text as "the *Louperkalion*."

These races were distinguished by a peculiar novelty: rather than driving their own horses, charioteers assumed the equine role and rode each other around the Hippodrome. Given the high status of the charioteer in Byzantine culture, these comically humiliating piggyback rides could offer a prototype for other rituals of assumed "foolishness" and social inversion typical of later Carnival. Constantinople's embrace of Lupercalia/Carnival as an arena of sport and absurd spectacle parallels medieval Roman celebrations in the following chapter. These descriptions of an extremely late celebration of the Lupercalia in the tenth century offer a promising thread of continuity between ancient Rome and the evolution of medieval Carnival, but one unfortunately cut short by the Turkish invasion of Constantinople in 1453, precisely the era when Carnival in the West was taking shape.

SATURNALIA

Carnival's aspect of social inversion, its elevation of the fool, glutton, and drunkard, are definitive traits. Given this, one Roman festival above all has suggested itself as prototype, namely, Saturnalia, during which masters famously became servants to their slaves.

But anyone with passing familiarity with the holiday also knows that it does not fit Carnival's calendrical frame. It was celebrated on 17 December during the Republic and, in Imperial Rome, over several days, December 17–23. Having earlier noted Carnival's slippery start date, we might for now concede the possibility that aspects of the pagan holiday not only filtered into the Christian Christmas (as is often discussed) but in the process shaped the customs of Carnival.

Carnival's reputation for riotous behavior also matches our received notion of *Saturnalia.* After all, we now find the word in dictionaries defined not only as the Roman holiday but also as a general term for wild revelry and orgiastic excess.

Let's look for a moment at the sources for this belief.

In Seneca's *Moral Epistles*, written around the middle of the first century, in a section on "Festivals and Fasting," he writes:

It is the month of December, and yet the city is at this very moment in a sweat. License is given to the general merrymaking. Everything resounds with mighty preparations—as if the Saturnalia differed at all from the usual business day.

Rather than a citywide orgy, this sounds more like the bustle around the last shopping days before Christmas. Even though license is given to set aside work in favor of entertainment, Seneca undercuts it all by comparing the occasion to a "usual business day" in the lively capital.

Nor does it appear that Saturnalia celebrations gained transgressive momentum over time. About a half century later, the Church Father Tertullian, someone from whom you might expect a frothing critique of pagan excess, offers little complaint on the subject. In his *De idolatria*, he comments only on the annoying "din of banquets."

Roughly a century after Christianity had become the religion of the Empire, a calendar published for the year 448 provides a final echo of the holiday, describing December 17 not as "Saturnalia" but as the "*feriae servorum*" (holidays of the slaves), referring presumably to elevated privileges granted on the day. Does this truly represent an anarchic upending of the social order, or might it denote only a day of small favors and considerations no more dramatic than National Teacher's Day? It couldn't have been too disruptive to the moral order as this last reference appears in a calendar created by the decidedly Christian writer Polemius Silvius for the Bishop of Lyon.

Our flamboyantly exaggerated notions of Saturnalia, by the way, can be traced to those Victorian and Edwardian writers and artists eager to project upon the pagan world all manner of forbidden pleasures, a fantasy of ancient license embodied in the literature and art of the period with particular frequency by the figure of Pan (cf. Arthur Machen's *The Great God Pan* etc.).

More soberly, this quest for what is natural and untainted by the accretions of Chris-

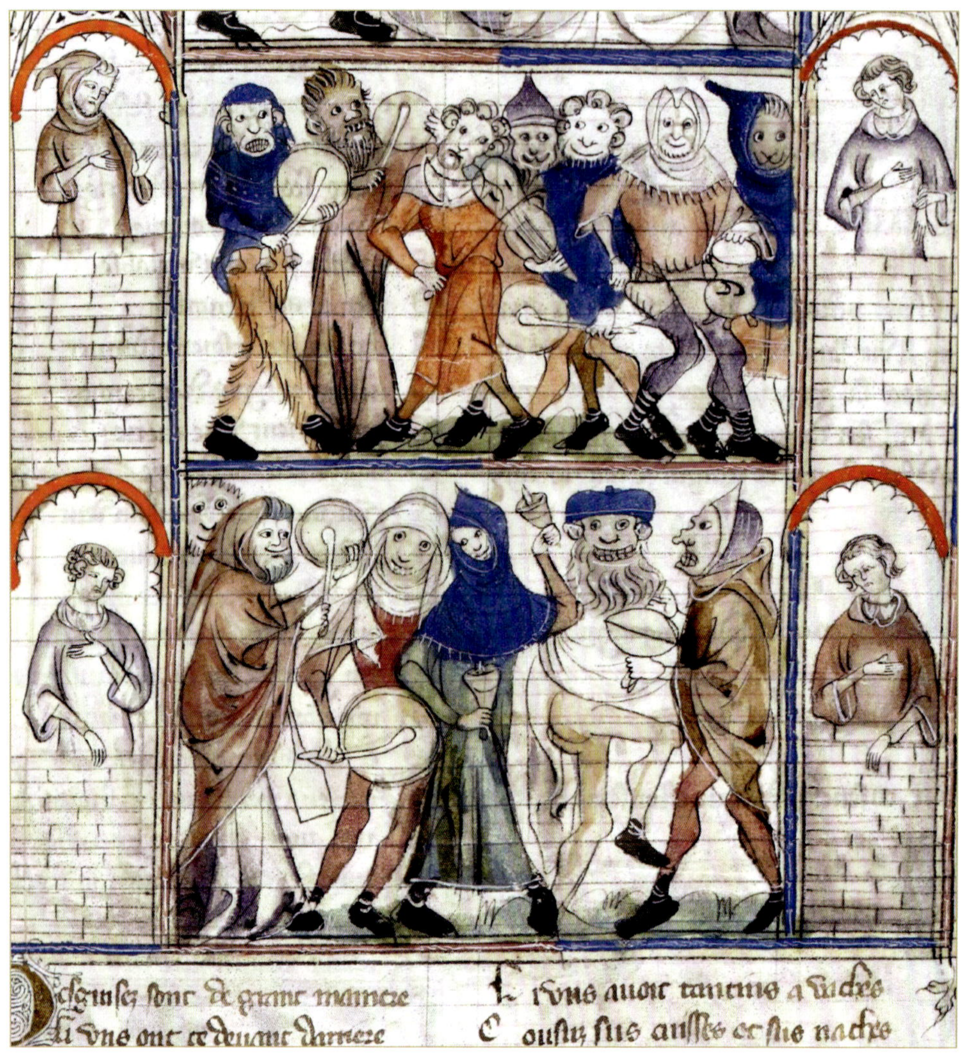

Illustration from *Le Roman de Fauvel*, c. 1300.

tian centuries gave birth to the anthropological approach to religion, as in the works of nineteenth-century writers like Edward Burnett Tylor, William Robertson Smith, and most notably James George Frazer, whose multi-volume study *The Golden Bough* (1890) saw in festive customs of the countryside traces of the ritual sacrifice of an ancient god-king. Long after Frazer's work was rejected by academics as unsupported by archeological and historical evidence, its reductive impulse lives on in popular interpretations of various customs, fed by the drama and righteous thrill of such "unmaskings." The modern commonplace that Christmas is but a whitewashing of the Saturnalia rests upon just such a foundation.

THE JANUARY KALENDS

For both the Saturnalia and Lupercalia to have significant influence in shaping Carnival, they would ideally be widely celebrated, not only in the capital but across the Empire. Lupercalia was exclusively a civic festival of Rome, symbolized by the quartering of the Lupercali in the Cave of the Lupercal, the she-wolf who raised the city's mythical founders, Romulus and Remus. The festival's later presence also in Constantinople was a unique Byzantine effort to recast that city as the "Second Rome."

Most, but not all, accounts of the Saturnalia come from Rome. But the festival did not share in the populism integral to Carnival; it did not cut across classes. References suggest Saturnalia was more a concern of well-off citizens, those who had servants and could host banquets.

The most influential Roman festival in fact was the Kalends of January. While the word *kalendae* designated the first day of any month, the January Kalends, as New Year's Day, was celebrated more widely and persistently than any other Roman holiday. Unlike our other contenders, attestations of Kalends celebration come from all over the Empire and are far more numerous.

Accounts of these celebrations not only continued into the fifth century, when Saturnalia and Lupercalia festivities ceased to be reported in the West, but in fact *increased* in number during the Christian era and continued to appear for another six centuries, as we shall see. Only after the tenth century, when Carnival first appeared, were the Kalends no longer mentioned, suggesting a partial supplanting of one by the other.

During the early Middle Ages, when the Lupercalia existed in Byzantium only as a burlesque horse race, and the banquets of Saturnalia were long gone, the Kalends was enthusiastically celebrated in a way instantly recognizable today as carnivalesque.

Festivities took the shape of processions of disguised participants, often wearing the skins and horns of animals or cross-dressing. True to the transgressive spirit of Carnival, the revelers earned the ire of Christian authorities, whose writings also happen to provide us description of the celebrations.

The obvious discrepancy, the calendrical mismatch between Kalends and Carnival, I will address shortly, but first let's look at some historical accounts of these festivities.

The first attestation comes from the fourth century, from Roman North Africa, and is found in a sermon by St. Augustine, "De calendis Januaris," in which he criticized "the din of silly and disgraceful songs" and "disgraceful merrymaking and dances" which typified "this false feast day."

The "disgraceful songs" are reminiscent of the mocking ballads of Lupercalia mentioned by Pope Gelasius, and even more characteristic elements are mentioned by the Eastern Church Father John Chrysostom, who around the year 400 complains of "all-night devilish celebrations" of drunken revelers, of "the tauntings, the invectives, the nightlong dances, this ridiculous comedy," a spectacle also marked by the appearance of costumed participants he describes as "demons marching in procession in the marketplace."

Also from Byzantine Turkey, Asterius of Amasea complains of rowdy door-to-door processions. Containing "vagrants and the jugglers of the stage," these groups go from house to house, particularly those of city officials, and demand hand-outs, he says. "Until late in the evening, there is no relief from this nuisance." While masks aren't mentioned, the inclusion of performers associated with the stage as well as the advisability of disguising oneself while harassing one's betters suggests masks were worn.

These comments come from two different sermons Asterius preached against the Kalends. In the second, from the year 400, he complains of a reveler who would

> *loose his tunic to his ankles, twine a girdle about his breast, use a woman's sandal, put a roll of hair on his head in feminine fashion, and ply the distaff full of wool ... and changing the tone of his voice utter his words in the sharper feminine treble.*

Two sermons on the subject were also preached in the early fifth century by Peter Chrysologus, Bishop of Ravenna, an Italian city strongly connected to the Roman East. In the first, he laments over men "who have made themselves equal to beasts, put themselves on a level with asses, made themselves up as cattle, masqueraded as demons," and in the second he complains that on this day "human beings are dressed as beasts, they turn men into women."

He adds another intriguing detail, referring to revelers creating images of pagan gods—Saturn, Jupiter, Diana, and the like—parading these about, adding that when Vulcan is dragged out, participants can be heard "roaring out tales of his obscenities."

"There is not enough charcoal that can blacken the faces of such gods," he writes, "and so that their appearance may reach the level of utter and complete terror, straw, skins, rags, and dung are procured from all over the world, and anything connected with human shame is put on their face."

The costumed figures again are described as visiting homes. He fumes, "This is what Christians gaze at, what Christians look forward to, what they allow into their homes, what Christians welcome in their homes."

During the fourth and early fifth centuries, accounts of Kalends become more frequent, with animal disguises prominent. In the late fourth century, Ambrose of Milan, in a sermon dedicated to Job and David, writes, "In the beginning of the year, by folk custom, the stag frolicked about." A few decades later, St. Maximus composed a sermon on the Kalends, writing,

> *Aren't they all false and absurd things, when men, shaped by God in His image, transform themselves either into cattle or other beasts, or even into other monstrosities?*

Later, in the sixth century, a *Life of St. Hilary of Mender* describes the saint confronting a group of villagers celebrating the Kalends who had "decked themselves out in the heads of stags to resemble in their appearance wild beasts."

A particularly vocal adversary of these practices in France was Caesarius, Bishop of Arles (470-543). In his "A Sermon Necessary in Parishes," he chastises those who "practice that most sordid disgrace of masquerading as a heifer or a stag."

"Playing the stag" is explicitly linked to the Kalends in his sermon "De kalendis Ianuariis," in which he condemns those who:

> *change their appearance for that of wild animals. Some are dressed up in the skins of farm animals, others put on the heads of wild animals, celebrating and leaping about.*

He then directs his ire at male revelers who:

> *make their manly strength womanish by means of girlish fashions, not blushing to put the arms of a soldier into the tunics of women. They show bearded faces but want to appear like women.*

He describes these cross-dressers singing "the praises of vices along with disorderly gestures and immodest songs." These troupes also engage in house visits, as he warns, like Peter Chrysologus of Ravenna, that Christians "should not permit a little stag, a heifer, or any other kind of monster to come before your homes."

These condemnations continue to appear in the seventh through ninth centuries, not only in Italy and France but in Spain, Germany, and England, where Theodore of Tarsus, Archbishop of Canterbury, in his *Poenitentiale Theodori*, compiled after his death in 690, condemns animal-masking similar to that described by Caesarius, prescribing for those who participated in this practice acts of "penance for three years because this is devilish." The same period of penance was again stipulated in 906 by the German abbot Regino of Prüm.

The late-tenth-century *Chronicon albeldense,* from northwest Spain, prescribed a single year of penitential acts for "dancing in women's clothes" and disguising oneself as monstrous figures such as the orcus (an underworld figure later possibly understood as an ogre).

Around 1015 in Germany, we see one of the last references to such activities, in a collection of canon law, *Decretum*, by Burchard of Worms. While such collections typically include older texts, Burchard makes a point of noting that the practice is still current. Part of the confessional he provides for priests setting penance asks:

> *Hast thou done anything like what the pagans did, and still do on the Kalends of January, in the guise of a stag or a calf?*

I've quoted these sources at some length as many of their details will be recognized in later Carnival customs described in the following chapters.

In particular, the Carnival practices found in more rural, more traditionalist communities still bear a surprising resemblance to Kalends customs. In these settings, costumed

The Month of February: Shrove Tuesday, Crispijn van de Passe I, 1580–1588.

troupes visiting houses to demand food and drink almost always include a cross-dressed figure and sometimes costumes employing animal hides or horns. In later chapters, we'll encounter many vaguely zoomorphic looks, not imitating a specific animal but evoking something decidedly wild and not human; examples include shaggy fur suggested by fluttering patchworks of rags, or voluminous suits crafted of straw. The faces blackened with charcoal in Peter Chrysologus's fifth-century account are still strikingly widespread in many regions to be discussed.

CARNIVAL IS CHRISTMAS IS CARNIVAL

Now to that sticky issue regarding the calendrical mismatch between the Kalends and Carnival's timeframe.

Festival of Fools, Pieter van der Heyden after Pieter Brueghel the Elder, c. 1570.

Asking how New Year's customs might move forward into February or March to "become" Carnival starts on the wrong foot. It would be better to consider how, in the old way of thinking, the festive seasons extended and overlapped in ways we may have forgotten.

Christmas was not a single day, but a season. It merely began at midnight Mass on December 25 and extended forward either to Epiphany, January 6, or all the way to Candlemas, February 2. The Kalends of January 1 was therefore part of Christmas (which may account for the exaggerated reputation of the Saturnalia as a celebration conflated with the Kalends).

Carnival, as noted, to this day in southern Italy starts on January 17, the feast of St. Anthony the Abbot. In France and Germany, Epiphany is said to begin the season (setting aside the German date of November 11, better regarded as a separate Winter Carnival preceding St. Martin's Lent). In Venice, as we'll see, the traditional start of Carnival was established as December 26, *within* the Twelve Days of Christmas. It's worth remembering too how the motif of Carnival's battle with Lent (as in Bruegel's painting) represented an adaptation of the earlier Christmas-versus-Lent motif in the poem "Bataller de Caresme et Charnage." In eastern European cases to be examined, there is even frequent confusion over whether certain terms are best interpreted as belonging to Carnival or Christmas.

Though it's obviously obscured today, historically and regionally, Carnival and Christmas overlay each other. It's not so much a question of one festival moving into another but of one big, tasty cake, which can be sliced a variety of ways.

THE FEAST OF FOOLS

During this extended medieval Christmas, January 1 continued to be celebrated with activities resembling those of the Roman Kalends. Often these revels are described with a sort of catch-all term, the "Feast of Fools." The term includes both the ecclesiastic celebrations, the actual "foolish" feast days, and the secular or folk customs which paralleled these. It seems likely that the Kalends practices, the processions of wild revelers, lived on in folk traditions alongside the ecclesiastical traditions and that these were regarded as simply two sides of a coin by the common people. Whatever feels exotic and "pagan" to us in descriptions of Kalends activities would not feel so to participants. The prevailing attitude is nicely sketched in a sermon by Peter Chrysologus:

Illustration of the tomb of the Boy Bishop, Salisbury Cathedral. From *Old England: A Pictorial Museum*, Charles Knight (1845).

But one of you says, "This isn't the deliberate pursuit of godlessness, these good-luck visits are just for fun; this is a celebration of a new beginning, not a superstition from the past; this is just New Year, not the threat of paganism."

Clearly Chrysologus disagreed, but the Church meanwhile seemed to celebrate its own species of irreverence in a series of "foolish" feast days. On these occasions, playful role-reversals took place during the Mass: deacons played priests, while priest were demoted to deacons, and on other days subdeacons and deacons switched roles, inversions that couldn't help but draw titters from those in the congregation. These inversions were staged on January 1 (St. Sylvester), December 26 (St. Stephen), December 27 (St. John), and possibly December 28 (Holy Innocents). Local custom in the French and German regions where the customs were most prominent emphasized some of these over others.

Even children would temporarily be elevated to clerical roles. December 28, the Feast of the Holy Innocents, which honors the infants slaughtered by King Herod in his attempt to kill the newborn Jesus, was chosen as a fitting occasion for this. Not only would a boy play the role of the priest but (in England and Germany) he could ascend to Bishop. This "Boy Bishop" tradition was later moved to St. Nicholas Day (December 6), thanks to that saint's association with children.

These celebrations in the Church were associated with secular activities, which could be quite unruly, echoing the "disgraceful merrymaking" Augustine peevishly noted in the Kalends. After Mass, the child cleric would be escorted through the streets by a noisy cortège in processions visiting homes of important citizens and inns where food and drink were to be provided.While it is tempting to imagine the spirit of unruliness associated with these droll ecclesiastic rituals evolving from ancient Kalends customs, the Church offered its own theological rationale for these inversions.

During the elevation of the Boy Bishop, for instance, the mitre would be placed upon the child's head at a significant liturgical moment—as the choristers sing the words of the Virgin upon realizing she carries the infant Christ within her: "He hath put down the mighty from their seat: and hath exalted the humble and meek." In this way, Christmas itself, with its exemplum of a Messiah born into a manger, carried the topsy-turvy seeds of Carnival in its own theology.

This is not to say that such rituals were imposed through top-down directives from Rome. However theologically sound it all may have been, extreme liberties taken in the rite's enactment could serve to vent resentments roiling within the Church, mocking its vaunted hierarchies at the same time the Protestant Reformation was taking shape.

As for liberties taken, one example should suffice: a complaint written in 1445 by the Faculty of Theology of Paris, lamenting such excess.

Priests and clerks may be seen wearing masks and monstrous visages at the hours of office. They dance in the choir dressed as women, procurers, or minstrels. They sing wanton songs. They eat black puddings at the horn of the altar while the celebrant is saying Mass. They play at dice there. They cense with stinking smoke from the soles of old shoes. They run and leap through the church, without a blush at their own shame. Finally, they drive about the town and its theatres in shabby traps and carts, and rouse the laughter of their fellows and the bystanders in infamous performances, with indecent gesture and verses scurrilous and unchaste.

Eventually, these tensions grew too great. Celebrations, in some cases, had become outright dangerous and even led to loss of life (detailed in my book *Krampus and the Old, Dark Christmas,* Feral House, 2016). Church leaders had also come to regard the festivities as an irreligious blight upon the holy season of the Nativity. Local bishops began cracking down on the fun, and by the fifteenth century the Feast of Fools was no more. Or at least those profane energies were redirected outside the holy season, into what the liturgical calendar calls "Ordinary Time, the period between Candlemas and Lent, a perfect time for a Carnival."

· CHAPTER IV ·

ROME

REVEALING

THE BLOODY ORIGINS

OF

ROMAN CARNIVAL,

PAPAL OVERSIGHT OF ANIMALS SLAUGHTERED, BULLFIGHTS,

PIGS ROLLED DOWN THE TESTACCIO HILL

&

OTHER CRUELTIES MAKING SPORT OF

JEWS, HUNCHBACKS, ETC.

ALONG WITH

DRAMATIC RACES
OF WILD BERBER HORSES
THROUGH ROMAN STREETS,

BUT ALSO

PLEASANT DETAILS RELATING TO

CONFETTI, GIFTS, & SWEETS

SHOWERED UPON SPECTATORS.

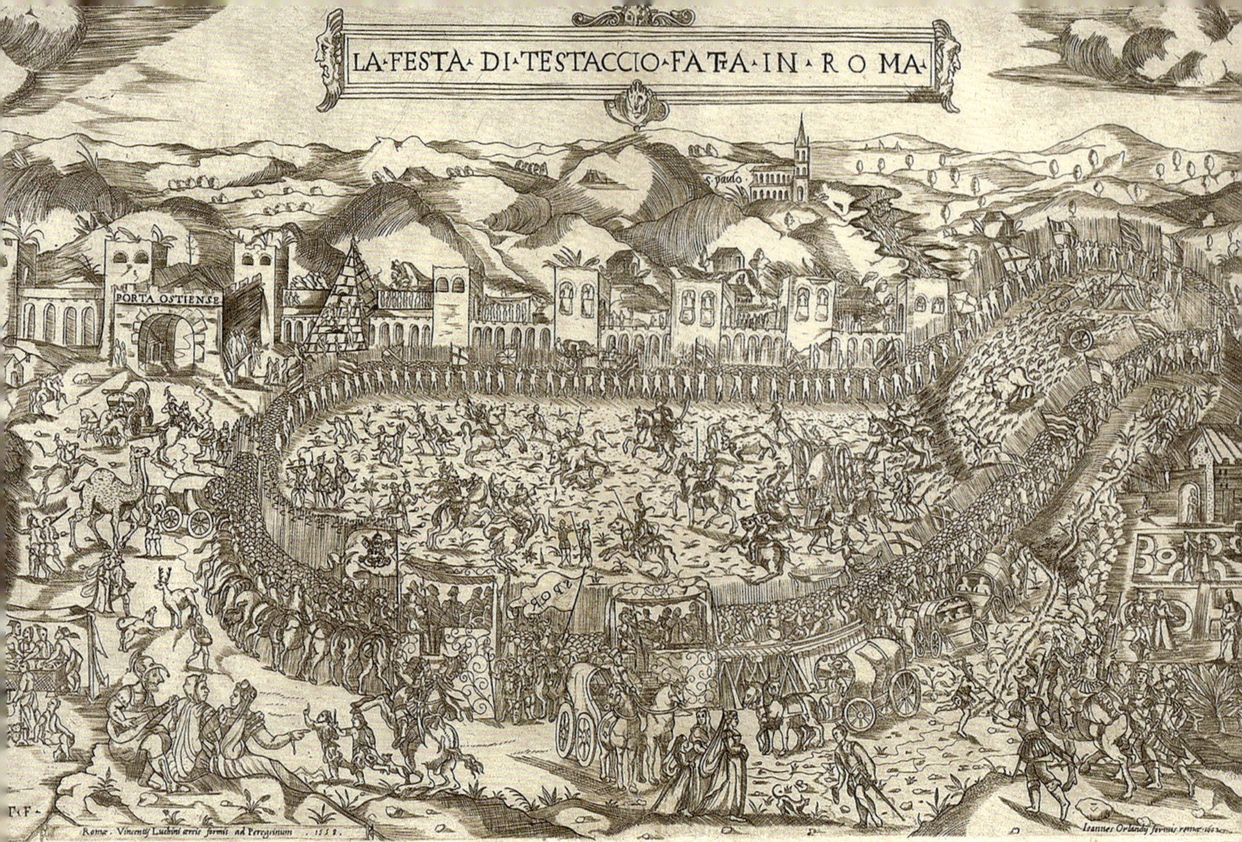

Illustration of Carnival games on Mount Testaccio in Rome, Vincenzo Luchino, 1558.

BLOODY RITES AT TESTACCIO

In twelfth-century Rome, Carnival was born, though not quite the Carnival you imagine.

It was there that the impending Catholic fast of Lent became the engine driving a new festival of eleventh-hour indulgence. In Rome, the term for private renunciation, *carne levare,* came to be applied to this public spectacle, one that held a grotesque mirror to the city itself, reflecting both the startling worldliness of the papacy and bloody memories of the Coliseum.

Around 1142, a Vatican canon by the name of Benedict wrote a book, *Liber politicus,* cataloging processional routes and rituals. In it, he describes "*ludus carnelevarii*" (Carnival games or performances) that took place around the Testaccio Hill. Also called the Monte dei Cocci (or the Hill of Potsherds), it was created out of the remnants of discarded oil amphorae and its namesake neighborhood for centuries was—more significantly—known as the "belly" or "slaughterhouse" of Rome.

In the afternoon "on the Sunday before Lent," Benedict writes, Pope Innocent II departed the Lateran Palace, riding with a prefect and various dignitaries to the Testaccio Hill, a site associated with Rome's establishment. What happened there is couched in the canon's language of moral allegory, but his analogies are drawn from a very real and brutal rite.

Previous: *Carnival in Rome*, Johannes Lingelbach, 1650, Kunsthistorisches Museum, Vienna.

Just as there the city had its beginning, so there on that day, the pleasures of our body have their end. They perform the game before the pope, so that no contention arises among them. In killing a bear, the devil is slain, who is the tempter of our flesh. When bullocks are killed, the pride of our pleasures is slain. In the killing of a cock, the lechery of our loins is slain, so that we may live chastely and soberly in the midst of the spiritual battle and so be counted worthy to taste the body of the Lord at Easter.

Though we don't again hear of the above allegory-friendly slaughter, scattered references in the fourteenth century imply that Carnival games (some bloody) continued on the site. Mention is made of a "festival of the bull" (bullfight) along with a race for a "*palio*" (a costly prize sash or banner) and equestrian tournament events, including "running at the ring." Certain games also appear at the Campo di Agone (later renamed the Piazza Navona), and processions between the two offered further pageantry.

Benedict's scene of slaughter is more strongly echoed in another game, sometimes called the "rolling of the pigs."

In a volume from 1346, *Polistoria*, the Roman canon Joannes Cavallino briefly mentions this peculiar Carnival rite at Testaccio. "From the top of the same hill," he writes, "wheeled carts containing wild bulls and other woodland animals are released, spilling them out."

The spectacle is more luridly described by Adam of Usk, a cleric visiting Rome from Wales. In his 1405 book *Chronicon,* he notes the "excessive drinking and unrestrained licentiousness" of Rome's revelers and describes the procession, equestrian competitions, and grisly aftermath of the four rolling carts, covered with scarlet cloth and containing eight live boars ... yoked to eight wild bulls. When the carts come down the hill they break up, and the animals are set free, whereupon it all becomes spoil for the Romans to fight over, and then everyone rushes upon the said beasts in unrestrained attack with his own weapon.

After the melee, they go away in meanspirited procession to their wives, some with little bits of animal, and others with intestines or dung, on the ends of their swords. Anybody who fails to bring home a piece of the spoil for his wife is regarded as wretched and senseless and is not allowed to lie with her until the feast of St. Pancras.

The last represents rather serious consequences, as the feast of St. Pancras is May 12, resulting in roughly three months of imposed abstinence.

BULLFIGHTS AT THE VATICAN

The bulls let loose at Testaccio were hunted down by horsemen armed with spears, within a bullring improvised at the foot of the hill via a circle of parked wagons, as represented in sixteenth-century etchings.

A bullfight (or hunt) was even held at the Vatican's Belvedere Courtyard on Shrove Tuesday of 1510 (along with a horse race), as well as on other occasions, such as royal weddings.

Even the Cardinal Cesare Borgia fought bulls at the Vatican on the Feast of St. John

The Start of the Race of the Riderless Horses (La Mossa), Horace Vernet, 1820.

in 1500. The Piazza del Campidoglio on the Capitoline Hill was also the site of a "running of the bulls" on February 25, 1536, roughly a week before Lent that year, so this was presumably presented as a Carnival entertainment.

THE RACE OF THE JEWS

In 1466, Pope Paul II, a Venetian, moved Carnival activities into central Rome. Races were added to the festivities and followed a mile-long course along the Via del Corso with their finish line in the Piazza Venezia near the papal palace. Eventually, there was a full week of races, both footraces and animal runs. The footraces don't seem to have been presented as displays of competitive athleticism but rather as a carnivalesque novelty. Very young children competed on the Tuesday before Mardi Gras, older youth on Wednesday, the elderly endured a grueling race on Thursday, donkeys raced Monday, and charging buffalo offered a finale on the final Tuesday.

By 1501, the races notoriously became an outlet for Roman antisemitism. Jews, who had already been compelled to finance the "rolling of the pigs," were now forced to compete in humiliating footraces. As an added touch of cruelty, the runners were weighted

THE HORSE RACE AT ROME DURING THE CARNIVAL, PAUL SANDBY, C. 1781.

down with great quantities of food forced on them before the race. Spectators along the way amused themselves by taunting the runners and pelting them with eggs and rotting vegetables.

By the 1580s, Jews were forced to run naked, and on certain occasions were ridden like horses. In the 1600s, the naked runners were allowed to don clothing—or, rather, costumes more likely intended to provoke laughter than save the runner's dignity. These shameful activities taking place in the capitol of Christendom were finally ended in 1668 by Pope Clement IX. This small mercy, however, had its cost, as a new tax was extracted from Jewish residents and used to finance the increasing cost of street decoration and other Carnival pageantry.

In 1501, the Borgia pope Alexander VI also added a race run by prostitutes, and in 1633 a race of hunchbacks running along the Via Giulia was added, along with another race for handicapped or deformed runners held in the Trastevere neighborhood.

RACING HORSES AND CANDLES

During Carnival, the Via del Corso was also the site of riderless animal races, or runs. From the sixteenth century, we see reports of donkeys and buffaloes charging along the Corso, but Berber ("Barbary") horses became a favorite and the *Corsa dei Berberi* was eventually repeated eight times over the final eight days of Carnival.

Carnival in Rome, the Feast of Moccoletti, Ippolito Caffi, 1852.

Particularly spirited and muscular horses from North Africa, the animals were whipped to a panicked frenzy by the screaming spectators crowding the narrow streets but also by "spurrs so placed on their backs, and hanging downe by their sides, as with their motion to stimulate them," a contrivance described by the Englishman John Evelyn in his Italian travel diary of 1644-45.

The end of the race in the Piazza Venezia offered its own form of drama. A curtain was placed at the spot where the Via del Corso opened onto the piazza, but this barely slowed many of the charging horses, so brave grooms, the *barbareschi*, were compelled to wrestle the maddened animals to a stop.

The Race of the Berbers remained popular for centuries, until 1874, when a young boy was fatally trampled, an event personally witnessed by King Victor Emmanuel II, who ended the races.

While other less humane races along the Via del Corso had ceased some time earlier, one peculiar footrace remained into the 1800s, the Candle Race or *Corsa dei Moccoletti*.

During this competition, short, burning candle ends (*moccoletti*) were carried along the route by participants moving as fast as they could while trying to keep the flame alight and at the same time extinguish the flames of those around them. To protect their flames, many participants took to mounting their candles in cups carried overhead on sticks, which apparently was within the rules. First held in 1773, the Candle Race flickered out toward the end of the 1800s though briefly returned for a 1999 encore.

The Carnival in Rome, José Benlliure Gil, 1881.

CARNIVAL ON VIA DEL CORSO

The Via del Corso was the site not only of races but of a parade kicking off Carnival. Between these events, it also served as the site of more impromptu masked promenades. As the environment became increasingly crowded, wild, and festive (or dangerous, when filled with charging horses), seating was rented out, while the upper classes preferred observing the scene from their balconies.

The inaugural parade featured lavishly ornamented parade wagons representing mythological themes, the glory of ancient Rome, or—most frequently—the glory of families blessed with secular and ecclesiastic power.

These same themes were also represented in short plays, usually comic, composed for the season and performed on mobile outdoor stages (as well as at indoor banquets hosted by the elites). Again, we have John Evelyn, commenting on the scene in 1644:

> *One thing yet is remarkable, their acting comedies upon a stage placed on a cart, or plastrum where the scene ... is made of bowghs, in pastoral and rural manner, this they drove from street to street with a yoake or two of oxen, after the antient guise: The streets swarming with whores, buffoones and all manner of rabble.*

Along with these, strolling revelers were entertained by musicians, acrobats, and poets. Particularly eagerly awaited were visits by wealthy aristocrats, senators, or cardinals,

19TH-CENTURY ROMAN CARNIVAL FIGURE, ILLUSTRATION BY BARTOLOMEO PINELLI IN *LETTRE DE M. MILLIN,... À M. LANGLÈS, SUR LE CARNAVAL DE ROME* BY AUBIN LOUIS MILLIN, 1812.

passing through in ostentatious carriages and throwing out treats en route or appearing on their balconies to do the same.

The most common projectiles were handfuls of comfits, which are sugar-coated nuts, fruit, or seeds. Today this might be most familiar as almond comfit, or Jordan almonds, but in the fifteenth or sixteenth century, coriander, anise, fennel seeds, or diced ginger would serve as the basis for the confection.

This gesture of showy largesse had a malicious parallel in the throwing of plaster pellets, possibly accompanied by loose handfuls of dry plaster or quicklime, presumably a deed more common to youthful pranksters than powerful individuals eager to curry plebeian favor. As this became more commonplace, masks of wire mesh were sometimes adopted as necessary Carnival gear.

George Stillman Hillard, an English visitor in 1854, described the dreadful sensation of being hit with this unpleasant comfit counterfeit in his book *Six Months in Rome*, writing,

> *the first sensation is as if the points of a thousand needles had been suddenly shot into the skin; and then a cloud of darkness settles down upon the eyes, which gradually passes off in a rain of tears.*

One might assume that even that expensive handful of Jordan almonds could also do some damage. For this reason, by the 1890s, a cheaper and harmless substitute of paper was innovated, namely *confetti,* the Italian word for its predecessor, comfits.

Even more desirable than sweets were the hollow balls occasionally tossed out, inside of which could be found various trinkets, money, or tokens for prizes, including food, wine, or (as legend has it) even deeds to valuable apartments. The scramble to obtain these could result in violent scuffles, suggesting that these acts of purported largesse were sometimes tinged with sadism. Occasionally, too, revelers might be sprayed by some beneficent passerby with a mist of cool water, or the scent of saffron, lavender, or balsam.

Called *sparsio* from the Latin for "sprinkle," the tradition of throwing such gifts or *sparsiones* has ancient precedent in customs associated with the gladiatorial games. The historian Suetonius, in his biography of Nero, describes how the emperor has "many thousand articles of all descriptions ... thrown amongst the people to scramble for; such as fowls of different kinds, beasts of burden, wild beasts that had been tamed." I'm having some trouble picturing a mule or ox thrown into the crowd, but Suetonius was a bit prone to exaggeration.

· CHAPTER V ·

CARNIVAL IN VENICE

HOW THE VENETIANS ALSO TORMENTED BULLS
& OTHER ANIMALS AT CARNIVAL, THREW EGGS
AS A FORM OF COURTSHIP & DONNED MASKS
ALLOWING CERTAIN LIBERTIES;

A DESCRIPTION OF THE MASKS

&

THEIR SOCIAL PURPOSE;

THE SPECTACLES

OF ST MARK'S SQUARE, INCL.
THE POWERS OF HERCULES & FLYING ANGELS;

MOCK BATTLES ON THE BRIDGES

&

A VENETIAN TRIUMPH RELIVED
THROUGH THE SLAUGHTER OF PIGS;
A PIRATE ABDUCTION OF BRIDES WHO
STRANGELY BECAME JEWELED EFFIGIES,

THEIR STATELY PROCESSIONS

LATER REVILED BY FICKLE VENETIANS
WHO PELTED THEM WITH GARBAGE.

BLOOD IN THE WATER

However cruel and bizarre descriptions of Rome's medieval Carnival may sound, they're a bit less jarring only because you've likely spent little time imagining Carnival in Rome. It's only Rome, after all, not Venice.

By the nineteenth century, Carnival in the Eternal City was already fading, and today its celebration is relatively anemic. But Venice had established a more tenable mode of survival, an elusive reality that was always conveniently beyond reach, celebrated by secretive gatherings and private masked balls.

The Venice Carnival we think of is less outward-facing than Carnival in Rome for good reason. While public races were considered a fitting celebration for almost any occasion in Rome or Constantinople, Venice did not have a Circus Maximus or Hippodrome to set that pattern. It did not have a history of triumphal processions staged for returning victors as an inspirational source for later Carnival pageantry (nor even the requisite roads, obviously).

But Venice did have public squares, or *campi*, where Carnival was outwardly celebrated before the eighteenth-century balls and banquets came to dominate and privatize the Venetian Carnival. In those *campi*, medieval celebrations of Carnival could be every bit as blood-spattered as those in Rome, and at times the violence spilled onto the bridges and *calle* that pass for streets. Now happily forgotten, the elegant festivities of "the Most Serene Republic" have roots in a more brutal world delighting in teams of bloodied men battling it out with sticks and fists, bull hunts, and other cruel games with animals, even a celebratory slaughter of pigs.

THE HUNTING OF THE BULLS

Around the time that Rome's bull hunts and sportive butchery at Testaccio were supplanted by the races on the Via del Corso, we begin hearing of bull hunts in Venice. Whether these were the original Venetian Carnival celebrations is more difficult to say, as the city's particularly long season (starting on either December 26 or February 2, i.e., Candlemas) overlay a variety of celebrations not necessarily initiated explicitly as Carnival activities.

The *Cazza del Toro* (hunting of the bull) originally began on December 26 and occurred in different *campi* every day of the week before Lent, excluding Fridays. Over time, however, the practice became less frequent, eventually restricted in the eighteenth century to either the last Thursday of Carnival or Shrove Tuesday.

Anywhere from six to eighteen bulls appeared in these wildly popular hunts, which began early in the afternoon and could run till midnight. While the animals are usually referred to as "bulls," these were hardly the bulls bred for Spanish bullfighting. They were oxen, usually those nearing the end of their useful lives as beasts of burden or even chosen from among those awaiting the slaughterhouse. Nonetheless, only the largest and

PREVIOUS: *A Carnival Scene at the Piazza San Marco, Venice*, Sebastian Vrancx, c. 17th Century.

The Bull Hunt in Campo Saint Paul, Joseph Heintz the Younger, c. 1632-1678.

presumably strongest of these were selected, and the animals would appear even more formidable as they sometimes charged into the *campo* with fireworks fixed to their horns, ringed in smoke and sparks and maddened by the pyrotechnics.

While the oxen in Venice would leave the square alive, they were restricted in their movement. Contemporary illustrations show them scattered among running spectators, but upon closer inspection one notes that they are controlled by pairs of men, *tiradori* in flamboyant plumed hats, who restrain the beasts via ropes tied to each horn (or only one horn if the *tirador* is particularly brave). And it was not men who fought the oxen but dogs, specially trained and guided during the fight by white-shirted *cavacani*. Similar to the bullbaiting of old England, the canine's aim was to bite or tear off the animal's ear. A particularly tenacious dog, refusing to release its grip on the ox, risked being crushed to the pavement or tossed through the air, and when the *cavacani* feared something like this was imminent, they would famously resort to biting the canine's tail to ensure his release, a source of terrific amusement to the crowd.

Oxen that had become difficult to control and were endangering the *tiradori, cavacani*, or spectators—or, more frequently, those who had been tortured to the brink of death by dogs—were dispatched by a trained butcher waiting in the wings. He wielded a heavy longsword capable of taking off the animal's head in single blow if his aim was good. For this purpose, each animal's spine was chalked with a target mark before entering the square. Should the swordsman succeed with a single blow, he was wildly cheered; if he failed, mercilessly taunted.

By the 1800s, spectators were restricted to bleachers, though safety here was not al-

THE RHINOCEROS, PIETRO LONGHI, 1751. CA'REZZONICO, VENICE.

ways assured, and in 1802 a frenzied ox knocked one of these down in the Campo Santo Stefano, killing or injuring spectators. The Austrians who ruled Venice at the time, and had long found the sport distasteful, happily terminated the practice.

NOT ANIMAL-FRIENDLY

Unfortunately, the cruelty toward animals did not end with bullbaiting. We know of quite a few other ghastly Carnival diversions from a collection of captioned engravings published in 1609 by the artist Giacomo Franco. His *Habiti d'huomeni et donne venetiane*

(*Dress of the Men and Women of Venice*), while focusing on fashions, includes alongside this a number of seasonal sports that would have seen the city burned by PETA.

Tying live ducks atop a pole as a trophy to be grabbed by competitors climbing to reach them was apparently considered fun. Another unfortunate avian, a goose, was tied and suspended head-down from a window over a canal. Competitors leapt up, trying to catch its head, ending up either in the canal or with a broken-necked goose as a prize. The most horrific involved head-butting a cat tied to a board. Contestants here first had their heads shaved to give the cat a fighting chance with its claws.

Elsewhere, a game is described involving an eel swimming in a barrel of water blackened by cuttlefish ink. Revelers attempted to seize the eel with their teeth. Dogs also might be tossed in blankets and cocks stoned to death as a test of marksmanship. The Campo Piazza Santa Maria Formosa was the main site of these atrocities, which persisted into the late eighteenth century.

A much more pleasant Carnival entertainment involving animals was the exhibition of Clara the Rhinoceros. She arrived in Venice on January 22, 1750, brought from India by a Dutch captain by the name of Douve Mout van der Meer. The novelty proved quite popular and was said to have earned her promoter 4,000 ducats, which would be about $6 million US today. Before visiting Venice, she'd already toured Holland, Belgium, Germany, Switzerland, Austria, and France and would later go on to visit Denmark and Poland, finally dying in London in 1758 at the age of twenty.

THE GAME OF THE EGG

While none of this is the sort of thing we now associate with Venice Carnival, or Carnival anywhere, it's worth noting that those beloved Venetian masks also originated with festival violence, albeit between human revelers.

Just as in Rome's Carnival comfits were thrown, Venice had its holiday projectiles, most famously eggs, though apples and oranges could be more injurious, especially when tossed from a balcony. One would also need to be on the lookout for handfuls of plaster comfit or flour. Egg throwing, or the *giuoco degli ovi* (game of the eggs), was an important feature of the Venetian Carnival from the beginning. This was not only a form of street mischief but—with the right eggs—could serve as a sort of flirtation when those shells were filled with rosewater, orange-blossom water, or some other perfume. Preparing these provided lucrative trade for vendors set up along the *calle* every season. Young men might toss these in the street, while females were more likely to throw from a balcony. A clumsier tribute, perhaps better suited to the timid, involved hurling eggs simply at the houses of the intended. During Carnival, families with young women likely to be thus wooed sometimes took the precaution of covering windows and balconies with netting. As the egg-throwing mania increased, even public buildings on certain squares ended up entirely covered in netting.

But there was also a market for eggs filled with ink or paint, and of course revelers also threw eggs filled with their natural contents—as likely as not, spoiled. As early as 1268, an

Maskers Throwing Scented Eggs in Venice, unknown artist, 17th century, after Francesco Bertelli.

edict went out forbidding the throwing of eggs in the Piazza San Marco, but the custom crept back into practice, surviving intermittent bans for centuries. Eggs weren't always thrown by hand: at least when targeting a balcony far overhead, a sling was used, and egg-throwers thus equipped were known as *frombolatore* (slingers), from *frombola* (sling).

This is where the connection with Venice Carnival masks comes in. A particular kind of multi-colored costume and mask became associated with the *frombolatori*. The mask would have offered a bit of protection from counterattacks, and the ensemble also became traditional to a Carnival character known as the *Mattaccino* (English: Mattachin). This character appeared in street demonstrations of various acrobatics and particularly a sort of sword dance resembling that of Britain's Morris dancers.

MASKS AND SOCIETY

Of course, the Mattaccino would primarily be interested in wearing a mask while egg-slinging for the same reason a bank-robber would—anonymity. The permissive spirit of Carnival became ever more permissive with masks; the upstanding citizen could freely slip into the bordello or the low-born gambler into a gaming hall of the wealthy. Beyond detaching actions from social repercussions, there was the sense of mystery and possibility masks engendered, the wild play of imagination they encouraged.

While the last has become a familiar cliché regarding the Venice Carnival, certain liberties they made available are more difficult to imagine today. Venice into the early modern period had some of Europe's strictest sumptuary laws, or restrictions on dress for various classes and occupations. During Carnival, those laws and the rigid hierarchies they enforced were lifted. The mask is incomplete without its traditionally paired wardrobe, and the entire ensemble, along with the character it represents, is spoken of as a "mask" (*maschera*).

If this strict pairing strikes you as further sumptuary law reinserting itself, consider the effect of more personalized choices and how a mix-and-match approach and individualized choices might betray one's identity. In contrast, the traditionally outfitted Carnival-goer steps into a ready-made type and, with this, anonymity.

THE CASINO, PIETRO LONGHI, C. 1720-1790.

The social utility of masks was recognized by Venetians in contexts outside of Carnival. The Ridotto, the city's storied casino (the first such public venue in the West), swelled with guests during Carnival and masks served to ease many of the social tensions that might otherwise beset that environment. They leveled the playing field. If one could afford the mask and cash for the wager, one was equal to all at the table. No taint of low birth or history of unpaid debts followed one. Anonymous players engendered no gossip about shameful losses, and vengeful losers could not know against whom to direct their retribution. Masks made the Ridotto a world safe unto itself, anticipating by centuries the wise maxim "What happens in Vegas stays in Vegas." Masks, therefore, were not merely an option at the Ridotto; they were required year round.

Masks worn during Carnival (at certain periods of the Republic) could be worn all the way till the Feast of the Ascension (May 8) as well as sporadically throughout the remainder of the year, i.e., for the feast of the city's patron, St. Mark, and that of SS. Vito and Modesto. Meeting the needs of all these masked festivities was a growing number of mask-makers, who came together to form a guild in 1436. As early as 1610, an annual promenade of masks (the *Liston di Maschere*) on the Campo Santo Stefano had become the traditional kick-off event of the season.

Illustration by Niccolò Cavalli (1750–1822) showing (L-R) man in bauta mask, woman holding moretta mask, and Arlecchino.

THE CLASSIC MASKS

Certain masks were also obligatory for other functions, particularly the *bauta* mask, an angular white mask covering the upper face and mouth while leaving the chin exposed. It was employed when votes were to be cast, as ceremonial formal dress when receiving dignitaries, or at banquets hosted by the doge. Like a Scotsman's kilt, it was also patriotic, expressing pride in the stable and wealthy Republic of Venice, *la Serenissima*.

Of various mask designs, the bauta came to the fore because of its utility, namely that it provided maximum anonymity while leaving the mouth free for conversation, drink, or food thanks to the squarish overhang that obscures the mouth without covering it. It is the traditional men's mask of Carnival, though it is now largely replaced by (and confused with) another mask, which extends down over the chin—the *volto,* meaning simply "face" and representing a white, almost featureless abstraction of the human face. Today, you find these decorated with any number of colors, feathers, and jewels, though the original was strictly white and was sometimes also called the *larva,* from the Latin for "ghost."

The bauta is never worn without a black silk hood; in fact, the word *bauta* more correctly applies to the hood from which the mask takes its name. The mask and hood are always worn with a black tricorn hat and a loose black cloak of the same color, the *tabarro*.

THE FORTUNE TELLER, PIETRO LONGHI, C. 1756. NATIONAL GALLERY, LONDON.

While women sometimes wore the bauta, the characteristic mask for females, never worn by men, is the oval-shaped *moretta.* It takes its name from the black or very dark velvet with which it is made (*moro* meaning "dark") and covers the center of the face, including the mouth. At first glance, the effect is rather startling, as if a neat oval has simply been excised from the wearer's face, leaving a black hole.

Very popular in the eighteenth century, the moretta would be quite surprising to see at today's Carnival, as the mode of fixing the mask to the face is highly inconvenient. Rather than a band or lace to be tied, the moretta was held in place with a button sewn on the reverse, one which is gripped in the teeth. This accounts for the mask's other name, the *muta,* meaning "mute."

Woman wearing a moretta shown in detail, from The Rhinoceros by Pietro Longhi. (Full image on page 48.)

What now sounds unthinkably sexist and oppressive in its day was perceived as offering the wearer a strange kind of freedom. In practical terms, the moretta was free of any hard-to-reach ties and could be whipped off or replaced at a moment's notice. But this is trivial compared to the powerful effect the wearer's silence could impose. She would remain, at her discretion, an object of mystery impossible to read and impossible to engage in conversation (if she so chose). A modern parallel might be recognized in the at once glamorizing and distancing effect of sunglasses worn strictly for style.

The effect of the stark black moretta against pale skin was also considered striking. The Venetian artist of Dutch descent Giovanni Grevembroch (Jan van Grevenbroeck) commented on this in his volume *Venetian Dresses of Almost Every Age Diligently Collected and Painted in the 18th century,* describing a woman who "had her face covered by a black moretta, which created such contrast to the whiteness of the flesh that it shone, making it highly visible."

The moretta, or something like it, was not unique to Venice but was simply a local example of a fashion present in France, England, and Scotland. Called a visard (or vizard), this sort of oval mask, held in place by either laces or the teeth, was particularly popular in Paris of the seventeenth century (though it had disappeared within the next century). Visards can be noted as far back as the sixteenth century, when they served as ladylike accoutrements protecting travelers against sunburn and discouraging unwanted attention.

Though largely restricted to Carnival season, the moretta, like the bauta, was worn at other times, not only as a mark of decorum but in compliance with certain laws. By the late eighteenth century, it was a requirement for females attending the theater, presum-

Parlor of the Nuns, the reception room of the nuns in San Zaccaria, on the day when friends and family members could visit the novices, Giuseppe de Gobbis, late 18th century.

ably because the theater was then regarded with a certain unease. Like the Ridotto's gamblers, theater-goers wearing the moretta were protected from gossip, thus encouraging their attendance and the growth of the institution.

The upper-class moretta, unsurprisingly, was initially forbidden to prostitutes, and violations could be dealt with quite harshly. In 1608, the punishment consisted of flogging and banishment for a period of four years. But the prostitutes in Venice were particularly ambitious in presenting themselves as members of the fashionable set. Thanks to these efforts, by the eighteenth century Venice had come to be regarded as the courtesan capitol of Europe, and by then prostitutes were no longer penalized for wearing the moretta but required to do so by law.

Venice has a noteworthy history of concessions to prostitutes, one that gave birth in the sixteenth century to two curious landmarks, the Ponte delle Tette (Bridge of Tits) and the nearby Fondamenta delle Tette (Canal Path of Tits). According to tradition, the names derived from a crisis faced by the working women via competition from a tide of homosexual activity. An appeal was made to Bishop Antonio Contarini in 1511 to rescue Venetian men from the sin of sodomy (and protect the prostitutes' earnings). The secret weapon in this battle was to be permission for the courtesans to bare their breasts in public. While such permission was not exactly granted, a blind eye was thereafter turned toward the rampant breast-baring that occurred on these sites, and Venetians soon christened the bridge and path with more memorable names.

Homosexual activity was, of course, one of the otherwise forbidden enticements sought out during the libertine season, and there was a particular mask worn to signal availability, one known as the *gnaga*. The name is presumed to come from the word *gnao*

Illustration of Arlecchino (M), his companion Brighella (L) and peasant woman (R) from *Grotesque Comedy in the Drawings of Ottavio Burnacini* (1636-1707).

(Venetian for "meow"), and the half-mask represented a feline's face. The male wearer dressed in drag and might carry a basket containing a mewing kitten, or would carry a toy animal and supply the mewing himself. It's said that Carnival tradition offered a curious loophole permitting an otherwise severely punished behavior: because one's behavior is expected to conform with the disguise chosen, and the *gnaga*-wearer is dressed as a woman, sex with a man represented a sort of righteous compliance. I somewhat doubt this ever was put to the test in court, but it's a splendidly carnivalesque bit of sophistry.

COMIC MASKS AND SNAKEBITES

While the bauta and moretta are the classic masks of Venice, representative of an old aristocratic ethos, they do not evoke the essential madness of Carnival as do the *maschere buffe*, the comic masks.

These half-masks are easily recognized by their grotesque features, like the long, pointed noses of the *Zanni* or *Scaramuccia* (Scaramouche) or the lumpy black grimace of the *Arlecchino* (Harlequin). A notable exception is the mask of Columbina, lover of Arlecchino, whose more delicate mask extends not far beyond the eyes.

These figures were borrowed from the *commedia dell'arte* of the sixteenth to eighteenth centuries, an early theatrical form devoted to comedy (as the name suggests) and performed by actors for whom acting was their profession or trade (*arte*). Our word *zany*, as well as the name of the Carnival mask, comes from the *Zanni,* originally applied to a comic servant character but later generalized to describe almost any sort of clown of the *commedia.*

Commedia performances made use of stock figures, like Arlecchino, whose appearance (mask and costume) and foolish or scheming propensities were recognizably consistent, if comically absurd. While performances usually followed some minimal script, much of the action consisted of improvisations around a time-tested routine, the *lazzo* (joke), whether it be a bit of physical comedy or some formulaic exchange of dialogue. Songs, dances, and acrobatic feats could also be incorporated.

"Entertainment given every day by the Charlatans of Piazza San Marco..." from *The Dress of Venetian Men and Women*, Giacomo Franco, c. 1610.

Commedia dell'arte was largely developed in Bergamo but quickly spread to Venice. The few days it might take a troupe to travel from Bergamo to Venice would be particularly worthwhile during the long Carnival season when the city swelled with visitors.

While always bustling, the Piazza San Marco during Carnival would have been famously jammed with entertainers and merchants vying for attention. Actors performed on temporary stages improvised over barrels and trestles. Strolling musicians wandered about. Puppet shows were performed and trained animals exhibited.

Carnival visitors would also encounter St. Mark's famous mountebanks. After drawing crowds with short warm-up performances by acrobats, musicians, or clowns, the charlatan would launch into his pitch for his favorite nostrum, often with as much theatricality as the entertainers preceding him.

The English traveler Thomas Coryat, in his 1611 book *Coryat's Crudities: Hastily Gobbled Up in Five Months of Travels in France, Italy etc.* paints a vivid picture of the Venetian mountebanks, who

> *do much to make this city famous ... because there is a greater concourse of them in Venice than elsewhere, and that of the better sort and the most eloquent fellows.*

Shrove Thursday celebration on Piazzetta, Gabriel Bella, c. 1779-92, Pinacoteca Querini Stampalia, Venice.

After describing a mountebank allowing himself to be bitten by "poisonous vipers" to demonstrate the miraculous efficacy of his cure, Coryat marvels over another remarkable performer, who would

> *hack and gash his naked arm with a knife most pitifully to behold, so that the blood has streamed out in great abundance, and by and by after he has applied a certain oil unto it, wherewith he has ... stanched the blood, and so thoroughly healed the wounds ... we could not possibly perceive the least token of a gash.*

While on the topic of quacks, it should be noted that the plague doctor mask now so firmly associated with Venice Carnival is not traditional and would hardly be welcome in a city that was famously devasted by the Black Death. My guess is that it's a twentieth-century creation by a mask-maker who noticed tourists calling his long-nosed Scaramuccia a "plague doctor" and capitalized on the interest.

FEATS OF STRENGTH AND DARING

From the sixteenth century onward, the Piazza San Marco was also the site of annual feats of daredevilry on Shrove Thursday (the Thursday preceding Shrove Tuesday).

The Powers of Hercules, Allegory of Fame, Francesco Guardi (attrib), c. 1730-40.

This event's original name was the Flight of the Turk in honor of a Turkish ropewalker who undertook to cross the square on a line anchored on one end to an anchored ship and the other to St. Mark's Campanile. After ascending the belltower, he made his way down, stopping at the ducal balcony to present flowers to the doge. The homage would have helped ensure municipal support, transforming the stunt into a respected and long-standing tradition. Over the years, other ropewalkers followed suit, adding various flamboyant gestures: somersaults on the wire, multiple synchronized performers, etc. After one aerialist floated over the square wearing angel wings, others stole his look and the event became the Flight of the Angel.

In 1680, an acrobat by the name of Sante da Ca' Lezze reportedly ascended the belltower on a horse, though I'm not sure how that was accomplished. In 1706, an aerialist riding a wooden satyr flew over the square, followed by another in a boat and a third with firework mortars fixed to him. On another occasion, a small child in a basket was sent plummeting down a zipline to present the doge with flowers.

The heroics came to a sudden end when in 1759 an acrobat belonging to a prominent family fell to his death, after which a large wooden dove replaced the human performer

A procession through a town square with figures dressed in Comedia Dell'Arte costumes, Venetian School, 18th century.

and the event became the Flight of the Dove. For nearly forty years, the mechanized dove showered spectators with rose petals and confetti, until the custom was abandoned at the fall of the Most Serene Republic in 1797. In 2001, however, the spectacle was resurrected as the Flight of the Angel, with celebrities and athletes recruited to suit up as angels and make the ride.

Another Carnival spectacle to be witnessed on the Piazza San Marco were acrobatic competitions known as *le Forze d'Ercole* (the powers of Hercules). Performed to musical accompaniment, these events saw two teams competing to build the tallest human pyramid, and some of them reportedly reached eight stories. Pyramids could be constructed in various ways, with performers assuming configurations bearing colorful names such as the Colossus of Rhodes, Bella Venezia, the Case of Mohammed, and the Duck. Begun in 1705, the event was also staged at times on barges and stages constructed over the Grand Canal.

THE BRIDGE BATTLES

Thanks to the city's unique layout, the obvious spaces for entertainment were the squares, but canal bridges could also serve the purpose. The curious name still designating one of these alludes to the particular game enjoyed there: Ponte dei Pugni (Bridge of Fists).

Since the thirteenth century, both fists and sticks were used in mock battles staged on these bridges for Carnival, New Year, and certain other occasions. Spectators crowded balconies and gridlocked the canals with boats to watch often bloody fights between the

Competition on the Ponte dei Pugni in Venice, Joseph Heintz the Younger, 1673.

Castellani and Nicolotti, representing neighborhoods on either side of the Grand Canal.

Staged on several bridges in addition to the namesake, these *battagliole* (little battles), were followed by Venetians with enthusiasm no less fanatical than that of modern football or soccer devotees. Their cheers, whistles, hisses, and waving handkerchiefs determined the winner (presumably guided by the relative amounts of blood shed or number of bodies shoved into the canal). At times, spectators also joined the melee or expressed their opinions by throwing tiles torn from roofs. Not infrequently, or surprisingly, the militia was called upon to break up these events.

To avoid these free-for-alls, team membership was clearly indicated by the opponents' red and black scarves. The Castellani (red) were largely sailors or ship-builders from the eastern neighborhoods around Castello, while the Nicolotti (black) were primarily fishermen from the western parish of San Nicolò dei Mendicoli.

These two factions also competed at forming human pyramids in *le Forze d'Ercole.* In fact, that competition was explicitly created in 1705 to replace these bridge events, after one of these mock battles got a little too real, devolving into stone-throwing and stabbings.

The Castellani–Nicolotti rivalry goes back centuries, with mock battles first noted in Venetian chronicles in 1369, though not taking place specifically on bridges until 1421. While fistfights were the order of the day after 1600, before this more brutal battles were conducted with sticks.

Fighters not only struck each other with sticks but sharpened the ends and used them to jab opponents. Often leather or wooden shields were employed, sometimes iron helmets. A few even armored their chests with leather, metal, or chainmail.

When an exhibition match was held for the visiting French monarch Henry III in 1547, the horrified king remarked, "This is too small to be war, but too cruel to be a game!" Unsurprisingly, these games were intermittently outlawed (but later reinstated).

The Venetian Carnival battles were not without parallel. Similar battles with wooden weapons took place in Pisa, and in Florence, from the sixteenth into the seventeenth century, guilds of dyers and weavers fought it out. In many ways, these sports were simply the plebeian equivalent of the jousts and tournaments of the aristocratic classes.

Professional soldiers likewise staged mock battles in Venice, as in 1458, when two troupes of seventy men clashed in the Piazza San Marco with the goal of capturing a model castle set up before the doge's palace. By 1480, when horses were banned from city streets, combats like this shifted to the water, with teams in opposing boats attempting to overturn each other with their oars.

While mock battles between professional soldiers served to test their readiness for war, battles with civilian combatants also assured rulers of their capacity to serve as soldiers. Perhaps more important to city leaders, the very real local rivalries offered political benefits. Following the ancient Roman principle *divide et impera* (divide and rule), these games made it unlikely that a united populace might organize a general uprising.

TWELVE PIGS MUST DIE

The political might of the Republic was celebrated in another strange and bloody festivity recreating a moment of Venetian triumph. Taking place on Fat Thursday, the killing and butchering of twelve pigs and a bull echoes both the Venetian bull "hunts" and to some extent the Roman events at Testaccio. The swine in this case were stand-ins for the twelve vassals of the Austrian Ulrich II von Treven, who was in turn represented by the bull. Ulrich was the Patriarch of Aquileia, an ancient Roman settlement roughly seventy miles northeast of Venice. Uncomfortably close to the Patriarchate of Aquileia lay the island of Grado, also home to a patriarchate ruled by Enrico Dandolo, member of a noble Venetian family.

There had long been conflicts between the two patriarchates, but by the twelfth century, with Dandolo's link to Venice, the stakes had risen, especially so since Ulrich of Aquileia was allied with the Emperor Frederick Barbarossa, who had an interest in acquiring Venice for the Holy Roman Empire.

In 1162, when Ulrich's men invaded Grado, Dandolo fled to Venice, seeking aid from Doge Vitale Michiel II. The Venetian forces were immediately dispatched against Ulrich, burned several of his castles in Friuli, and took hostage the Patriarch of Aquileia and his twelve vassals. Through the intervention of Pope Alexander III, however, Ulrich was released.

According to legend, the condition for this release would be a symbolic tribute offered annually by Aquileia, namely one bull, twelve pigs, and twelve loaves of bread. The bull went to the doge, the pigs went to the Republic's senators, and the bread was to be provided to prisoners. This payment was first made on Shrove Thursday of 1162. Conveniently, this allowed for five days of feasting on the meat before Lent.

The doge himself was said to originally be the one to kill the bull, while the swine were dispatched by senators, but later we hear of blacksmiths doing the job with their hammers and butchers standing by to cut up the carcasses. Dogs were also used to torment and tire the animals before they were killed. It's said that the people of Venice so enjoyed the spectacle that the Republic continued to provide the animals once the pope abolished the patriarchates of Aquileia and Grado, creating in their place the Patriarchate of Venice. Other accounts also mention the doge and senators destroying small replicas of Ulrich's castles.

By the sixteenth century, it was officially members of the Butcher's Guild tasked with killing the pigs and it was the strongest member of the Guild of Ironworkers who decapitated the bull with a special sword forged by guild members.

It was a matter of crowd-pleasing importance that this be done with a single stroke of the massive sword. And ideally the head would be severed from the spouting neck without allowing the blade itself to touch the ground. Later in the century, the pigs were no longer slaughtered, but the Fat Thursday bull execution remained traditional until the fall of the Republic in 1797. This gory spectacle made such an impression upon citizens of the Republic that it is still remembered in a Venetian expression meaning, "Let's get to the point," i.e., *"Tagliamo la testa al toro"*—let's cut the head off the bull.

FESTIVITY OF THE MARYS

Another ancient Carnival celebration, resurrected (after a fashion) in 1999, is the *Festa delle Marie* (Festivity of the Marys). It was celebrated over several days from the eve of January 31 to February 2. Its beginning on January 31 is connected by Venetians not to the new year but to the transfer of the relics of the city's patron, St. Mark, from Egypt to Venice on January 31, 828, both a civic and an ecclesiastic holiday for the city.

February 2 today is usually said to mark the start of the Venetian Carnival, though in the Middle Ages, when the season began on December 26, the *Festa delle Marie* would have fallen in the middle of the season.

The confusing nomenclature around February 2 (Candlemas/Feast of the Presentation/Feast of the Purification) comes from the biblical story in which the infant Jesus, in accordance with Jewish law, is presented at the Temple along with the prescribed sacrifice of two doves, offered by his mother to ritually purify herself after pregnancy. The reference to candles just denotes the day as one on which church candles are blessed. While candles and the infant Christ played their role in the Venetian holiday, it was the figure of Mary celebrated in the *Festa delle Marie*—and not just the one Blessed Mother but a multiplicity of Marys in a festivity also sometimes called the Feast of the Twelve Marys.

The significance of the *Festa* is likewise confusing, as there are multiple legends explaining its origin and meaning differently. The celebration recreated in 1999 is simply

a cross between a beauty pageant and a historical costume pageant during which twelve unmarried women ("Marys") in Renaissance garb parade and make appearances throughout the city.

LEGEND ONE: DOWRY GIFTS AND MASS WEDDINGS

The stipulation that the women be unmarried connects the modern recreation to an origin legend emphasizing gifts presented by the doge to brides-to-be on January 31. The doge's beneficence not only honored St. Mark on the date of his relics' translation but also was meant to assist families otherwise unable to provide dowries necessary for marriage.

These gifts are usually described in terms of lavish jewelry donned by the women in the celebrations or items otherwise ostentatiously displayed. This detail is important to another legend woven into the story by the fifteenth century.

BRIDES OF VENICE, JOZEF VAN LERIUS, 1871.

LEGEND TWO: PIRATES AND MASS WEDDINGS

This elaboration has pirates—tempted by the exhibition of riches and beautiful young women—swooping in to steal both. In short order, they are naturally defeated, women and riches are rescued, and Venetian heroism exemplified.

An earlier thirteenth-century version emphasizes the abduction of the women over any dowries. This tale asserts that mass weddings were part of January 31 celebrations and that the women assembled at the cathedral were abducted during the middle of wedding ceremonies by a band of Adriatic pirates led by a certain Gajolo or Gaiolus.

Whatever the origin story presented, the glorious victory of the Venetian Republic is key, as is the number of women rescued—always twelve.

AN ACTUAL HISTORICAL TRADITION

The widely circulated pirate abduction tale makes for a good story but is almost certainly just a bit of mythmaking. Nor is there necessarily evidence that the *Festa* ever involved gifts of dowries. Inspiration for that idea might be found in lavish communal displays of largesse which accompanied the first day of the *Festa*. But these did not come from the doge, Church, or city coffers but were assembled by particular *contrade* or parishes.

Every year, two *contrade* were chosen to host the events of the *Festa*. Given the number of *contrade* in the city, this meant that duties fell to a parish only every thirty years. This provided plenty of time to bank resources and lent a sort of go-for-broke quality to the festivities. For participants it could be a once-in-a-lifetime opportunity to best their neighbors.

Martin(o) da Canal, in his *Les estoires de Venise*, written between 1267 and 1275, describes two sequential *contrada* processions on January 30, the eve of the celebration of St. Mark's relics. Festivities held on the Piazza San Marco featured trumpet players, flag-waving children, a choir, and the parish priest outfitted in gold velvet, carried in an ornamented chair. Male youths bore silver trays stacked with sweets and silver jugs brimming with wine, sharing these most eagerly with marriageable women but also with the presiding priest and choristers. Perhaps the young males' preferential treatment of single women is somehow related to the purported dowry tradition, but it's hard to know.

Festivities on January 31, according to da Canal, featured two groups representing the two *contrade* processing from the Piazza San Marco to the Church of Santa Maria Formosa. The festive groups again featured trumpets, silver platters, and children with flags, accompanied now by banner carriers and more than a hundred older children bearing silver crosses. Bringing up the rear in one procession was the parish priest borne on a litter and this time costumed as the Virgin Mary. The two would later in the day appear in a play representing the Annunciation, in which Mary is told by the Angel Gabriel that she is pregnant with the infant Christ.

AT LAST, THOSE "TWELVE MARYS"

In the evening, twelve feasts were hosted in parish homes by six families chosen from each *contrada*. The centerpiece of these was an exquisitely adorned statue of the Holy Mother. Da Canal describes the

> *twelve Marys dressed so richly and so beautifully, that it is a wonder to see. They each have a crown of gold on their heads, with precious stones, and are attired in clothes of gold, and on all the clothes are ornaments of gold, with precious stones and pearls in abundance.*

Hosts of the Marys opened their homes on the following day to further exhibit the statues, and on February 2 a festive cortège of twelve boats (six per *contrada*) bore the figures through the canals. Four of the six boats displayed the statues accompanied by a company of women and girls. Bishops, priests, and deacons in rich vestments rode in another, and the last bore a troupe of armed guards. Some have speculated that the guard was there to protect the statues, or at least the jewels adorning them, which were lent from the city treasury.

While this all sounds very dignified and elegant, a rather different picture emerges roughly seventy-five years after da Canal provided his account. In 1349, the Grand Council passed legislation regulating the event, demanding,

> *...that scandal-provoking conduct cease .... [F]rom now on, the throwing of turnips or any other object is, on pain of a fine of 100 deniers, banned for the duration of the festival.*

It's quite possible that the heated rivalry between *contrade* led one group to pelt the other's procession, but this could just as easily represent general spillover from the Carnival sport of egg-throwing. Aside from reverential processions, there were, after all, other more carnivalesque entertainments associated with the *Festa delle Marie*, that is, the *ludi mariani* (games of the Marys) including races, hunts, and dances.

Venetian efforts to control the wilder side of Carnival eventually prevailed over the following centuries. By the 1800s, the idea of Carnival had crystallized into the image we know today. Gone were the medieval bull-hunts, butchered pigs, and bridge battles. Even the "game of eggs" was forgotten. Frozen in time, Venice Carnival offered only a backward-looking fantasy of masks, cloaks, and coquettishness.

While this refined eighteenth-century memento may now be the best known image of the European Carnival, we'll next explore a very different path taken in Germany, where fools and wild men became the season's heroes.

· CHAPTER VI ·

GERMAN FOOLS

HOW A TWELFTH-CENTURY SHIP HAULED OVERLAND
BY BACCHIC REVELERS
IS FALSELY LIKENED TO CARNIVAL;

TRUE ORIGINS
OF
CARNIVAL PARADES

REVEALED IN THE SCHEMBARTLAUF OF OLD NUREMBERG,
ITS COSTUMED PARTICIPANT INCL.

THE WILD MAN

& HIS WIFE,
ITS WONDROUS FLOATS CALLED "HELLS,"
ITS SHIP OF FOOLS & DEVILS INSPIRED BY A BOOK;
THE DEVILISH CARNIVAL FOOL & THE MEDIEVAL CHURCH;

ATTRIBUTES OF THE

SWABIAN-ALEMANNIC FOOL,

HIS MASK, COSTUME, BELLS, & BOOK;
HOW HE IS ACCOMPANIED BY
BEARS, DEVILS, WITCHES, GHOSTS

SPIRITS OF FOLKLORE.

INTO THE WILD

A goal of this book is to trace the history of Carnival to its unfamiliar roots. The examples of medieval Rome provided this in spades as its celebrations are virtually unrecognizable as Carnival. Our look at Venice found startlingly unfamiliar medieval customs alongside the early use of masks. While masked balls after the Venetian model later became extremely common where Carnival is celebrated, it is impossible for a city uniquely built on canals to offer a complete and universal prototype for celebrations. With this chapter's discussion of historical German celebrations, we'll examine, among other things, the origin of annual parades that helped give shape to Carnival as we now understand it.

Another goal of this book reflects a personal bias that motivated me to write my earlier book on the Krampus—a fascination with the monstrous, grotesque, and fantastic. We have already seen a trickle of this in the history thus far, but in Germany that trickle becomes a stream. The half-human figure of the Wild Man becomes prominent, echoing the Kalends beasts of the Dark Ages, and we witness the birth of the Carnival Fool, a figure grotesquely mirroring and inverting all that is proper and prudent.

Unlike the urban Carnivals of Rome and Venice, the German Carnival (specifically in the southwest) also demonstrates a yet unseen connection to rural traditions and folklore. The absurd backwards ways of the Fool reach into medieval tradition and mock the aristocratic Enlightenment-era milieu of the Venetian Carnival and its masked intrigues.

PAGAN WAGONS

Folkloric, or backward-looking, qualities of the German Carnival have prompted some scholars to seek its origins in ancient heathen tradition. For those, a tantalizing passage in Tacitus's *Germania* offers a prototype for Carnival parades.

Tacitus, describing the situation at the end of the first century, writes that certain Germanic tribes:

> *share a common worship of Nerthus, or Mother Earth. They believe that she takes part in human affairs, riding in a chariot among her people ... After that, the chariot, the vestments, and (believe it if you will) the goddess herself, are cleansed in a secluded lake.*

A "Mother Earth" designated by the name Nerthus is not to be found in any other texts, and no consensus has been reached as to whether that name might represent some permutation of a known deity. However, the ritual use of wagons among Germanic peoples is supported by archeological finds, such as the ceremonial Dejbjerg wagons discovered in a bog in western Denmark.

PREVIOUS: FASTNACHT AMUSEMENTS IN THE BLACK FOREST, ILLUSTRATION FROM *ILLUSTRIERTE CHRONIK DER ZEIT*, G. HEINE, 1890

CARNIVAL FLOATS ON THE MEIR SQUARE IN ANTWERP, ERASMUS DE BIE, 1670.

Unfortunately, the religious nature of the Nerthus procession has little in common with the Carnival parades appearing in Germany in the fourteenth century. And there is also that small matter of those thirteen intervening centuries.

There are, however, certain accounts from that interim period that sometimes draw comparisons. Writing in the sixth century, Gregory of Tours, in his *Gloria confessorum*, describes a Burgundian bishop encountering rural folk "drawing this statue about in a cart, for the prosperity of their fields and vineyards." He relates this (erroneously or not) to another anecdote involving a long-lost statue of Berecynthia, identified with the Great Mother, Cybele. It's a tantalizing "pagan survival" anecdote but not easily related to other Germanic customs and particularly unrelated to Carnival.

Much more intriguing, and certainly more carnivalesque, is the anecdote related by the Flemish abbot, composer, and chronicler Rudolf of St. Trond in his *Gesta abbatum trudonensium* (*Deeds of the Abbots of Trond*). It describes a "diabolical trick" instigated in 1135 by an unnamed German "rustic":

> *Having gotten the confidence of the magistrates and help from frivolous men who delight in jokes and novelties, he constructed a ship in the nearby woods, and having attached wheels to it, made it movable on land. He also got the authorities to allow it to be dragged by ropes over the shoulders of the weavers from Kornelmünster to Aachen.*

PERFORMERS OF THE SWABIAN-ALEMANNIC FASTNACHT IN BAD HINDELANG, BAVARIA.

After dragging it for roughly seven miles between these German cities, the weavers haul it another twenty-five miles over the border into the Netherlands, where it's fitted with a mast and sail, and then roughly forty-six miles further into Belgium, toward Sint-Truiden, where the abbot from the author's monastery gets word,

> *hearing that the ship, so unpropitiously assembled, was approaching our city without aid of mast or oar, with a display of such paganism, was preaching in a prophetic spirit to the people that they should avoid involvement with it because they would be ensnared through this in the deceit of the evil spirit.*

He repeatedly preaches to the citizens of Sint-Truiden, sharing his misgivings about the "idol of evil." But they pay no heed.

Instead, filled with excitement and enthusiasm, they installed this fatal "Trojan Horse" in the middle of the city square. The weavers of the city received the invitation to come without delay to the sacrilegious vigils before this idol.

The abbot speculates that the ship is a:

> *dwelling—whether of Bacchus, Venus, Neptune or Mars, I do not know, or, perhaps better, of all the evil spirits—a gathering of various musicians singing filthy songs unworthy of the Christian religion.*

Just as evening was coming on, just as the moon was rising, a mass of women, drop-

SNOW CANNOT STOP THE ROTTWEIL FASTNACHT.

ping all womanly modesty, hearing the racket of this merrymaking, came out with their hair let down, some half-undressed, some wearing only their shifts, and broke in and shamelessly joined those leading the crowds around the ship. You might see there sometimes a thousand of both sexes singing an outrageous and shameless sea-chantey until the middle of the night.

The festivities continued for more than twelve days, until the town council demanded that it be removed. Planning to next haul the ship to Louvain, they are forbidden entry to the city. After this, the narrative redirects to conflicts between Louvain and its neighbors, and we sadly hear no more of the devil-ship.

I hardly know what to make of this incident, assuming it has some basis in fact. That it was actually some kind of pagan temple on wheels seems to me primarily the writer's pious way of explaining behavior he finds devilish. Was it rather an insanely involved lark on the part of the weaver's guild? There's no reference to Carnival in the passage, but various guilds did historically fund and produce Carnival entertainment—but this only within an organized municipal framework, not as an improvised journey of no return. In any case, it does seem like a good time.

FASTNACHT AND FOLKLORE

Words used for Carnival in Germany reflect different styles of celebration. The Latinate *Karneval* is used mostly in the western Rhineland (excluding a pocket in the southwest). East of that, the alternative is *Fasching*, derived from *Fastnacht*. Though linguists now debate this, until the twentieth century the etymology of *Fastnacht* was commonly derived from *Fastenzeit*—Fasting(time) and *Nacht* (eve)—thus, Lenten Eve. This is hardly the only word used in these regions; local dialects insist variously on *Fasnacht*, *Fassenacht*, and especially *Fasnet*.

The uniquely folkloric quality of German Carnival mentioned earlier is associated with areas where the term *Fastnacht* (or variations) are used, i.e., southwestern Germany, specifically Baden-Württemberg, Franconia (northern Bavaria), and Hesse, as well as the German-speaking region of Switzerland and into western Austria. More specifically, this style of Carnival (the primary focus of this chapter) is called the Swabian-Alemannic Fastnacht. The name refers to the Germanic tribes settling in these lands, the Swabians and Alemanni.

While the Rhineland's *Karneval* features bands marching in military-style uniforms and floats heavy on political and social satire, the Swabian-Alemannic Fastnacht is characterized by its carved wooden masks representing wild men, witches, devils, and legendary creatures. The figure of the Carnival Fool, however, appears in all German celebrations, *Fasching*, *Fasnacht*, or *Karneval*.

In the nineteenth century, when Germany's Carnival customs assumed their current form, *Karneval* regions reflected the dominance of Prussia and its love of uniformity, but Swabian-Alemannic customs reflected highly localized traditions, preserved especially in more rural regions. The aesthetic was also influenced by romanticism's enthusiasm for "primitive" pre-Enlightenment cultures, the growing interest in folklore, and obviously by early folk-tale collectors such as the Grimms. While the Swabian-Alemannic Carnival customs consolidated in that era rarely represented an unbroken tradition from the past, they embraced these elements with newfound enthusiasm.

"GROTESQUE GAMES"

The earliest reference to Fastnacht ("*vasnaht*" in the text) appears in a story written between 1200 and 1210, the medieval romance *Parzival* by Wolfram von Eschenbach. The section is headed: "How the women around the castle of the Counts of Hirschberg-Dollnstein performed grotesque games."

The comic episode involves Parzival's friend and fellow knight Gawan (Gawain) who, at the beginning of the tale, is intimately engaged with the Princess Antikonie when suddenly they are attacked by the townspeople of Schampfanzun. Fleeing to a tower, they discover an immense chessboard, which Gawan employs as a shield. As they begin hurling the heavy stone chessmen down on the angry mob, von Eschenbach comments on Princess Antikonie's manner of fighting, saying, that she

> *acquitted herself there like a true knight, she was seen fighting at Gawan's side with such spirit that the peddler-women at Dollnstein never fought better at vasnaht, for they do so as a frolic and exert themselves without cause.*

The text seems to refer to mock battles or games engaged in by women of a certain

"Storming the Schembart Hell of 1539" from the Schembartbuch of the Pickertschen Collection, Nuremberg City Library.

class (peddlers perhaps selling goods from the country). That the activities are restricted to women reflects Carnival's spirit of inversion, with women assuming the aggressive role in medieval society.

The tradition of a Carnival exclusive to women (a *Weiberfastnacht*) persists in modern Germany. In the Rhineland, it's celebrated on the Thursday before Ash Wednesday, the day on which Carnival begins in earnest. A tradition of the day involves women snipping off neckties worn by men, a custom that has not disappeared even in these casual times, when men will happily don neckties just for the occasion. The Swabian-Alemannic traditions include a *Weiberfastnacht* on days varying by region, and the town square of Dollnstein regards the women of von Eschenbach's text as local heroes, boasting a "peddler woman" sculpture atop a fountain in its town square.

THE SCHEMBARTLAUF

In the fourteenth century, Nuremberg played host to a dramatic explosion of Carnival activity called the *Schembartlauf.* These costumed parades were beautifully documented every year in visual catalogs, the "Schembart books," eighty of which still exist in museum archives and provide illustrations for this section.

CARNIVAL TOURNAMENT WITH ACCOMPANYING FOOLS FROM MARX WALTHER'S *TOURNAMENT BOOK WITH FAMILY CHRONICLE FOR 1506 TO 1511*.

Those familiar with the unruly processions of costumed devils known as a *Krampuslauf* will recognize the latter part of the word as meaning "run" or "walk." The other part of the word refers to the masks worn by those taking part in the processions. *Schem* can be related to the modern German word *Schemen*, for a silhouette, shadow, or ghost. *Schem* compares with *Larve*, another old German word for masks, taken from the Latin *larva*, which also means "ghost." Both German- and Italian-speaking regions tend to use this Latin designation (in Italian, *larva*) exclusively for Carnival masks of the carved wood variety. *Schemen* is also the source of the name of a masked Carnival procession in the Austrian town of Imst, the *Schemenlaufen*. It's been suggested that the *bart* in *Schembart* simply carries the modern German meaning of "beard," but masks depicted are rarely bearded, so that issue stands open.

As with the weavers' guild said to have been responsible for the mysterious wheeled ship earlier discussed, it is the butchers' guild of Nuremberg that staged the first Schembart activities. This consisted of a large dance in the town square. Illustrations show several dozen dancers formed in long chains linked by rings which look like sausage. Along with sausage, products of their trade (beef and mutton) are represented by an ox and a sheep depicted on standards held by dancers at each end. Other figures of more cryptic significance include three hobbyhorses, including a ram and unicorn, something like a donkey holding in its mouth a goose, and a man holding an apple tree or Tree of Paradise. In certain illustrations members of another guild indispensable to the butcher's art, the knife-makers, parade with brandished knives.

The first of these dances, held in 1349, was supposedly staged to honor the butchers for their loyalty to the town council. During a period of riots instigated by other guilds, the butchers are supposed to have warned council members of an assassination plot. In another version, a butcher provides refuge to a councilor fleeing a murderous mob and is joined by fellow butchers in fighting them off.

In return for the butchers' risk to life and limb, so the story goes, permission was

Costumes from 15th-16th century. Schembart Books.

granted to hold the public dance. This seems a rather onerous price to pay for the privilege of offering public entertainment, and it's more than possible that this origin story is merely a fable told to encourage general allegiance to the council.

A more plausible explanation of the festival's origin involves the Lenten fast. As the meatless days approached, appreciation of the city's butchers and their products would automatically increase—as would their revenues. Wishing to show their gratitude for these seasonal profits and as a public relations gesture, the butchers may have used the money to finance public entertainments. Conversely, the impending loss of income over Lent might spur the guild to organize events as a form of last-minute promotion of their trade. Later accounts also mention money directly collected by costumed participants.

"Artichoke" pyrotechnic device depicted in Schembart Book, 16th century.

The original dance did not showcase those masked figures that came to dominate the Schembartlauf. It was only toward the middle of the fifteenth century that the focus was on the runners ("runners" being a standard translation for *Läufer*, those in the *Lauf*).

Originally, the runners only provided crowd control and cleared the square for the dance. To do so, they employed fireworks (always an excellent means of dispersing crowds!). Rather than scattering these on the cobblestones, runners shot showers of sparks

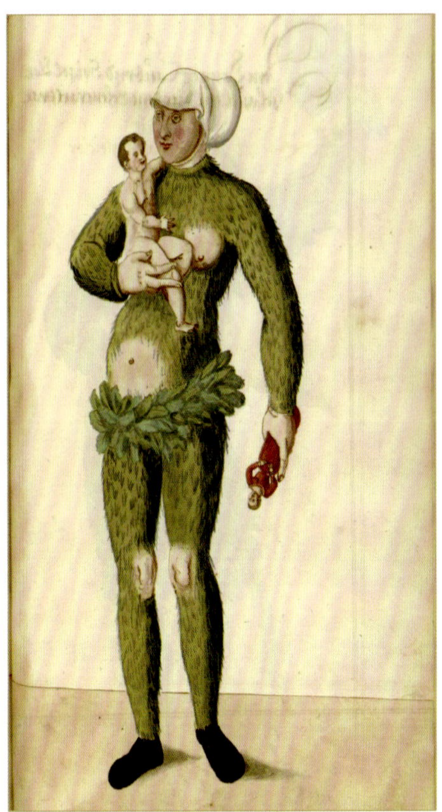

Costumed wild man and wild woman with child depicted in the Schembart book, 1600.

from handheld launchers that look for all the world like impossibly large artichokes. Some have interpreted these objects as bundles of green leaves containing pyrotechnics. (This strikes me as highly unworkable, but if anyone can explain to me how a bundle of leaves is charged with powder or pyrotechnic loads, ignited, and recharged, I'm all ears.)

These puzzling "artichokes" are at first more prominent in the Schembart books than the masks. In fact, it is easy to not at first recognize the masks as such, as they are easily mistaken for the runners' own faces; only when one notices their expressionless uniformity do they read as masks.

Early costumes are less elaborate, usually white suits with straps of bells worn at the waists and beneath the knee. In numerous images, the runners' identity as butchers is indicated by a small meat cleaver worn on the chest. As a teasing reminder of the meatless days ahead, some of the runners are seen carrying baskets of fish or crabs, proffering fistfuls of salted herring. Several books from the late 1450s show another runner wearing a money box, apparently for soliciting donations to the guild.

By the middle of the fifteenth century, interest in the Schembartlauf had grown to such an extent that those outside the butchers' guild were also eager to participate. Eventually young men from aristocratic families bought their way in and began vying to create

Wild Man and Wild Woman, Hans Guldenmond, 1545. Woodcut is based on illustration by Hans Schäufelein accompanying Hans Sachs's *Lament of the Wild People over the Faithless World.*

more impressive costumes. In Schembart books, they appear masked but recognizable thanks to the family arms accompanying their images. They are often shown holding "artichokes" but also pikes, with which they apparently marched. Their white linen suits are now painted with rosettes and twining branches, diamond patterns, stripes, suns, moons and stars, shamrocks, flames, and thistles.

Alongside these are more striking figures dressed in suits encrusted with nuts or dice,

"HELL" FLOATS FROM NUREMBERG SCHEMBART BOOK, C. 1590-1640: DRAGON AND GIANT FOOL.

fluttering with peacock plumes, or covered in a shaggy layer of documents fixed with wax seals. There are also mythical beings: a hairy devil with devil child, a bristly boar-headed monster, a bird-headed creature with female breasts. Particularly prominent are the beings from the forest, the wild men and wild women. The male is majestically bearded, wearing a mossy suit and a crown and girdle of ivy. Slung over his shoulder is an uprooted tree, with a tiny human dangling from its branches for scale. The female is similarly mossy and girdled but, strangely, wears a bonnet and maternally cradles a child.

Forest-dwelling beings play a role in the legends of many countries, but the wild man became especially important in Germany in the fourteenth to sixteenth centuries. While German folklore is replete with woodsy, leafy, mossy beings (e.g., *Schratten, Holzleute, Moosleute*), the wild man and his wild woman (the *Wildleute*) were not regarded as beings of the fairy realm but rather another tribe or race of humans. While his legendary strength led to him becoming a frequent emblem in German heraldry, the species also was known for those more human traits exemplified in the maternal wild woman cradling her child.

In northern Renaissance culture, the *Wildleute* came to be regarded as a sort of pure Edenic race. In 1513, the German poet and playwright Hans Sachs composed a poem expressing precisely this view. His "Lament of the Wild People over the Faithless World" not only enumerates the evil propensities of mankind but presents these woodland races as having once belonged to civilization but having withdrawn to the forest to avoid mankind's corruption. Sachs was a citizen of Nuremberg at the time it hosted the Schembartlauf and was known for writing plays presented at Carnival, so it's easy to imagine his poem presented theatrically by an actor borrowing a moss suit and beard from one of the runners.

But in reality it seems wild men weren't always exemplars of virtue. In 1469, the mayor and town council decreed "neither the wild men nor others, shall run after people to make them give money, sizing them up, or using force." He goes on to complain about

"HELL" FLOATS FROM NUREMBERG SCHEMBART BOOK, C. 1590-1640: COCKATRICE AND ELEPHANT.

other actions of the runners (not necessarily the wild man), decrying "licentious, immodest," and "uncivilized" behavior, including "skits and rhymes" using "impolite words and gestures." Some of this may have occurred in taverns or other localities runners were known to visit outside official activities on the square. In one of the illustrations, we even see a runner looking up at a balcony poised to throw an egg in a sort of German version of the *giuoco degli ovi.*

THE HELLS

By 1457, the Schembartlauf entered its golden age with the introduction of spectacular floats pulled by the runners. The first of these came in the form of a tremendous dragon, probably augmented with pyrotechnics. The fiery special effects and fearsome imagery these tended to present led to them being referred to as *Höllen* (hells). Those pictured in the Schembart books include a giant shaggy devil devouring women while gripping a severed head, an ogre gobbling children, and a giant fool or jester devouring tiny fools in matching outfits. The towering figures were usually perched atop a castle to magnify their scale. Along with pyrotechnics, they were likely enhanced with mechanically moving parts or puppetry. Costumed devils might ride on the hells, march alongside, or board them as they entered the square.

Less infernal motifs included a battle elephant saddled with a howdah firing cannons, a Fountain of Youth flowing with real water, windmills, towers, a cannon firing an old woman from its mouth, a sort of playground with trees between which acrobats leapt, and an oven into which jesters shoved children.

At least twice, a ship crewed by fools and devils was wheeled into the square. An illustration from one year shows the ship assailed by soldiers and mounted knights as the

SCHEMBART FLOAT OF 1539 CAPTAINED BY LUTHERAN PREACHER ANDREAS OSIANDER WITH CREW OF FOOLS AND DEVILS. DEPICTED IN NUREMBERG SCHEMBART BOOK, C. 1590-1640.

motley crew defended the ship, throwing projectiles from the crow's nest, etc. We even see a pair of wild men getting into the action, aiding the knights and armed with tree trunks. Fireworks might also figure into these sorts of battles, as all the hells were eventually burned or blown up in front of the town hall on Ash Wednesday, as the finale of a theatrical performance.

Many of the hells served as sets for plays, which might explain the illustrations of less remarkable floats lacking spectacular dragons or cannibalistic giants, e.g., those representing the Fountain of Youth, a garden house, and a marketplace. 1518 saw the appearance of a hell representing the legendary Venusberg, the mountain setting for the tale of the knight Tannhäuser, who was seduced by Venus and kept for seven years within her subterranean pleasure palace. A reference in one of the Schembart books lists sixty characters associated with this hell, who are probably performers in a Venusberg play presented for Carnival.

ONE HELL TOO MANY

But in 1539 there arrived one hell too many. That year the Schembartlauf boasted the largest participation ever, with 150 performers, and anticipation was at an all-time high as the event had been on hiatus for the previous fourteen years due to war and plague. There had been other turmoil too. The Protestant Reformation instigated by Martin Luther in 1517 had gained followers in Nuremberg, and many in the city council were not keen on reviving old Carnival customs with Catholic associations. But Nuremberg was hardly of a single mind here.

The hell that rolled into the city square that year was an old favorite, a ship manned by fools and the devil. Among the crew, a black-gowned scholar was positioned as captain. The foolish scholar was a comic standby beloved by the people and had appeared among the fools on deck in the past surrounded by his books, globes, and astrolabes. This scholar, however, was different; he was a theologian, and of the Lutheran variety. In retellings of the incident, this captain either preached a comic sermon while waving a Bible or waved a backgammon board in place of a Bible. In any case, spectators recognized him at once; he was Nuremberg's most prominent Lutheran preacher, Andreas Osiander.

It was a gross miscalculation on the part of the organizers. Osiander was already a divisive figure, and Carnival was already a volatile season. Over the next days, while crowds amused at the targeting of the preacher took to the streets singing popular ballads mocking him, Osiander threw about his considerable weight, scolding the city council for permitting these Catholic frivolities and demanding an end to them. When the people learned that the council was poised to forever ban their beloved Schembartlauf, they formed a menacing mob outside Osiander's home, and troops were called out to disperse them.

While Carnival festivities of a sort continued in Nuremberg, nothing like the Schembartlauf was ever seen again.

SHIP OF FOOLS

The Schembart ship-hells embodied a well-known trope of the day, one popularized by a satirical work written in 1494 by the Swiss humanist and theologian Sebastian Brant, *Das Narrenschiff* ("the ship of fools").

Title page of the 1497 Latin translation of Sebastian Brant's *Ship of Fools.*

Already a popular motif when it was written, the device is used by Brant as a launching point for a series of 112 short satiric poems examining man's vices and foibles. Only appearing in a few of these, the titular ship is manned by 100 fools and bound for the fictional land of Naragonia ("Foolagonia" or "Fool's Paradise" in translations). Brant's yen for wordplay is also responsible for the invention of a St. Grobian (from the German word for "vulgar" or "uncouth"). *Das Narrenschiff* was generously illustrated with over 100 woodcuts, roughly two-thirds of which have been attributed to Albrecht Dürer.

The work was immediately popular, quickly published in several German cities after its original Basel printing, and within four years was translated into Latin, French, and

OPPOSITE: *Ship of Fools*, part of *The Pilgrimage of Life* triptych, Hieronymus Bosch, c. 1494-1510.

THIS LATE MEDIEVAL RELIEF ON THE TOWN HALL OF NÖRDLINGEN, GERMANY, REPRESENTS THE FOOL'S MIRROR. THE FOOL GAZES AT THE SPECTATOR, SAYING (IN THE INSCRIPTION) "NOW THERE ARE TWO OF US."

English. It's often said that either it inspired a triptych of the same name by Hieronymus Bosch, or the book's frontispiece drew inspiration from the Dutch painter's work. The Alsatian preacher Johann Geiler von Kaysersberg made use of Brant's book in his homilies, while in that same region the Franciscan poet and satirist Thomas Murner drew inspiration from Brant for his 1512 publications *The Muster of Fools* and *The Guild of Rogues*.

FOOLISH DEVILS, DEVILISH FOOLS

The playful tomfoolery that comes to mind when one thinks of a Carnival fool only partially describes the figure as conceived in medieval Germany. There is (as with so many things German) a dark undercurrent, in this case an association between the fool and the devil. For this reason, Nurembergers witnessing Brant's *Ship of Fools* visualized as a Schembartlauf ship-hell would not have been surprised to see its crew equally divided between fools and devils. They recognized a bond between the two, that devils were foolish and fools devilish.

With this equation, Carnival's celebration of the fool would seem to welcome diabolical influence, making the upheaval of the season dangerous not only to the social order but to the soul. A secular rationale might justify this period of chaos as a necessary social safety valve releasing chaotic energies in a non-destructive way, but medieval thinkers recognized a different value in Carnival, a theological method in the madness.

A term for Carnival in German is *Narrenzeit*, meaning "time of fools," a season also described by medieval thinkers with the phrase *mundus inversus* (world upside down). The world properly oriented, the godly order of things, St. Augustine analogized as the *Civitate Dei* (City of God), opposing this to the *Civitas diaboli* (City of the Devil). During the upside-down time, the City of God is thrown down and the City of the Devil arises. But this is transitory and false, a passing spectacle of masks and costumes, a sort of participatory mystery play engaged in by the whole community.

Accordingly, the common practice of burning an effigy representing King Carnival on the eve of Ash Wednesday enacts the inevitable end of the devil's reign. The ashy cross

Dance of Death: Death and the Fool, (attrib) J.A. Chovin (1720-1776), after the Basel Dance of Death.

the Christian receives the following day reminds him of the dust to which he will return and the need to put his hope in the eternal City of God, not the transient temptations of the illusory City of the Devil.

In art of the period, Eve's surrender to the devil's temptation is foolish as well as sinful, and this becomes a prototype for a figure known as Mother Folly or the Fool Mother (*Narrenmutter*), a symbolic representation of foolishness inherited like original sin or, more proverbially, passed "in the mother's milk."

Pieter Bruegel the Elder, in an engraving from 1512, depicts one such character nurturing a basket of infant fools while their older siblings frolic awkwardly. Similar allegorical figures appear carved in a French church stall at Corbeil Cathedral and in a German pew of the Church of the Holy Cross in Rottweil. A sixteenth-century fresco on the walls of Coira Castle in South Tyrol shows a fool squatting on eggs just beginning to hatch tiny beings in jester costumes.

Fool's Plate, Circle of Jörg Breu the Elder, 1528.

THE FOOL'S PLATE

A particularly vivid example of this motif is provided by the *Narrenteller* (fool's plate) found in the *Wunderkammer* (cabinet of curiosities) of Ambras Castle in Innsbruck, Austria. Crafted in Augsburg, Germany, in 1528, this painted wooden plate depicts a central Mother of Fools wearing a gold jester's head as a pendant and surrounded by her seven foolish sons playing out scenes along the plate's circumference.

That the number of her sons is seven is significant. It connects the Fool Mother to Eve, or at least the Edenic couple, via a nursery song common throughout Germany, translated as:

Adam had seven sons, seven sons,
They didn't eat, they didn't drink,
They didn't know what to do.

The song accompanies a sort of "Simon Says" game involving comic gestures appropriate to sons too foolish to even feed themselves, and the phrase "The fool had seven sons, seven sons were fools" is also shouted by members of the Fool's Guild (a Carnival troupe) in Rottweil, Germany.

On the plate, the foolish offspring of the Fool Mother are depicted in scenes reminiscent of those performed in comic Carnival plays. A popular scene in these performances involves an unhappy victim enduring an enema (usually at the hands of a fool-doctor), and this is represented twice, once with a normal syringe and once with oven bellows. A medical procedure of another kind also appears: a team of fool-surgeons cutting into a patient's head, probably referring to attempts to remove the "fool stone" once believed to be the seat of madness. Other scenes depict a fool's baptism by fool-priests, coopers constructing a barrel around a particularly rotund fool, and a fool-farmer sowing seeds over a field from which sprout baby fools. The latter is a motif enacted in the Carnival of Wilflingen, Germany, in which a Fool-Seed-Sower leads the procession, scattering the "foolish" version of seed, that is, its opposite, chaff. *Narrensamen* (fool's seeds) is also used by German Carnival troupes as a playful reference to children too young to don adult masks and costumes.

Fool with bladder balloon. Illumination from Carrow Psalter, 13th c.

CLUBS AND PIGS' BLADDERS

Some of the earliest depictions of the fool come from medieval psalters, or psalm books. The 14th and 53rd chapters of the Book of Psalms both open with the phrase: "The fool says in his heart, 'There is no God.'" The opening letter of this opening verse is often illuminated with an illustration of this fool. Earlier images may show a demon whispering foolishness into his ear, but more frequently he is depicted with attributes also used to indicate madness in the Middle Ages, meaning he is naked, or barely clothed, and carries a club. He's also often depicted holding a round object, apparently bread referred to in the fourth verse, in which the foolish or iniquitous "devour"

Bladder balloons brandished by a member of Fools' Guild of Elzach, Germany.

the Lord's people "as men eat bread." Over time, psalters portraying this fool show him more fully clothed and without the bread, but the club remains. With time, this figure comes more and more to resemble the Carnival fool or jester.

Two figures of the Rottweil Fastnacht, the Fransenkleid (fringed dress) and the Guller (from a local word for "rooster")

Occasionally, as in the thirteenth-century Carrow Psalter from East Anglia, that club becomes an inflated pig's bladder tied on a stick. While all but forgotten in England, this medieval children's toy became a classic attribute of the Carnival fool, particularly in Germany, where it is still used to playfully strike at spectators. This *Saubloder*is traditionally fixed to a dried bull pizzle, giving the "weapon" a bit more heft and spring. The pig's bladder itself carries unexpected meaning. It's been related to the Latin *follis* for "windbag," both in the sense of "bellows" and in that of "empty-headed babbler." *Follis* also happens to be the source of the words for "fool" in French (*fou*), Danish (*fjols*), and English.

More frequently, the fool's club in medieval illuminations is made to resemble the marotte of a court jester, a parody of the king's scepter topped by a small replica of the jester's head. While this comic prop would afford the court fool with opportunity to engage in absurd dialogues with himself, in Christian interpretation it represents the fool taking

Animal attributes: donkey ears and cock's comb shown in Jacob Cornelisz van Oostsanen's *Laughing Fool*, c. 1500.

Fox tails are required attributes of the Faselhannes character of the Waldsee Fools' Guild, Bad Waldsee, Germany.

counsel only from himself (rather than from God) as well as a sort of self-involvement or self-love that characterizes his unredeemed nature.

ANIMALS AND ATTRIBUTES

The traditional jester's cap, widely associated with Carnival, also carries its own symbolic meaning with the two-pointed protrusions representing the ears of a donkey. While depictions of such a cap only date to the thirteenth century, the equation of donkeys with fools is obviously older, as Latin uses the word asinus to describe both, and the animal was likewise symbolic for the Greeks, used to embody stupidity in at least twenty of Aesop's fables. A variant of the donkey-eared cap attaches a rooster's comb between the ears, thus adding a medieval symbol of lust to the fool's ignorance.

In Germany, the jester's cap is only worn in the Rhineland, not by fools of the Swabian-Alemannic Fastnacht, who instead wear cowls. While donkey symbolism plays no real role either in Fastnacht, the lusty rooster appears in Rottweil's Carnival as the *Guller* (Swabian for rooster), represented by a hobbyhorse-style figure given to charging after female spectators.

Even more widely represented is the fox, another animal representing human foibles, in this case deceit, flattery, and greed. While these associations with the fox are proverbial and all but universal, it is specifically the fox's tail that adorns many costumes of the Swabian-Alemannic fools, usually fixed to either side of a mask but also pinned on cowls, cloaks, and tunics.

The fox tail was historically used as a stigmatizing marker hung on the deceitful or ignorant. In sixteenth-century France François Rabelais, in his satire *La Vie de Gargantua et de Pantagruel*, for instance, has a character by the name of Panurgi mock scholarly windbags by pinning fox tails to their backs. In Germany of that same era, fox tails show up in numerous satirical broadsheets, including a 1535 woodcut of that name, *Foxtail,* by Erhard Schön. But it is its connection with flattery that remained strongest in that country, with modern German still using the word *Fuchsschwänzer* ("fox-tail-er") meaning a flatterer or one who "strokes with a fox tail."

While many theories have been floated to explain the symbolic meaning of bells worn on the fool's costume, none seems particularly compelling since function here obviously trumps meaning, i.e., they're there to draw attention. Bells are quite prominent on Swabian-Alemannic Fastnacht costumes, though the small jingle-bell variety typically decorating the jester's cap is not used. Instead, two types of bells are worn. *Rollen* are larger bronze or copper sleighbell-style bells (some as large as small grapefruits) worn on bandolier straps crossing the torso. Slightly less common are the heavier *Schellen*, squarish or oval bells like cowbells worn on a belt at the waist. Fools wearing these, as in the Imst Schemenlaufen in Austria, can be named for the bells worn, i.e., *Scheller* and *Roller.* The type of bell worn will dictate to some extent the performance, with the *Scheller* adopting a stylized hopping movement that causes the heavier cowbells to swing rhythmically.

SWABIAN-ALEMANNIC MASKS

While all the above attributes help define the fool of the Swabian-Alemannic Fastnacht, most important is the mask and the suit that belongs to it. As with Venetian Carnival figures, Swabian-Alemannic presentation is strictly dictated by tradition.

A fool's "guild" (troupe) consists of a few characters played by several, dozens, or even hundreds of nearly identically outfitted performers, usually exclusively male, though exceptions to this are slowly becoming more frequent. These may be accompanied by a much smaller set of adjunct characters with their own fixed costumes, masks, and attributes.

Costumes and masks not only are reused year after year but may be handed down over generations or donated to the guild. Some masks kept by guilds today date to the seventeenth century.

The fool's costume, known as a *Häs* (plural: *Häser*), is handmade within the guild. Available suits may be rented to new participants whose membership has been approved but need to be purchased after two years. Guilds will not sell suits to non-members, and guild members wishing to hand off or resell their suits must receive permission from the guild. Should you wish to make your own suit (according to specifications), many guilds will only hand out sewing instructions in person. These instructions are very exacting, stipulating for instance that the fox tail hanging from your cap cannot come from a grey or silver fox, only the red.

A classic mask worn in the Rottweil Fastnacht is the grimacing "Biss" (from the word for "bite").

The mournful "Briekere" mask of the Rottweil Fastnacht derives its name from the Swabian dialect word for "cry."

Masks also strictly conform to traditional models. While a few guilds make use of tin or painted wire mesh, the typical Swabian-Alemannic *Larven* are carved from wood, usually linden.

There are several general categories into which these are classed.

GLATTLARVE

The first is the *Glattlarve* (smooth mask) characterized by a sort of smoothed-out neutrality of expression, a look somehow cherubic and somehow a bit sinister at the same time. The foreheads, which are unsettlingly large like a child's, are framed by two horsehair braids tied with ribbons, in a manner suggesting a baroque wig. While the earliest surviving *Glattlarve* can only be dated to about the mid-1600s, a painting created between 1545 and 1550 and displayed on a family tomb in Munich's Frauenkirche depicts a mask immediately recognizable as a *Glattlarve*. It happens to be held in the hand of a devil, whose disguise of innocence is undone as Christ defeats him in the painting.

SCHANTLE

Another classic Swabian-Alemannic mask superficially resembling the *Glattlarve* but with a more expressive, defined, and individualized physiognomy is the *Schantle*. An example is found in the Rottweil Fastnacht's *Briekere* (meaning "cryer"). Only appearing at the close of Carnival, the crying face of the *Briekere* laments the ending of festivities, though even here the carved wooden tears trickle over a classically impassive mien. Generally, the *Schantle* lacks the infantilized, sexless quality of the *Glattlarve* and looks more like an older male burgher.

BISS

Rottweil's *Biss* (bite) pushes this look a bit further with its almost pained grimace, and the *Fratz* of Elzach, Germany, presents something similar, a mild scowl carved in a more angular, primitive style.

GROTESKLARVEN

Other classes of Swabian-Alemannic masks include the animal masks, witch masks, and *Grotesklarven*, those which push the designs toward the grotesque. These can include assorted legendary beings like the wild man, *Butzen* (bogeymen), or the *Hoorige Bär* (shaggy bear).

WHITE FOOLS

The fools of the Swabian-Alemannic Fastnacht can also be classed by the type of costume worn with the mask. Here there are two main categories: the white fool and the fringed fool.

The white ensemble, which is usually worn with the *Glattlarve* or *Schantle,* consists of loose white linen pants, smock, and hood, and is attached to the mask. Sometimes these

"White Fool" style hand-painted suit and *Rollen*-style bells worn by "Narro" characters of the Villingen Fools' Guild.

Postcard "A Remembrance of the Villingen Fastnacht," 1900. Note the overstuffed Wuescht (Wuascht) figures being attacked on upper right!

are draped with an additional shawl or colorful silk scarves. As no skin or hair is to be left uncovered, gloves are also worn. The white fabric is painted with designs in oils (or occasionally embroidered). In the Rottweil Fastnacht, for instance, subjects allowed by tradition include images of Bacchus symbolizing the season's liberal enjoyment of drink, tendrils of ivy, and images of folklorically attired Tyroleans and Turks.

These may be rendered as portraits on the back, but each pant leg (front and back) also requires a standing figure in the guild's code. Some half-hearted explanations have been advanced to explain the specific need for Turks and Tyroleans, but these most likely merely represent popular subjects of the day when suits were first created.

The Wuescht

Embodying vanity, that foolish quality passed from the Middle Ages, the white fool is generally considered a sort of comical dandy, especially in Villingen, Germany, where he wears a distinctive ruff collar. An interesting inversion there is found in the character known as a *Wuescht* (coming from a word for "ugly"). He wears the same white fool costume beautified with decorative painting, but it's stuffed to bursting with straw, so much so that the figure can barely walk. The suit may also be dirty or tattered, and his *Glattlarve* may likewise be in sorry shape and, even worse, not properly worn but held away from the face, overtly violating the fool's imperative to never remove a mask in public.

These egregious violations make the *Wuescht* a literal target. On his back, he wears a

A FRINGED FOOL WEARING HIS FLECKLESHÄS (TAG SUIT), MEMBER OF THE PLÄTZLERZUNFT WEINGARTEN.

board at which kids, or anyone so inclined, may throw snowballs or pinecones gathered for the occasion. Mercifully, the *Wuescht* has some control over all this via a broom he carries. Turning it upward signals readiness for the assaults; downward means ceasefire.

The *Wuescht,* or several of them, always march at the end of the procession, symbolically signaling that the fool's ultimate and final duty is to make fun of himself.

FRINGED FOOLS

The fringed fool wears another kind of suit more familiar outside of the Swabian-Alemannic region. The jester's motley, meaning a patchwork suit of variegated colors, is a tidied-up version of the fringe suit, with diamond-shaped cloth pieces sewn into a single fabric. The diamond pattern of the Italian *Arlecchino* (later French *harlequin*) is another "tidied up" version of the fringe suit.

In sixteenth- and seventeenth-century Britain, a motley sewn together of cloth scraps or "tags," could also be referred to as "tag and rag" and "rag-tag," an expression that's come to mean not only haphazardly constituted but also disreputable. Interestingly, German offers a similar evolution in the word *Lumpen*, first used for "rags," later for a person of low character, and finally, in Marxist jargon, as the "*Lumpenproletariat,*" an underclass unenlightened by class consciousness.

Perhaps more palatable than the word *Lumpen*, the word *Fetzen* ("shreds" or "tatters") is the preferred word used for the cloth tacked to suits and hanging in fringed rows. These tags are of multiple colors, arbitrarily arranged, and often diamond- or tile-shaped, creat-

WHEELED RATCHET NOISEMAKER OPERATED BY THE FOOLS OF THE DINGELI-SPÄTTLE GUILD OF ORTENBERG, GERMANY.

ing a covering almost like the feathers of a bird or scales of a reptile. Sewing an entire suit of this type can easily take a seamstress forty hours or more.

The suit of the white fools has an obvious precedent in the painted linen suits of the Schembart runners. But the fringed look also echoes the Schembart suits covered not in rows of cloth tags but in other materials—the nuts, dice, peacock plumes, and sealed letters mentioned. These also have more direct parallels in modern Swabian-Alemannic characters, the Nutshell Hansele of Wolfach, Germany, whose suit is encrusted with more than three thousand shells or the Snail-Shell Narro from Zell am Harmersbach, Germany. (Narro, from *Narr* for "fool," is a moniker often given these characters, and Hans or Hansele is a generic everyman name, used as English uses *Jack* in *Jack in the Green* or *jack-o'-lantern.*)

TOOLS OF THE TRADE

Aside from parading in a lovely suit, mask, and (often) jangling bells, what does the Swabian-Alemannic fool do?

He might teasingly flick spectators with that bladder-balloon left over from the Middle Ages. Certain fools carry treat baskets, into which a spectator is occasionally allowed to dip. In Rottweil, it's a metal tin, called the fool's "snuff box." Chocolates or candies may be thrown from the baskets, though oranges have been outlawed here and there for

"Stretch scissors" employed by a member of the Gole Fools' Guild of Riedlingen, Germany.

fear of black eyes. Another tasty projectile is the pretzel, which fools carry on long sticks skewering stacks twenty or thirty pretzels high. Confetti is also thrown but is much more associated with regions outside the Swabian-Alemannic zone.

"Stretch-Scissors" are a common and eye-catching prop seen at Fastnacht. Hinged like pantographs, they surprisingly expand six feet or more when opened to menace spectators or even to pluck away a hat or scarf. Noisemaking wooden ratchets are another bit of clever Carnival engineering adding to the bell's clamor. Ratches come in all shapes and sizes, some as large wheelbarrows pushed along on geared wheels which drive the clacking. Whip-cracking is also traditional in some areas.

You'll also hear "fool's calls" shouted at Carnival. This is a sort of call-and-response greeting shouted both by fools and spectators. While each region in Germany has its own distinctive fool's call, in the Swabian-Alemannic zone "Narri Narro!" and "Narro Narro!" are often used:

The straw bear of the of the Poppele Guild in Singen is known as the "Hooriger Bär" (hairy bear). The suit here is made from peastraw rather than that from a grain crop.

Call: Narri!
Response: Narro!

"Narri Narro!" can also serve to punctuate what's known as a "fool's saying," a mostly nonsensical rhyme recited by fools as a sort of en route performance; an example would be the "Adam had seven sons" verses referred to earlier. Another performance possibility would involve something called the "fool's book." This has become increasingly rare but is preserved in the traditionalist Rottweil Fasnacht.

Handmade and illustrated by the performers carrying them, these books portray events of the year deserving of satire. These can range from community-level failures to more personal embarrassments. When the fool spots a victim, he taps him with his fool's sausage (a stuffed leather baton resembling a sausage) and he is compelled to follow along as the fool points and recites his way through the embarrassing and comic scenes. For good reason, these books always begin with the motto, "To everyone's joy and no one to hurt," though it's easy to imagine a certain discomfort being involved.

Going back to mocking songs of the ancient Roman celebrations, Carnival has been widely regarded as an opportunity to satirize breaches of conduct within the community. While this is an important part of the Rhineland Karneval and is gently remembered in the fools' books of Rottweil, this sort of satire is not particularly characteristic of Swabian-Alemannic Fastnacht.

BEARS

The embrace of rural folkloric traditions that distinguishes the Swabian-Alemannic Fastnacht is best represented in figures such as the wild man and other "shaggy" costumes understood to be an earlier, rougher version of the suit worn by the fringed fool. Rather than tags of cloth sewn onto a garment, suits such as these use leaves, corn husks, reeds, or tied hanks of straw to create their look. The wild man in today's processions, presumably like his predecessor depicted in sixteenth-century Schembart books, is covered in leaves and moss in this way.

Particularly in rural regions, where materials like straw would be plentiful but a single suit of clothing was worn throughout the year, it's likely that decorative material would be temporarily tacked to garments and removed after the celebration. Within more recent memory, this is the case with early Krampus or Percht suits improvised from coats with fur lining turned inside out and other materials improvised into hoods or masks later returned to normal use.

Unlike a suit constructed of tags of cloth, one made of shaggy and loose materials adds volume to a costume, making a man into a monster, and a material like straw easily suggests the fur of a beast, in particular a bear. The German Carnival features these in some variety: the *Hoorige Bär* (shaggy bear), *Strohbär* (straw bear), or *Erbsenbär* (pea-straw bear), and so on with rye-straw, oat-straw, etc. While especially common in the Swabian-Alemannic region, the tradition extends throughout Germany and was formerly

The straw bears of the of the Poppele Guild in Singen.

practiced in Czech Bohemia where Germans settled. An odd detail regarding these bears is the rarity of bear masks worn with them. Most, instead, wear masks suggesting more the face of an ogre or wild man, something more human. This probably is the result of the costume originally being worn with no mask at all (since the trade of mask carving was slow to spread outside larger cities). When masks became fashionable and more available, they were carved to resemble not a bear with his snout but a more human face which had become associated with the costume. Carnival "bears," as we'll see in the upcoming chapter, are often just as much monster as bears.

The impression of an actual bear, however, may be reinforced by a performer guiding the straw bear with a sort of leash, as would be the case with live bears formerly exhibited at fairs. On a more practical note, the cumbersome nature of the suits makes it helpful for the performer to have assistance close at hand. In Empfingen, Germany, where these bears are sometimes marched door to door rather than in a procession, the "bear-trainer" dresses in top hat and tails, doffing his hat to receive money from those visited.

DEVILS AND WITCHES

The devils that parade in the Wilflinger Fastnacht offer an interesting comparison with some aspects of the straw bear. With a history extending to the seventeenth century, the devil suits, which consist of long (two- to three-foot) dangling strips or shreds from old garments, make the impression of a sort of transitional stage between the neatly tiled cloth tags of modern fringed suits and the more unkempt bulkiness of shaggy suits made of straw. Another comparison is offered by the carved masks. Guild documents record that before the seventeenth century the devils did not wear masks but appeared with faces blackened with soot. When masks were introduced, they were painted black, imitating the earlier look, the same process I've suggested for the straw bears with no bear masks.

While the Wilflinger devils are older than the many other devils found among the guilds of the Swabian-Alemannic Fastnacht, older still would be those presented in the Schembartlauf. Not only in Nuremberg but in other cities, as noted in council records, masks used in Carnival were borrowed from the Church, which employed these in their religious dramas.

Witches, that is men in drag and wooden *Larven*, arrived in the Swabian-Alemannic Fastnacht at a much later date. Here and there, one can find reports of late-nineteenth-century Carnival witches, but it wasn't until the mid-1930s that they really had a presence. This began with the *Hexen* (witches') guilds of Offenburg and Gengenbach, Germany, who donned satisfyingly folkloric wooden masks, though it's worth noting the strong resemblance of these masks to the witch from Disney's *Snow White*, just released in 1937. An interesting addition to the costume is a bright red hood resembling a cross between a crone's headscarf and a double-peaked medieval bonnet (or escoffion). The witch ensemble consists of a short jacket, skirt, petticoat, and cartoonishly striped socks. The traditional shoes worn with this are a type of peasant shoe made of straw.

The devils of Dorauszunft Saulgau make ample use of fox tails.

Another way to fly using witches' brooms. Stegstrecker Fools' Guild of Pfullendorf, Germany.

Typical witch mask of the Swabian-Alemannic Fastnacht displayed in the Black Forest Costume Museum in Kinzigtal.

During Germany's postwar occupation by France, when no Carnival activity was permitted in the streets, the Offenburg *Hexen* devised an interesting alternative, which became an ongoing tradition. The *Hexenfraß* (the witch feeding), as it was called, saw costumed witches popping out of windows or appearing on balconies to toss smoked sausages and rolls to pedestrians below.

Witches tend to play the role of comic villain in the Swabian-Alemannic celebrations, partly thanks to their storybook persona but also because they are relative newcomers to the scene and therefore less bound by tradition. Favorite pastimes include unlacing and stealing spectators' shoes, catching up young women, or anyone likely to shriek, and running about with the victim slung over a shoulder, or putting children in cages à la Hansel and Gretel. Outfitted with wheels for the processions, these cages are also often rigged to spin on their axes, meaning captives are whirled mercilessly before being released. Wheeled tubs full of confetti also sometimes roll alongside the *Hexen*, providing ready access should a spectator need confetti dumped down the collar. Children small enough to fit in the tubs are often thrown in to be "bathed" in confetti. A particularly elaborate stunt contrived by the Gengenbach *Hexen* involves a device used to apply netting to Christmas trees before transport. The Gengenbach *Hexen* have adapted this mechanism as a means of thoroughly restraining small children and young women. The witches' obvious preference for targeting females serves as a reminder that the performers under the masks and skirts are quite male.

LEGEND FIGURES

Around the same time the witches appeared, new figures from local folklore also began to parade alongside traditional fools (increasingly so after the war). In 1934, the fools' guild of Markdorf, Germany, added to their ranks *Kaujohle,* a pitiless forester who, with his hound, would hunt down starving villagers foraging for mushrooms in the lord's forest. After his death he was condemned to haunt the lands he guarded in life. The performers playing him don suits painted with oak and beech leaves and particularly grotesque masks, each carved with a different configuration of goiters and warts.

The Murrhardt, Germany, fools added Night Raven, a traditional nocturnal visitor of children who refuse to come in after nightfall. Raven wings are suggested by expansive black shawls (though the masks are actually decidedly vulpine). A second folklore figure, the *Hotzenklingenstoffel,* a hostile forest spirit targeting those who chose ill-advised woodland shortcuts. The mask is a monstrous assemblage of boar bristles, fox tails, and roe antlers.

In Furtwangen, Germany, they welcomed the *Bodenwälder,* another forest guardian who dons a suit of moss and lichens, a gnarled mask, and a bird's-nest hat. He may at times carry about a taxidermized weasel.

Particularly charming are *Lauratalgeister,* ghosts of the Laura Valley wearing white gowns and conical hats painted with bats, owls, and strawberries—the last because they

Mask of the Lake Forest Goblin of the Friedrichshafen Fools' Guild Seegockel.

A friend of brewers, the leafy Hopfennarr (hops fool) is a legendary figure represented by the Fools' Guild of Tettnang, Germany.

Legendary figure from Bad Cannstatt: the Brunnengeist of the Felben Fools' Guild represents the spirit dwelling in the town's fountain.

Sad wandering souls. The Lauratalgeister (ghosts of the Laura Valley) are legendary figures represented by the Plätzler Guild of Weingarten.

The Rottweil Federhannes mid-vault.

represent the spirit of a young woman said to have stayed out to long during a strawberry-picking excursion during which she got lost and died in a storm. The tragedy of it all is emphasized by the wooden tears streaming down their mournful masks.

THE ROTTWEIL POLE VAULTER

The town of Rottweil has been frequently mentioned in this chapter as it represents a sort of gold standard when considering the Swabian-Alemannic Fastnacht. An ever-growing number of participants (four thousand at last count) parade each year through the town's charming medieval center to celebrate Fastnacht, or *Fasnet*, as it's locally known. The three parades taking place on Shrove Monday and two on Shrove Tuesday also have a distinctly regional name: *Narrensprungen* ("fools' jumps"). This is not just a bit of linguistic whimsy; it's a reference to two kinds of jumping that take place. The first, mentioned earlier, is the halting, hopping gait employed by bell-wearing fools to synchronize their bell-ringing. The second refers to a type of pole-vaulting.

Federahannes is the pole vaulter and a sort of icon not only for the Rottweil Narrensprung but for the Swabian-Alemannic *Fastnacht* generally. The name means something like Feather Jack, referring to the white feathers decorating his cloak and pants, possibly a reference to his efforts to fling himself, birdlike, into the heavens. Less easily explained are the prominent boar's tusks jutting from the mouth of his otherwise human mask. His pole-vaulting is done with a walking staff tipped with a dangling calf's tail, of all things, and the stunt does not exactly conform to track and field standards. It's just a brief skyward swing done without releasing his pole but can make for a startling effect. A final curiosity regarding this curious Federahannes—that calf tail dangling from his pole is doused in perfume throughout the parade and used to tease spectators who presumably have no particular interest in smelling perfume-saturated animal parts.

· CHAPTER VII ·

GOOD-LUCK VISITS

IN WHICH CARNIVAL
IS DIFFERENTLY CELEBRATED,
VIZ.,

HOUSE VISITING CUSTOMS

SAID TO BRING

LUCK & FERTILITY;

HOW THESE VISITS ARE CONDUCTED
IN EASTERN EUROPE;
THE POLISH CUSTOM OF

"KILLING THE MARE"

&

THE CZECH PLAY IN WHICH DEATH DIES;

ANIMAL GUISES,

INCL. GOATS & STORKS;
THE ASH MAN WHO ARRIVES AT MIDNIGHT.

RURAL WAYS

While Swabian-Alemannic Fastnacht customs harken back to the eighteenth century and echo aspects of the even earlier Schembartlauf, the general form they take is the same as contemporary Carnival celebrations, namely, the municipal parade.

Nuremberg of the Schembart era was a thriving commercial center and, along with its neighbor Augsburg, a hub of the Northern Renaissance and home to a circle of influential artists and thinkers—in a word, urban. The Swabian-Alemannic Fastnacht, developing later, did not replicate the spectacular floats and aristocratic support of the Schembartlauf. Evolving in somewhat smaller cities and towns, its traditions were nonetheless cultivated in a well-connected world of tradesmen's guilds, within a network of artisans and merchants, rather than in rural areas of scattered farms.

Moving from the familiar to the unfamiliar in this chapter, we turn from municipal processions to a different form of Carnival typical of less densely populated agricultural regions, the "good-luck visit." While we'll be examining this practice in the context of Carnival, its modernized, vestigial form is already familiar to readers as Halloween trick-or-treating or Christmas caroling.

LUCK, MAGIC, & BEGGING

The good-luck visit is undertaken by small groups (traditionally young unmarried men) who present at each home some type of performance: a song, dance, music, short skit, or recited rhymes, all of these in forms passed down through the generations. This performance is said to bring good luck to the home and its occupants. Participants are typically masked or costumed to convey the notion that this blessing originates not with familiar neighbor boys but from an outside source. In its original form, the visitors represented beings of a supernatural order, e.g., spirits of the fields and forests, God and his angels, or the ancestral dead.

In exchange for the luck-bringing performance, householders are expected to offer food, drink, or money. While any number of foods can be offered, the most traditional would be those foods to be banned during Lent and hence those to use up during Carnival, e.g., eggs, sausages, or doughnuts and other pastries (made with butter and eggs). Bacon and pork fat or other pork products were also once given out.

Those who fail to reward the visitors not only do not receive good luck but risk bad luck for offending the presiding spirits. In certain cases, the exchange is more about protection from bad luck or evil, as in cases where costumed visitors represent the unsettled dead, witches, and the like.

Over time and in less traditional regions, the masked visitors are less associated with a supernatural order and merely embody the goodness of the good old ways. Where

PREVIOUS: Slamění ("straw") figure of Vostatky troupe on his rounds in the municipality of Hamry, Czech Republic.

the supernatural promise is diminished or forgotten, emphasis shifts from the blessing given to the payment expected. Rather than "good-luck visits," these activities are then referred to merely as "begging customs" (in German, *Heischebrauch*).

A further evolution sees good-luck home visits transformed into the municipal parade. In this process, individual troupes formerly visiting homes on their own schedules and route are marshalled into a single procession through a central area. The Carnival activity described throughout the remainder of this book generally follows this form, with good-luck visits sometimes existing alongside an evolving municipal parade.

GERMAN CASES

In some regions of Germany, one can observe the later phase of such a transition. In Upper Bavaria, the Alpine town Mittenwald and others nearby host a week of processions featuring bell-ringers, bears, and dancers in traditional dress—all in lovely wooden *Larven*. But alongside this exists a tradition known as *Gungl*, visits made by multiple groups of costumed participants to centrally located inns. Accompanied by accordion and guitar, they perform traditional dances at each stop, inviting female patrons to dance with them. Though patrons are less inclined to accept this offer today, in the past it was a special honor eagerly sought. A century ago, *Gungl* troupes visited homes rather than inns.

Straw bears also are more likely than other Carnival figures to be associated with house visits. In Empfingen, as mentioned, a bear and his "trainers" seen in municipal processions can do double duty, splitting off into "free groups" to visit homes.

EASTERN EUROPE

It is in eastern European countries that house visits are most frequently a part of Carnival. One probable reason for these differences is the slower penetration of the Church into these regions. While Christianity was quickly adopted in the fifth century by the Franks of what is now France and western Germany, the Saxons of the German northeast held to their pagan beliefs into the ninth century, and it was only at this time that the East and South Slavs began to accept the faith. Even later, the West Slavs of Poland held out until Christianity was forced upon them during the Northern Crusade of 1195. The two countries we examine in this chapter are Poland and the Czech Republic, another area settled by the West Slavs.

In these countries, the old medieval blurring of Christmas and Carnival customs is also pronounced. Epiphany, while technically the beginning of Carnival in most of Germany, is more strongly associated with the Christmas cycle in most of Europe. The appearance on that day of the three kings who followed a star to Bethlehem is marked in Germany, Poland, and the Czech Republic by house visits of costumed groups singing carols and led by an individual holding aloft a star. Czechs, for instance, may refer to this as a custom of *Masopust* (Carnival) rather than Christmas. The songs they sing are considered *Masopust* carols, and similar processions continue into the Carnival season. The

Vostatky troupe in Eastern Bohemia (Czech Republic) make their rounds in the municipality of Hamry prior to the "Killing of the Mare."

same is the case in Poland, where Carnival is known as *Zapusty* or *Mięsopust* (etymologically related to Czech *Masopust*). Slovenes and Croats also use related words. Versions of the Latin-derived word *Carnival* have been adopted throughout eastern Europe, but they tend not to be used in describing local customs.

KILLING THE MARE

While Carnival good-luck visits are best documented in Poland, we'll first look at an example from the Czech Republic, where enthusiasm for masked Carnival festivities is expressed in the old adage "*Masopust* without masks is like bread without flour."

In eastern Bohemia, in Hlinsko and surrounding villages, there is a tradition of house visits known as *vostatky*. On Shrove Tuesday, one can see troupes of twenty or more performers taking to the roads in colorful costumes decked with fluttering ribbons, baroque lace collars, cuffs, and clownishly oversized cravats. Most impressive is the array of headgear, including towering constructions adorned with flowers, foxtails, feathers, and ferns. The colorful procession is followed by a brass band and perhaps a dozen tag-alongs, excited kids from the neighborhood and curious adults.

The performance at each house consists of traditional music of the season and accompanying dance, but there are also unscripted interactions between the costumed characters and those visited, all of which symbolically bestows prosperity, specifically thriving crops and healthy livestock.

VOSTATKY TROUPE IN EASTERN BOHEMIA (CZECH REPUBLIC) MAKE THEIR ROUNDS IN THE MUNICIPALITY OF HAMRY PRIOR TO THE "KILLING OF THE MARE."

The central figure of the procession is the "Mare," represented as a hobbyhorse, or a horse figure attached at the performer's waist, intended to resemble a rider and his mount but looking more like a man in a hoop skirt impaled by a miniature equine. The rider wears a cocked hat and carries a horse whip, which he frequently cracks.

Also prominent is a figure known as the *Ras*, who sticks close to the Mare. He also cracks a whip and would seem to function as a trainer, but that is not exactly his role. *Ras* is Czech for "knacker," a largely archaic term for one who picks up dead or nearly dead livestock to sell to rendering plants.

As they arrive at each home, a figure known as *Strakatý* (meaning "spotted") in a polka dot suit and impossibly high conical hat serves as master of ceremonies. Asking first for permission to perform, he then reads a rhymed greeting wishing a happy holiday to the occupants, after which he asks what tune they might prefer for the dance to be performed. Strakatý is accompanied by his "wife," played by a young male in drag.

The brass band strikes up a tune, and the dance commences, performed by the "Turks," several men crowned with flamboyant hats resembling lampshades streaming with ribbons. They twirl handkerchiefs as they dance in a circle, leaping higher and higher as the song progresses. The jumping is said to awaken the earth's fertility, causing flax and grain to grow as high as they might jump.

Grain is quite literally represented by the Straw Man, a figure encased in a knee-length tunic of straw, wearing a tall straw headdress and carrying a whip of braided straw. It's said that plucking some straw from his suit and feeding it to the poultry will increase their

Member of Vostatky troupe in the Easter Bohemian municipality of Hamry (Czech Republic).

health and fertility, and the women of the household can increase their own fertility by submitting to his attempts to embrace them and roll with them on the ground.

While music is played outside, another set of figures, the Chimney Sweeps, enter the homes and pretend to clean the hearth, usually resulting in ashy mess mischievously kicked up with their brooms. Their faces are blackened (as is the Straw Man's) and they wear dark suits, lace collars, and flower-decked hats. The last, it might be noted, are often plastered with racy pictures of women clipped from magazines (since procreation is the theme of the day, after all). To convey fertility, or at least good luck, they also tag as many residents of the house as possible with a greasy smear of black soot.

Meanwhile, the Knacker inquires after the health of the livestock (or pets or family members if no livestock is kept). Feigning disappointment that there's nothing to haul away, he nonetheless wishes continuing and increasing health to all. Other optional characters representing a bear, Gypsies, and Jews may also circulate about, engaging in comic schtick with the residents. The visit concludes, of course, with the group receiving doughnuts, pancakes, or other treats along with plenty of vodka and slivovitz.

Once the rounds are done, the troupe makes a final appearance at a tavern or public space where a play is performed. The troupe clears the floor, forming a ring in the middle of which the Mare paces nervously. The Knacker reads of a list of fanciful sins for which the Mare is to be executed, followed by a (not disinterested) declaration of the rightful recipients of the horses' body parts.

Chimneysweep characters are part of the retinue accompanying the straw bear on his house visits in Poland. Taken in the Upper Silesian village of Droniowice.

1978 PHOTO OF COSTUMED DEVILS TAKING PART IN THE "TRIAL AND EXECUTION" OF DEATH IN JEDLIŃSK, POLAND.

The Knacker then begins stalking the Mare, cracking his whip and goading the horse with a prod. As they circle, the costumed figures ringing the performance then yell louder and louder until the Mare hits his knees, bows his head, and is struck "dead" by the Knacker's goad. The performers pile their hats around the body in a beribboned floral mound, throw their arms around each other, and sing a sort of dirge.

But then, alcohol comes to the rescue! The Knacker administers a shot of vodka, and the Mare leaps up, hats are again donned, and the play ends with a cheerful tune and more booze.

DEATH GOT DRUNK

In Poland there is another festive execution enacted on Shrove Tuesday in the town of Jedlińsk, about sixty miles south of Warsaw. The condemned in this folk play is Death herself (the Polish word for death is feminine, so she's traditionally represented as a skeletal hag in a white shroud—later a black robe). As in our Czech example, the characters in the Jedlińsk play once did double duty circulating on house visits and also performing in a play given in a central location, but over time the house-visiting custom fell into disuse. The play, scripted in rhymed verse, is still presented annually in the town square.

The story begins with townsfolk announcing that Death was seen passed out drunk in a riverside meadow where she has lost her scythe. A colorful procession of characters proceeds to the site to take advantage of this situation, tie her up, and lead her back into

CHARGES ARE READ AGAINST DEATH IN THE CARNIVAL FOLK PLAY IN JEDLIŃSK, POLAND.

the marketplace (all performed in the same market square). Later she appears in court, her crimes are recounted, and Death is sentenced to death. She is marched to the executioner as a somber dirge is played. Her head is lopped off and displayed to the crowd, and, according to the script, ashes fall from the head and a black cat representing her soul flees from within her robes to its place of eternal punishment. An angel then steps up with a final monologue, warning the audience that Death will return to claim more souls and that now is their time to live good lives.

The play then turns into a festive funeral procession around the town square. It's headed by bride and groom and includes devils, a Gypsy, a Jew, chimney sweeps, a policeman, a fisherman, and city officials. Aside from the city officials and the fisherman (specific to Jedlińsk and its riverside fish farms), these costumed figures are traditional to many Carnival processions in eastern Europe, a sort of microcosm of the village world with bride and groom given a place of honor as symbols of spring fertility. The costumed figures, and by extension the celebration generally, are known as *kusaki*.

While the play today is performed in the town square on a stage with amplified sound, its source is genuinely old. It was first mentioned in an 1860 article by the parish priest Jan Kłoczowski, who also enthusiastically documented local folklore and customs. While it's not clear if he actually witnessed the play, he at least heard it described by locals and recreated his own version in verse composed in 1868, the script still used for the productions today.

MAGICAL ANIMALS

Outside Jedlińsk, *kusaki* customs had largely died out by the 1960s, but within the next decade revivalist efforts were made here and there and continue to this day, often encouraged by folk-dance groups or musicians with overlapping interests. One such area just to the west of Jedlińsk are the rural villages between Przytyk and Przysucha. But in cities also, younger people are embracing again a modernized version of these customs.

The figures mentioned in the Jedlińsk "funeral" procession are typical of *kusaki* processions elsewhere, though a grandfather and grandmother are also frequently present as representations of the ancestors. A prisoner and a soldier are also sometimes included just to round things out.

Along with the bride and groom, the most frequently seen *kusaki*, however, are Death, the devil, and one or more animals. Death and the devil do not play an easily defined role in these visits and seem to be vestiges of much older morality plays or religious plays borrowed into folk theater.

TURONIE (PL. OF TUROŃ) DISPLAYED IN THE ETHNOGRAPHIC MUSEUM OF KRAKOW, 1926.

A goat is often included among *kusaki* as a symbol of fertility. His appearance might be accompanied by the chanted verse:

Where the goat walks,
rye is born there,
Where he turns his
horns, haystacks rise.

The concept of fertility extends also to humans, with the desire to see babies born and the daughters well married giving us another verse associated with the goat:

Where the goat goes,
the maiden gets
married.

Traditionally, the animal was impersonated by a young man throwing over his back an inside-out fur-lined coat, hide, blanket, or bedsheet. He held a stick emerging from the covering and topped with a carved wooden head, adorned with real goat horns and perhaps a bit of goatskin. The finishing touch would be a livestock bell worn on the neck to jangle when the character dances. The jaw was hinged and fixed with a string, so that as music played it could clap along. A stork was also a common fertility bringer, thanks to its association with birth. Women whom it pecked were destined to become mothers. Its jaw was usually mechanized like a goat's. Occasionally, horse characters (hobbyhorses) might accompany the troupe (as in our Czech example). Bears also might join the *kusaki*, formerly in straw suits of the type mentioned, but now they tend to be disguised in a fur costume of some kind.

Turoń head with hedgehog skin on snout. From Stary Sącz, Poland.

While some of these animals are part of similar Carnival or Christmas processions in other regions (Scandinavia, northeastern Germany, the Czech Republic), a uniquely Polish processional animal is Turoń. This does not represent any known animal, though in the past its identity was spuriously linked to an extinct species of wild cattle (aurochs), thanks to a purported etymological link. As it doesn't represent an actual animal and is a character unto itself, the name Turoń is used as a proper noun.

Though Turoń's appearance differs by region, it's generally a sort of dark, bull-like monster, impersonated with the blanket and clap-jaw wooden arrangement but with the head held close to the performer rather than on a stick. The head is usually equipped with actual bull horns.The symbolic, or magical, purpose of Turoń (as you might guess) is to confer fertility, and it's done with a poke of those horns.

Turoń is a particularly rambunctious performer. Upon entering a home, he proceeds to chase any women present, but he is distracted from this when music is played, clumsily dancing along, stomping and braying like a donkey. At some point during all this, he keels

Polish Carnival mask representing a seller (and maker) of wood-tar, a cure-all once hawked by traveling merchants, a localized example of the quack-doctor character found elsewhere in Carnival troupes.

over, leaving the other performers desperate to resuscitate him, declaring that he's been hexed. Hay might be burned as a sort of hex-dispelling incense, but, even with the house filled with smoke, he refuses to arise. Again, alcohol comes to the rescue. When a shot of vodka is poured down his throat, he leaps up and this ends the visit on a happy note. The same scene may also be acted out with the goat. Goats are known to faint, after all.

"UNDER THE GOAT"

Goats and fertility figure into another Carnival game or ritual once practiced in central Poland called *Podkoziołek* (literally, "under the goat.")

One version of the game involved unmarried men parading about town with a goat, this time represented not by a costume but by some sort of makeshift goat effigy, either fixed with wheels or hauled on a cart. The group would stop at the houses of young women, demanding that they come out and dance. Hopes ran high that, under the spell of the goat, the dance might lead to love and marriage.

Another version gave women the initiative. In this case, unmarried men and women (along with musicians) gathered at a tavern. Women would buy dances with the desired suitor by placing coins "under the goat," being either the same effigy hauled around town or something custom-made for the occasion—a figurine, likely of wood, but occasionally made of turnips or carrots. To drive home the mating angle, the goat was often equipped with an oversized penis. The band then struck up a tune and one would just hope for the best.

Shrove Tuesday *Podkoziołek* festivities in the tavern would end at the stroke of midnight, when the arrival of Ash Wednesday was celebrated by patrons sprinkling each other with ashes. Even better, an ash-filled sieve secretly suspended by the innkeeper might be dumped on patrons with the pull of a string. A third possibility would come in the form of a young man hobbling through the door disguised as the old Ash Man, a character outfitted in old-fashioned clothes and a long flaxen beard and holding a rod with a bag of ash on the end. Any unmarried woman who'd failed to slide her coins under the goat (thereby buying her way out of the courtship game) would be shamed for her non-participation with a shower of ash shaken from his bag. Sometimes, it would be a hobbyhorse performer who might "ride" into the inn and more indiscriminately scatter ash on guests. Herring might also be tacked up around the ashy tavern as a bitter reminder of the meatless Lent into which they'd now entered. Poles know how to party!

· CHAPTER VIII ·

FERTILITY RITES

HERE WE CONSIDER THE FORGOTTEN

PLOW RITUALS OF CARNIVAL;

REVEALING THE SHAMEFUL SECRETS OF UNWED YOUTH
YOKED LIKE HORSES & THEREBY MADE TO WED & REPRODUCE;
HOW LOGS WERE LATER DRAWN INSTEAD OF PLOWS

THE MOCK WEDDINGS

THAT ATTENDED THESE;
A SPECTACULAR ALPINE LOG-PULL
WITH MASKED PARTICIPANTS;

AN ITALIAN EVENT DESCENDED FROM SUCH CUSTOMS
BUT

*SO STRANGE AS TO
DEFY EASY DESCRIPTION;*

UKRAINIAN CARNIVAL LOGS
FÊTED WITH VODKA & DUMPLINGS,
BAPTIZED, DRESSED,
AND GIVEN CHRISTIAN BURIALS.

Illustration of the "fool plough" from *The Costume of Yorkshire* by George Walker (1814).

PLOUGH MONDAY

It is with great sadness I must inform you that this chapter does not mention a single human sacrificed in a wicker effigy or describe scenes of lusty peasants copulating in the fields. Though less thrillingly cinematic in form, the pursuit and celebration of fertility is nonetheless the driving force behind the folk rituals to be discussed. Unlike in previous chapters, these practices are not driven by Christianity's imposition of the Lenten fast. Instead, it is the Biblical injunction "Be fruitful and multiply" that lies behind most of these traditions. Cycles of the natural world also figure in, as Carnival happens to overlap with the beginning of the plowing season and of agricultural labors generally.

In Protestant Britain, Carnival is usually only recognized in the vestigial celebration of Pancake Day on Shrove Tuesday, but this represents only the Lent-driven aspect of the season. An echo of Carnival's other form concerning itself with fertility is to be found in celebrations of Plough Monday in the north and east of England.

Plough Monday is the first Monday after Epiphany. This early January date might exclude it from consideration as a Carnival event today, but, as we've seen, the season in earlier times began immediately after Christmas. Situated at the intersection of these two seasons, on the day before plowing traditionally began, the celebration of Plough Monday could represent either the last hurrah of the Christmas season or the initial festivity of Carnival.

PREVIOUS: Moss Man of the Blochziehen (log pull) of Fiss, Austria.

Star of the Straw Bear Festival, Whittlesey, England.

In either case, the traditions associated with that day are very much those of the good-luck visit. Boys or young men on this day would decorate a plow with ribbons and drag it from house to house. At each home, they would offer a song, recite some rhymes, or perform a play or dance. Often the performance included capering by a "Plough Fool," or a cross-dressed character known as a "Bessy" or "Molly." At each house, the group received money from homeowners aware that the failure to do so could result in their yard being plowed up.

Decorated plow pulled in the Whittlesey Straw Bear Festival procession, England.

While most of these customs died out toward the end of the nineteenth century, since the 1970s there have been efforts to revive them, often by Morris dance sides (troupes), as in Leicestershire, where the holiday is celebrated by the Hinckley Bullockers (*plough bullockers* being a term for those pulling the plow door to door).

In some regions, in place of a fool or Bessy, the group might be accompanied by a straw bear. This is the origin of the Whittlesea Straw Bear Festival in Cambridgeshire, in which several straw bears process through the streets on the Saturday after Plough Monday. While it's the straw-clad figures that are showcased today, a much-sidelined ribbon-decked plow still finds its place among the many Morris dancers and musicians swelling the ranks. The procession as it exists today represents a reforming of the tradition during its 1980 resurrection. The pattern is familiar: a municipal parade has replaced earlier house-visit customs, which had died out seventy years earlier.

Straw bears, cross-dressed performers, and fools very much align Plough Monday with continental Carnival customs, but it's not just these. The plow too is an element of lesser known but widely spread Carnival traditions found in Germany, Austria, Italy, and Slovenia—all of which are symbolically dedicated to the promotion of fertility.

YOKED FOR LIFE

In Jakob Grimm's *Deutsche Mythologie*, a reference to German plow rituals or games appears in the context of his discussion of the wagon dedicated to the goddess Nerthus

WOODCUT BY ERHARD SCHÖN ILLUSTRATING HANS SACHS'S 1532 PLAY *THE MAIDENS AT THE PLOW.*

and that mysterious wheeled ship hauled by twelfth-century weavers (see Chapter VI). The two bear little more than a superficial thematic connection, but the plow ritual Grimm cites makes explicit the connection with Carnival. It's from 1592, from the *Chronicles* of the Bavarian town of Hof (now Saale) and reads:

> *On Shrove-Tuesday evil-minded lads drove a plough about, yoking to it such damsels as did not pay ransom; others went behind them sprinkling chopped straw and sawdust.*

The mock "seeds" tossed behind the plow are clearly analogous to the chaff still scattered as "fool's seeds" in the contemporary Carnival of Wilflingen. The "ransom" paid to avoid being yoked to a plow might be compared to moneys paid British Plough Boys to ensure one's yard isn't plowed up. But we needn't look that far afield for comparison. The playwright Hans Sachs, mentioned earlier for his wild-man verses, wrote another Carnival farce in 1532 titled *The Maidens at the Plow.* It begins:

> *To the plow they now are driven,*
> *Into Fastnacht hands are given"*
> *The maidens who remain . . .*

These maidens would be those of marriageable age who've remained unmarried until the last day of Carnival. Though it was not a custom in Sachs's Nuremberg, in other parts of Germany (and elsewhere) such women were hustled out their homes and forced to pull a plow through the streets. The young bachelors responsible for playing out the custom would often crack whips or wear eye-catching masks or costumes to make more of a spectacle of the process. Whether a woman might buy her way out of this embarrassing game with a bit of food, drink, or money would vary by region.

What may have passed as a bit of rascally horseplay in its day (and today strikes us as impossibly cruel) should be considered against the backdrop of similarly minded Carnival practices involving public mockery—the singing of derisive ballads, satirical "fool's books," and the like. In those less romantic times, a woman's choice of mate would have been a matter of collective responsibility, and a failure to see daughters married off when expected or holding out on suitors considered acceptable by the community created a tension released through this bit of coercive humiliation. Concerns would have been heightened by the fact that Carnival was a popular window for marriages, as weddings are forbidden over the coming forty days of Lent. The humiliation inflicted was justified by its perceived goal: ensuring the welfare of the individual and community, achieved through the time-tested path of marriage and parenthood. Concerning itself with the generative process, the plow ritual can be regarded, among other things, as a fertility rite. It was about making babies.

Such ritual has been preserved, after a fashion, in a few German Carnivals. In Fridingen, a small town on the Danube, the fool's guild presents a plow procession, replacing the unfortunate women of the sixteenth century with costumed fools. Dozens of these are stationed along a single rope, at the end of which is a plow guided over the street by a performer in folkloric dress.

"Fool's seed" (chaff or sawdust) is also scattered, as in our sixteenth-century account. A plow-pulling ritual (*Pfluagziachn*) is also included in the Carnival of Stilfs in South Tyrol (the German-speaking region of northeastern Italy). It also makes use of sawdust as "fool's seed" but is otherwise rather different as the antique plow used there must be dragged not over straight streets but up and down the winding medieval lanes of the hillside town. Unsurprisingly, the uncomfortable sixteenth-century significance of the ritual has been replaced in these modern incarnations by an emphasis on the simple "foolishness" of fools dragging a plow in the streets.

PULLING THE LOG

A Carnival tradition related to the German plow ritual is *Blochziehen*, or log-pulling. The log here would be a recently felled tree stripped of its branches and placed on a wagon and decorated in some way. Those hauling the log (like the plow) would again be unmarried women, or also unmarried men as the practice evolved. The custom is rare but still practiced in certain regions of Germany, Austria, Switzerland, Slovenia, Croatia, Poland, Russia, and Ukraine.

Blochziehen is mentioned at a particularly early date in what is now the Austrian Tyrol. In 1460, the account book of Sigismund, Archduke of Austria, mentions his donation of two gulden to the women of Hötting (now a part of Innsbruck) "who drew the log on Ash Wednesday." A few years later, in 1473, it's mentioned that the "noblest people," including the duke's wife Eleanor of Scotland, attended the event. In 1569, the log-pulling was moved by princely decree to a date *before* Ash Wednesday, fitting it to the traditional Carnival calendar, and the custom continues to receive passing mention in documents from intervening centuries.

WITCH AT THE "CHILDREN'S BLOCHZIEHEN," AN OFF-YEAR VERSION OF THE EVENT HELD IN FISS, AUSTRIA.

BLOCHZIEHEN IN FISS

By the nineteenth century, as interest in folk culture grew, the custom itself was dwindling, found only in the Tyrol's Upper Inn Valley (Oberinntal). The next century saw the tradition disappearing even from this region, except for the town of Fiss, where it was resurrected in 1909 as part of centenary celebrations of the Tyrolean Rebellion against Bavarian rule. After wartime disruptions, the event returned to continue to this day, encouraging other towns of the Upper Inn Valley to recreate the tradition, as with the *Larchzieh'n* in Umhausen. Certain towns in Styria, Austria, have also lately embraced the idea.

As would be expected, such modern recreations do away with any connection to the community's expectations regarding marriages, framing the tradition instead as a theatrical battle between good and evil folkloric figures, who serve either in the army of Winter or in that of Spring struggling to return. A bride and groom character may be present, but more as an excuse to enjoy the entertainments of a wedding party.

Every four years, tourists now descend on the Alpine town of Fiss to witness a cast of over three hundred costumed performers hauling a pine log more than a hundred feet long through the streets of this picturesque town. Several days before the event, the tree is felled in the forest, moved to the edge of town, and placed over an arrangement of three or four sledges. Over the first of these a "witch house" is built and decked with pine boughs. It serves both as home to a costumed Witch Mother during the procession and as a guard house for male youths who will, ostensibly, protect the log overnight from at-

Bell men lean into it at the Blochziehen of Fiss, Austria.

The Bear and Moss Man of the Blochziehen of Fiss, Austria.

The Bear is a central character of the Blochziehen of Fiss, Austria.

Moss Man of the Blochziehen of Fiss, Austria.

Witches at the Fiss Austria Blochziehen.

tempts by rival villages to steal it. While this may indeed have once been a custom, given the size of the log and the fact that Fiss hotels are booked full of tourists expecting the event, theft isn't really in the cards, meaning that witch house is really more of a clubhouse for overnight drinking.

At noon on the day of the event, a jester character called the *Bajatzl* announces the start of the event, assisted by the *Schnacker*, a masked figure wearing bells. Some declarations in old-fashioned rhymed verse are read, and the log begins slowly to move into town. The Alpine elevation and date in early February or late January mean streets are covered in snow, assisting the movement of the log on its sleds. Yoked to the front drawbar are two costumed figures embodying the power of the natural world: the bear and the Moss Man, a sort of wild man wearing a suit of "moss" (actually lichen). Joining the two on the drawbar are the Hunters, who will recapture the bear as he occasionally escapes.

Not just the more fantastic characters such as the Moss Man but all the performers, even human characters such as the hunters, wear carved wooden masks. Other secondary figures aid the forward movement by gripping the log itself. All these players, outfitted in traditional Tyrolean costume, represent the collectivity of the undertaking and the full spectrum of nineteenth-century village life: farmers, tailors, carpenters, millers, Gypsies, musicians, nightwatchmen, tinkers, and beggars. When the log stops at various stations, each of these engages the crowd with a certain characteristic comic routine. Somewhere among these are the bride and groom.

THE SCHWOAFTUIFL ("SWINE DEVIL") ATTEMPTS TO IMPEDE THE LOG'S PROGRESS IN THE FISS, AUSTRIA, BLOCHZIEHEN.

Other characters that circulate among the spectators throughout the event include the *Giggeler,* a man costumed as a rooster who (true to his medieval symbolism) pursues the women in the crowd. At intervals, the Bajatzl climbs to rooftops to sweep snow down onto the crowd while shouting witticisms.

Progress of the log is symbolically impeded by costumed witches and the Schwoaftuifl (swine devil), a shaggy Krampus-like figure who pulls backwards from the end of a trailing rope. The witches tease spectators with their brooms and perform dances, as well as verses satirizing embarrassing community events.

At the end of the day, the log arrives in the town square and there is music, food, and drinking, as well as an auction during which politicians and others endowed with the funds and desire to curry public favor bid for the particularly expensive wood into which the log will be rendered at the sawmill.

THE EGETMANN PROCESSION

A rather spectacular procession combining elements of the plow and log-pulling rituals can be found a couple hours south of Fiss, in South Tyrol. The town, built on winegrowing, has both an Italian name, Termeno, and a German one, Tramin, from which the Gewürztraminer grape variety gets its name.

The event, which takes place on Shrove Tuesday in odd years, is called the *Egetmann* festival. A connection to plow rituals is present in the name, as the German word *Ege*

Wedding wagon at the Egetmann Procession of Tramin, South Tyrol, Italy.

(Tyrolean: *Eget*) means "harrow," a cousin of the plow used for lighter cultivation. The central figure, the *Egetmann,* the plowman (or harrowman, for sticklers), is presented in the procession as an effigy of a groom about to be married, echoing the old plow rituals' association with marriage imperatives.

The Adige valley, where Tramin is located, formerly was home to many similar rituals documented with particular frequency in the 1870s. In Meran (Merano), one of the Adige valley towns less than an hour to the south of Tramin, there was a plow-dragging ritual through city streets involving the strewing of the fool's seed in the form of sawdust.

The Austrian poet and scholar Ignaz Vincenz Zingerle, who lived in Merano at the time, described a ritual common both to Tramin and to the adjacent town of Neumarkt, then called the *Egerthansel* (*Hansel* here used like *Jack* in English, as in *Plough Jack* or *Jack of the Plough*). In his 1871 book *Manners, Customs and Thought of the Tyrolean People*, he writes that on Shrove Tuesday

> *The lads make a tall man, called Egerthansel, out of straw and old, ragged clothes, and carry him around on a specially prepared stretcher. They stop in squares and at various houses and ask the straw man for news. On behalf of the doll, a boy replies and announces all the offensive stories of the day. Finally, the Egerthansel is bestowed as a bridegroom on an old but nonetheless marriage-loving maiden and hung up on the front door of her apartment to loud laughter. Then the boys go to the inn to music and dancing and have a happy day.*

Laundry wagon of the Egetmann Procession of Tramin, South Tyrol, Italy.

Cooks' wagon of the Egetmann Procession of Tramin, South Tyrol, Italy.

One of the "gypsy" wagons. Egetmann Procession of Tramin, South Tyrol, Italy.

The Wudele (Schnappvieh) of the Egetmann Procession of Tramin, South Tyrol, Italy.

Into the tub on the laundry wagon. Egetmann Procession of Tramin, South Tyrol, Italy.

THE WUDELE (SCHNAPPVIEH) OF THE EGETMANN PROCESSION OF TRAMIN, SOUTH TYROL, ITALY.

Fishermen's wagon of Tramin's Egetmann Procession. Fishermen stand high above the reedy bank and cast their lines among the spectators.

Cross-dressed Egetmann performer with bladder balloons, Tramin, Italy.

One of the "gypsy" wagons. Egetmann Procession of Tramin, South Tyrol, Italy.

While it's sometimes said the Egetmann dates to the sixteenth century, this would only refer to customs as generally represented in German-speaking culture. The event actually took shape in the late 1800s, and by the mid twentieth century had grown into the elaborate form seen today.

The Egetmann is not like other Carnival celebrations. It grows larger every year, with nearly eight hundred costumed participants taking part today. Given that all of these must be male residents of Tramin, this represents nearly half that demographic. While some walk in the procession, at least as many ride on one of many wagons representing scenes of village life or local lore.

For three or four hours, they roll through narrow cobblestone streets pulled by chugging trucks and antique tractors: wheeled constructions representing taverns and cobbler's, tailor's, and blacksmith's shops—a whole village rumbling through a village, every wagon wildly thrown together from weathered lumber, rusted tin, and old barrels, some draped in leafy boughs, others clattering with pots and pans, all filled with clambering performers screaming, laughing, playing music, drinking, eating, and cooking on little fires. Every wagon has its own kitchen, and each leaves a trail of greasy smoke in its wake. Food and wine are passed to spectators, who are also tagged with the same sooty paste that blackens the faces of many performers, muddling distinctions between the two. And the whole scene is lost in immersive clouds of confetti, flour, hay, and sawdust, liberally tossed out by performers on the wagons.

At the opening of this procession, the old plow ritual is suggested as figures known as "path-makers" symbolically open a path through the crowd, pantomiming their tasks with rakes and scythes and driving oxen pulling a plow and harrow. Along the way they scatter into the crowd the familiar "fool's seed." They are followed by the nuptial wagon, the *Egetmannhansl* effigy dressed in a groom's top hat and tails, and a younger male costumed as the bride.

These figures are followed by the carriage of more formally dressed dignitaries playing town councilors, whose job it is to read from an oversized book, known as "the Protocol." In fact, this is the local version of a "fool's book," full of rhymed embarrassing rumors and scandals of the year. Nothing too intimate is included, only community-level offenses are acceptable these days after an insinuation of adultery saw a jealous husband produce a gun and fire into the crowd.

FIGURES AND FLOATS

There are also now familiar figures like the wild man, who in Tramin is pursued by a hunter. Besides the bear at the drawbar, there are two bears of odd colors, one white and the other green, to represent Winter and Spring. At one of the processional stops, the winter bear is pursued and killed by a hunter, to reinforce the triumph-of-Spring motif. And the same happens at another square where the hunter shoots down the wild man he has captured after he goes just a bit too wild.

Unique to Tramin and something of a mascot for the parade are strange figures known as *Wudele* or *Schnappvieh* (snapping cattle). These are towering creatures with shaggy horned heads and immense jaws lined with wooden teeth. The jaws loudly clack when bounced by the performer hidden under a burlap robe that serves both as neck and shapeless body. At once cartoonishly silly and imposing, *Schnappvieh* stand ten or twelve feet high and roam in herds barely controlled by a butcher who pantomimes killing one every time the procession stops at a square.

As you will have noted, the pantomimed killing of an unruly costumed beast is common among Carnival performances. The tendency to explain this in terms of seasonal death and resurrection, or Spring's triumph over Winter, can be a bit overextended. Even with the butcher killing off *Schnappvieh,* you'll see this put forward, as if there weren't already a simpler and move obvious explanation, namely the comedic excitement provided. Given the monstrous scale of these "cattle," it also satisfies a Carnival fantasy of gorging on meat before Lent.

The scenes of village life rolling past the spectators constitute the bulk of the procession. Along with those mentioned earlier, there are barrel-makers, wine-tasters, moonshiners, a wagon of "rich Gypsies" and one for "poor Gypsies," fisherman on an enormous wheeled ship, tinkers and iron workers hammering away on metals, knife-sharpeners throwing off

Mechanical toy version of the "Old Women's Mill" (1880s) on display at the Mühlviertel Palace Museum, Freistadt, Austria.

sparks from grinding wheels, a laundry with laundresses splashing the crowd with suds and water, and bakers, who naturally throw flour. There are also performers circulating on foot amongst the crowd: dancing witches with steaming pots, a tailor sewing together the coats of unwary spectators, a cobbler who fixes shoes with a squirt of shaving cream down the ankle, and the like.

THE OLD WOMEN'S MILL

The final wagon of the procession is the Old Women's Mill, a white semi-trailer with its name and images of grinding wheels painted on the sides. Atop it stand a half-dozen white coated millers. While it's one of the least interesting wagons visually, this is made up for by the antics staged around it when it stops: the millers leap into the street to pursue a shrieking "old woman" (as always, a cross-dressed male, hamming it up as if his life depended on it). She makes it down the street a block or so till she's captured and thrown into a flour-filled wheelbarrow. It's rolled back to the Mill, thundering down the cobblestones, and the kicking and screaming victim is hooked to a cable and hoisted up toward the millers. At this point, the activity becomes hard to decipher, but it hardly matters since the aerial antics on the cable are really the climax, and besides, the crowd already knows the storyline.

SLOVENIAN "PINE WEDDING" RITUAL ENACTED DURING THE 1962 CARNIVAL IN PTUJ.

The Women's Mill of Tripstrill is a popular Carnival play written by a Swabian teacher, poet, and composer, Georg Anton Bredelin, in 1781. The original musical he wrote is sung every five years in Wolfach, but it's also represented as a float in other parades in Reckendorf, Bad Reichenhalt, Hohenfurch, and Schönsee.

In the story, the Mill is a sort of Fountain of Youth; old women ground through its gears come out young. Vain women submit to it encouraged by their lecherous husbands, who are then spurned by their regenerated mates. The play's satiric treatment of our more shameful tendencies is well suited to the lampooning spirit of Carnival, and all the slapstick stunts help distract from any eighteenth-century misogyny.

PINE WEDDINGS

Another type of Carnival procession similar to the German plow and log-hauling customs takes place in Slovenia and Croatia, in the southern region of Austria bordering Slovenia, and among Slovenes and Croats settled in Hungary. It goes by a number of names, but the most common is *ženitev z borom*, or "pine wedding." Like other log and plow rituals, the event was usually held when there had been no marriages in the village the previous year or between Christmas and Shrove Tuesday. The pine wedding replaced earlier Slovenian and Croatian plow customs like those of sixteenth-century Germany.

Slovenian "Pine Wedding" ritual enacted during the 1962 Carnival in Ptuj.

Slovenian "Pine Wedding" ritual enacted during the 1962 Carnival in Ptuj.

SLOVAKIAN ASH WEDNESDAY CUSTOM OF "WALKING WITH THE LOG."

In the earliest reference to a pine wedding, from 1689, it's the unmarried women of the village tasked with the log-dragging, but later that duty fell to young bachelors. As you might expect, any current survivals of the custom are no longer tied to what marriages may or may not have occurred.

Ever since the job of log-pulling was relegated to males in the 1880s, it's been an important male rite of passage, so much so that it's taboo for the uninitiated to sit with the initiated in the tavern. The log becomes a sort of aspirational symbol, a stand-in for the perfect male suitor. The thickest and longest tree is chosen as a suitably "virile" groom. After it's felled, it's stripped of its branches, loaded on a wagon, and decorated with ribbons, paper flowers, and wreaths or even whitewashed.

Originally, a mock wedding service was performed in the forest where the tree was cut down, and there was a bit more mockery in this mock wedding, with the tree regarded as sort of a booby prize, a wooden spouse married off to young people who'd failed to secure a mate as expected. Today, a younger male may play the bride. Or there may be effigies of a bride, or figures of bride and groom fixed to the wagon as a nod to the ritual's original intent.

On the way from the forest, or while the pine rolls through the town, members of a "wedding party" run alongside or perch upon the log. The group includes those playing groomsmen, bridesmaids, a priest, magistrate, or other dignitaries. Accordionists are usually present to provide the music. In a few cases, additional characters representing the village types (as with Egetmann) may be included. Sometimes all of this is dispensed with and it's just a stripped-down rite of passage in which participants in work clothes test and show off their logging skills.

While the modern pine wedding in Slovenia and its neighbors has mostly shed its socially coercive aspect, the ethnographic literature describing the Croats of old Hungary mentions some pointedly coercive Carnival customs directed at young women who do not marry as expected. This includes tying to the victim a smaller log or another encumbering object (like a pig trough), which must be dragged a certain distance. Logs might also be simply deposited in the victim's yard or leaned against doors and gates as a humiliating gesture.

THE ASH WEDNESDAY LOG

In Poland, there is the related tradition of the "Ash Wednesday log" (*Popielcowe klocki*). As soon as the midnight bell rang out Carnival, unmarried young women (and, in some regions, men) were at risk of being harnessed to the log or at least of having a Log of Shame deposited in their yard. It was possible to buy one's way out of this game by providing the mischief-makers shots of vodka upon arrival. If drinks weren't speedily forthcoming, the victim would be compelled to drag the log to the nearest house of another unmarried woman, thus perpetuating the game into the wee hours. While there was surely an element of humiliation involved, the Ash Wednesday log could also be used by would-be suitors as a way to show a more *personal* interest in changing the victim's status from unmarried to married. In cities like Krakow, this custom was scaled down into a sort of indoor party game or Carnival prank. Instead of a log, tiny bits of wood or sacks of ashes or other items were covertly attached to the victim's back. More distasteful objects were also used, such as dirty rags, herring bones or heads, or chicken feet.

THE LOG IS CARNIVAL, CARNIVAL IS THE LOG

Similar customs were to be found among the East Slavs of Russia, Belarus, and Ukraine. The game was especially important in Ukraine, where the word for "log" or its plural, *Kolodii* (*Колодий*), was in some regions the term for Carnival. The tradition was practiced into the twentieth century until discouraged by the Soviets, at which point Russian Shrovetide practices were promoted over those of Ukraine.

Refreshingly, the victim dragging the log here is male rather than female. On Shrove Monday, married (rather than unmarried) women of the community would visit the houses of bachelors who they believed should have found themselves brides in the previous year. The "logs" used were relatively small, decorated blocks of wood and would be tied not only to the legs of recalcitrant bachelors but also (in some regions) to those of parents who had failed to arrange mates for their children.

As with related customs, the young man might buy his way out of the humiliation with gifts or money. The following Easter, the girl was then obliged to present the reluctant bachelor with several dyed eggs tied in an embroidered handkerchief.

In explaining the custom, it's often noted that blocks of wood were sometimes tied to the legs of livestock to prevent them from jumping over fences and that, during the permissive days of Carnival, a feisty bachelor might be particularly inclined to jump over a fence (like a billy jumping in with the nanny goats) were it not for the block reminding him of his better intentions. In some regions, the log was replaced by less cumbersome, even amorous, tokens such as ribbons, scarves, or flowers.

A block also served as a focal point of a final feast of the Ukrainian Carnival, one celebrated exclusively by older married women. Gathering at an inn or tavern, each guest brought her own block, which would be placed amid a potluck of traditional Carnival dumplings (*varenyky*) as well as cheeses, eggs, and other foods soon to be forbidden. Should a male intruder show his face, he would immediately be tied to a block unless he provided another round of vodka for the women.

In some regions, the feast was the culmination of a week-long celebration of the block, with different days representing different stages in the cycle of life. On its "birthday," the block would be swaddled in diapers (which must be acquired from three different houses). It was "baptized" the following day and "christened" on the next (the two rites are separate in the Orthodox Church). When all that was done, it was able to "die" on the following day, providing an opportunity to stage a funeral complete with much singing of mournful vodka-soaked dirges so dear to the Slavic soul.

· CHAPTER IX ·

THE KURENT AND THE PLOW

PRESENTING THE MONSTROUS

SLOVENIAN KURENT;

HOW HE APPEARS AT A CARNIVAL OF GROWING REPUTE;
HIS STRANGE SHEEPSKIN COSTUME
ADORNED WITH FEATHERS & HEDGEHOG SPINES;

HOW HE BRINGS LUCK

WITH HIS PLOW;
HIS REPUTATION AS

A SLAVIC GOD

QUESTIONED

CONNECTIONS TO
GERMAN CUSTOMS REVEALED.

KURENTOVANJE IN PTUJ, SLOVENIA.

THE EVER-GROWING KURENTOVANJE

One of the most exotic and visually impressive European Carnival figures is the Slovenian *Kurent* (or *Korant*). It's increasingly well-known thanks to the circulation of images online and the growing popularity of a festival in the town of Ptuj, the *Kurentovanje*, which showcases the figure.

This event is now one of Europe's largest Carnivals, drawing several hundred costumed performers and more than sixty thousand spectators for the weekend procession on the Sunday before Shrove Tuesday (Shrove Sunday).

Ptuj even recently added an interactive museum, Kurent House (Kurentova Hiša), where you can take a souvenir selfie with a friendly Kurent digitally composited into the shot. Back around 1995, there was even talk of a theme park, Kurentland, but that seems to still be on the drawing board.

All this may sound like a long, strange trip from our discussion of village plow rituals, but in fact the Kurentovanje is connected with these. The fast forward occurred in 1960, when the Ptuj historian Drago Hasl gathered a variety of regional Carnival characters into the Ptuj town square for a procession. As the figures paraded, a narrator on loudspeaker furnished background on each custom represented while a local band provided music. The

PREVIOUS: KURENT IN LJUBLJANA, SLOVENIA.

KURENT IN LJUBLJANA, SLOVENIA.

program was well received, and the next year traditions from elsewhere in Slovenia were added (including "pine wedding" performers). The festival continued to expand representing other eastern European Carnival traditions and eventually even occasional performers from Austria, Italy, and Japan. The local hero, the Kurent, however, remained the favorite.

The Slovenian Kurenti begin their activities on Candlemas, February 2. On that night many of the performers gather for a large bonfire lit at midnight. As the flames rise, they don their bells and hoist their clubs for the first time. The suits and masks, however, are not worn till the week preceding Ash Wednesday.

In 2001, the Ptuj Kurentovanje added the Candlemas bonfire as an opening ceremony, though other activities (smaller exhibitions of folk customs) fall during the week preceding the two large processions on Shrove Sunday and a slightly smaller encore on Shrove Tuesday.

While the Ptuj festival represents a glorious all-in-one opportunity to see *Kurenti* (plural of Kurent) in action, by its scale it necessarily has decontextualized things a bit. As seen elsewhere, the processions in the town square represent a municipal translation of the old door-to-door good-luck visits still traditional to the villages around Ptuj.

A Kurent on the march in Ig, Slovenia.

Devils accompanying Kurent group in Ljubljana, Slovenia.

SHEEPSKINS, BELLS, AND TURKEY FEATHERS

So, what is a Kurent and what does it look like?

The costume has evolved over time to become more elaborate, but the style proudly shown in the Ptuj festival consists of a tunic of sheepskin, which is made from a long-hair breed, so that it nearly doubles the size of the wearer. This reaches only to the tops of the ankles, which must be covered in red leg-warmers. A crowning headpiece features two hornlike sticks spanned by a string of bright ribbons and turkey feathers. In certain regions, an actual set of horns (bull) is preferred to the headdress with feathers and ribbons.

Most Kurenti wear masks, topped by masses of draping sheep fur and featuring long snouts made of leather. Usually the face is dark, but occasionally may be red or orange with painted eyes. Beneath this, there is an extremely long, dangling tongue made of red cloth, sometimes decoratively embroidered. It's so stylized that to the untrained eye it may read more as necktie than anything else. Above the tongue can be seen a row of teeth made of beans and a stiff, jutting mustache fashioned from stalks of millet grain. The mask may also feature tusks like a boar's.

Each Kurent has around his waist a chain hung with five cowbells and silk handkerchiefs, which are offered as a sort of tribute by female spectators, whom the Kurent tends to chase. In villages, the performers must be unmarried males, but the international festival has recently made way for some female performers. Another near universal is a club called the "hedgehog" (*ježevka*), as the end is traditionally wrapped in the spiny hide of that animal. As a final touch, the Kurent may also carry pincers with which he seizes unwary female onlookers.

THE GOOD-LUCK VISIT

The plow is central to traditional Kurenti good-luck visits and for the occasion is festooned with paper ribbons and flowers, mistletoe, boxwood, or pine boughs. In some cases, it might even be topped with something like a small Christmas tree.

The plow is guided by a Kurent and pulled by two or three pairs of performers referred to as "horses" or "oxen." They wear tall black boots, white smocks and aprons, shawls, and either headdresses decorated with paper flowers or conical caps trailing long ribbons. The "horses" may be preceded by a performer in a decorated hat and high boots who cracks a whip, and other Kurenti bounce along behind the plow, clattering their bells. Carnival carols may be sung along the way.

In many troupes, there is also a young man in old-woman drag who carries a basket of symbolic seed (sawdust) to be scattered behind the plow. Or there may be a performer in old-fashioned costume who carries a rake and basket, the latter used not for "seed" but to collect donations made by those visited.

Arriving at the door of each house, the basket-carrier accompanied by a Kurent asks the householder for permission to plow the yard. This isn't a threat as it would be in Britain's Plough Monday (see Chapter VIII). The Kurent's plowshare rolls on wheels rather

Kurenti of Lancova Vas in eastern Slovenia.

Kurenti of Lancova Vas in eastern Slovenia.

KURENTI OF LANCOVA VAS IN ARE REWARDED ON THEIR HOUSE ROUNDS.

than cutting the earth, and the symbolic act is promised to ensure good crops and grow "fat turnips" (as the request is traditionally formulated).

When this is affirmed, the whip-cracker offers a dramatic display of his skill, after which the "horses" begin drawing the plow in circles over the yard, followed by the leaping Kurenti ringing their bells and brandishing their clubs. The higher the Kurent leaps, the higher the millet will grow, it's said.

A final member necessary to the troupe is the devil (*tajfl*), who embodies the bad luck chased away by the ritual, but in practice he can also serve as a sort of conductor, directing the plow and the movement of the Kurenti. He wears a red or occasionally black suit accented at the cuffs with fur or the black feathers of a crow. He wears a mask largely like the Kurent's, but with horns replacing the beribboned headdress. He may also be equipped with a pitchfork and net (with which to "capture souls").

At the end of the visit, the group receives money, drinks, or food from the homeowners. A sort of buffet table is often set up outside to facilitate the process.

All these customs can vary by region, as can the costumes. Unlike the much-photographed figures of the Ptuj festival, Kurenti elsewhere may wear less resource-intensive costumes. Instead of luxuriant sheep fur, suits may be patched together from scraps of animal hides or improvised with winter coats turned outward to show fur linings. This more modest approach is also seen in older photos. In earlier years, masks weren't even always part of the costume.

"PLOWING PROCESSION" BY JURIJ ŠUBIC. ILLUSTRATION FOR *THE AUSTRO-HUNGARIAN MONARCHY IN WORDS AND PICTURES*, VOL.12: *STYRIA*, 1890, VIENNA.

THE KURENT IN HISTORY

The earliest rendering of a Kurent is in the 1890 German-language encyclopedia *The Austro-Hungarian Monarchy in Word and Image*, an illustration of a house-visit showing a single Kurent guiding a plow drawn by team of "horses." The basket-carrier (with rake) and whip-cracking performer are also present—as are some rather frightened children.

The fear that accompanied the Kurent's visit is emphasized in the earliest description of the custom, from the 1887 chronicle of Ptuj, written by the clergyman Matija Slekovec. He provides a few details on the costume, mentioning the inside-out coat and leather mask (painted white rather than red or black), and then goes on:

> *With such a cap on his head, the "kurent" looks as if he has just escaped from hell. To announce himself from afar, he has a cowbell tied to his back. For defense, he has a strong pole in his hands, on the end of which is nailed a hedgehog skin. Thus made, he marches powerfully through the village, leaping and leaping as if twinned with Lucifer himself. Of course, the children are afraid of him, the club even more than him, but they all run after him. But if he runs into someone, he screams and runs away.*

Orači (Plowmen) and Kurenti near Markovcih, Slovenia. 1959.

Other references to nineteenth-century Carnival figures in Ptuj are more general. A "masked carnival ride" is mentioned as occurring in Ptuj on Shrove Tuesday 1873, and there are intermittent bans on activities recorded in the nineteenth and early twentieth centuries to prevent sometimes lethal fights between bands of revelers, which have been assumed to refer to rival Kurent troupes. An even older ban, from 1610, mentions "un-Christian" Carnival behavior with no specificity but has been eagerly interpreted as referring to Kurent customs. Those searching for evidence have even pointed to an ornament on a particular pilaster of a particular house in Ptuj built in the 1700s, identifying this as an early representation of a Kurent—very much an eye-of-the-beholder matter.

All that is definitively known about the original Kurent customs is restricted to mid-to-late-nineteenth-century references. Not surprisingly, however, there have been attempts to enlarge upon this, making of him a sort of ancient fertility god or Slovenian equivalent of Bacchus, who teaches man the art of viniculture and encourages the enjoyment of its fruits at Carnival. This aspect of the Kurent was first described in an 1858 issue of the Slovenian weekly *Neven*, in a story contributed by the historian Janez Trdina.

Trdina also published *The History of the Slovenian Nation* (1850), as well as collections of folk tales and reflections on Slovenian ethnic identity. His tales of the Kurent gave birth to a body of literature portraying the Kurent as a fiddle-playing trickster, a sort of man-in-the-moon character, or (most often) an ancient Slavic god, one condemned by the

Orači (Plowmen) and Kurenti in Ptuj, Slovenia, 1960.

Church but sometimes said to have been retained by the peasantry under the name of a saint (St. Korant). It's unlikely, however, that these depictions describe actual folk traditions. Instead, they are just original works of fiction crafted in a folkloric style.

This tradition continues to evolve into the present day with the Kurent as a subject of literary folk tales, poems, and the like. In 1909, the Slovenian literary light Ivan Cankar turned the Kurent into a human observer of the contemporary plight of Slovenes in his satiric novel *Kurent*. There's even a horror film about the Kurent currently in development, *The Moon of the Kurent*, to be directed by Tomaž Gorkič. The growing prominence of Ptuj's Kurentovanje festival has only fed this modern expansion of the mythology, and today the assertion that the Kurent is an ancient Slavic fertility god is to be found everywhere online.

A SLAVIC GOD?

I am by no means convinced that the Kurent is an exclusively Slavic figure, much less ancient. But reimagining the Kurent thus would have served as a cultural response to a late-nineteenth-century situation, namely desire of some in Slovenia, then an isolated territory of the Austro-Hungarian Empireto affirm their cultural ties to South Slavs, Czechs, and other subject peoples.

However, in embracing the Kurent as a sort of nationalist embodiment, its local context and certain particulars are lost. The area around Ptuj at the time the Kurent and plow customs are first recorded was largely German-speaking (86%, according to a 1910 report). The word used for the devil in the plow troupe, *tajfl,* is clearly a derivation of the German *Teufel,* and it's even suggested that the word *Kurent* comes from the German *Kurrende,* used to describe Christmas carolers (from the Latin *currere* for "run"). In western Slovenia, masked Carnival characters are referred to as *lavfarji,* from the German *Läufer* (meaning "runner"). While an etymological argument for a German origin is by no means definitive, other details also cry out for comparison, notably the dangling tongue reminiscent of the Krampus and the bells reminiscent of both Krampus and Percht.

The Austrian *Percht* (plural: *Perchten*) particularly shares much with the Kurent. The Percht can function both as a luck-bringer during Epiphany house-visits and as a *Kinderschreckfigur* (children's terror figure), as with Frau Perchta, who punishes bad children. The latter aspect is present in the earliest Kurent accounts, in which the fear he inspires in children is emphasized. The hedgehog-spine-covered club carried by the Kurent is an oddity of the ensemble, which tends to go without comment or explanation but becomes less puzzling if compared to the switch or whip carried by the Krampus or Percht. The author of the Ptuj *Chronicle* of 1887, after all, comments that children "are afraid of him, the club even more than him."

Especially relevant to the Kurent is the Percht's identity as a luck-bringer associated with fertility. Like those representing the Kurent, performers representing the Percht wear bells said to drive evil from the homes they visit on Epiphany (the start of Carnival). In some regions, Perchten also engage in hopping dances said to aid the growth of crops, a process described in the folk saying "So high the Percht leaps, so high grows the flax," as with the Kurent and Slovenian millet.

None of this is to say that the Kurent tradition is merely a Slovenian version of Percht customs. Rather, it seems that aspects of the Kurent ritual absorbed certain elements of Percht customs found in neighboring Austria and that this was melded to other Carnival plow rituals as well as other customs.

THE BUSÓ

WHEREIN WE MEET ANOTHER CARNIVAL MONSTER,

THE HUNGARIAN BUSÓ;

HIS FROLICS IN THE TOWN OF MOHÁCS
DRAWING INNUMERABLE SPECTATORS;

HOW HE APPEARS IN SHEEPSKINS &

FEARSOME HORNED MASK

& IS FURTHER EQUIPPED WITH BELLS, MACE & RATCHET;
THE FEMININE "BEAUTIFUL BUSÓK"
WHO ARE ELEGANTLY DRESSED

JANKELE

WITH HIS BAG OF ASH;

THE BUSÓ ARRIVING BY BOAT ON THE DANUBE
AND LATER CONVEYED IN FANTASTIC RUSTIC WAGONS;

HIS MAGIC BLESSING OF HOUSES;

A QUESTION OF IMPROPER CONDUCT;
A MARVELOUS TALE OF BUSÓ TERRORS
INFLICTED ON THE TURKS
SHOWN TO BE UNTRUE.

THE BUSÓ GOES WALKING

In Mohács, Hungary, a Danube town near the Croatian border, another eastern Carnival celebration rivals the popularity of the Ptuj Kurentovanje. It is the *Busójárás*, or "*Busó*-walking," a procession of more than two thousand performers in massive sheepskin coats and horned wooden masks called *Busók* (the plural of *Busó*).

More than eighty thousand spectators attend the six-day event featuring multiple processions, the largest of these on the Sunday before Shrove Tuesday, as in Ptuj. Alongside the processions are multiple bonfires in the town square, exhibitions of local folklore, traditional dances, choral performances, lectures, culinary events, and more. There is also a dedicated Busójárás museum (the Busóudvar), opened in 2013 for those who visit Mohács before or after the festival (though no booth for a digital photo with a Busó, it seems).

The Busójárás is not a custom of Hungary's native Magyars but is Slavic, originating with the Šokci people settled in the region, a subgroup of Croats found also in eastern Croatia, northern Serbia, and parts of Romania and Bosnia and Herzegovina. Sometimes, rather than *Busójárás*, the activity of going about in Carnival costumes is described with the Serbo-Croatian term *poklade*. While the Busójárás is recognized as a Šokci tradition, the population of Mohács, according to a 2011 census, was only about 4% Croat, so it seems safe to say that membership in the more than fifty Busó groups in the city would not be exclusive to that ethnicity. Only citizens of Mohács, however, are allowed to don the costume, and formerly this was also restricted to males over eighteen, however now one occasionally also sees children dressed in diminutive Busó suits.

THE COSTUME

The Busó's costume, like the Kurent's, originally made use of an inside-out winter coat (or just a vest) with sheepskin lining, but today coats are custom-made for the Busójárás and the extravagantly long fur of select sheep breeds is preferred. The coat falls halfway to the knee over loose white trousers, traditionally stuffed with straw to bulk up the figure. Colorful woolen leg-warmers cover the leg below the knee. The Busó's oversized wooden mask, carved in a decidedly naïve style (traditionally from willow wood) is worn with a large sheepskin hood and topped by a pair of horns—usually from a bull, but ram or goat horns are also used. The masks are usually black, but also painted dark red in accordance with a tradition claiming they were once painted with animal blood. Teeth and eyes are always delineated with bright white paint, and the chin is usually long and carved to suggest a beard. There is also a mustache, either carved, painted, or crafted from hemp or horsehair. Taken together, the visage is comically frightening, or frightfully comic, an odd mix described in the saying, "The Busó can't be a clown and can't be a horror."

PREVIOUS: Busó with ratchet noisemaker in Széchényi Square, Mohács, Hungary.
OPPOSITE: Busó having a nip.

At the Mohács Busójárás.

Hanging from a rope at his waist, the Busó wears a bell or two, but these are barely heard at festivities, and Busók do not adopt the stereotypical hopping gait used to set bells ringing elsewhere. The more indispensable noisemaker is a handheld wooden ratchet, which clicks and clacks as it's constantly spun. Some of these can be quite large, up to two feet in length. He might also accessorize with other items: a haversack slung over the shoulder and a water gourd at the belt, or he might carry a wooden walking stick or pitchfork. The Busó's most common tool is a whip made of dried bull pizzle, though this is more symbolic than anything, used mainly for pointing or, on rare occasion, to surprise an unwary spectator with a harmless tap. Another item occasionally carried for symbolic effect is a wooden mace, topped by a starburst intriguingly assembled from interlocking pieces.

OPPOSITE: Buso taking a load off.

BEAUTIFUL BUSÓK, BAGS OF ASH

A couple other characters may be seen in the Busójárás. The Szépbusók, or "beautiful Busók," are women dressed in the traditional Šokca attire, colorfully embroidered skirts and shawls, with lace veils held in place by slim eye masks. Their job is to help guide the Busók, whose vision is impaired by the awkwardly fitted masks. This role was formerly played by cross-dressed men.

Jankele is a less common figure, dressed something like a scarecrow in ragged clothes and with some sort of mask improvised from a cloth bag or remnants. These are usually younger performers, playfully referred to as "Busó students." His job is to guard the Busók from pesky children and unruly spectators, smacking them away, when necessary, with a cloth bag weighted with sawdust or flour. Sometimes a handful of the latter is thrown or rubbed on spectators. In less genteel times, this smacking-bag was more aggressively weighted with rocks and ash or even contained decomposing rats, cats, or other things equally repulsive.

Busójárás troupe, The Danube Passage Group, preparing to cross the Danube.

BUSÓ'S BIG DAY

Festivities begin early on Carnival Sunday with a number of troupes from the southern part of the city crossing the Danube in small boats. After greeting spectators and other Busók on the docks, they join a procession to Kóló square, a historical center of Šokci culture, and from there march to the larger Széchényi square, the main staging ground of the festival.

The parade through the city includes a multitude of decorated wagons pulled by old tractors and mules. Atop these are built shacks seating more performers amid cornstalks, gourds, and other farmyard trappings. Other wagons contain giant noisemaking ratchets the size of pianos. Some Busók pull handcarts on which sit wooden tubs containing Busó dolls or effigies. The Szépbusók hand out candy, and all costumed characters throw feathers into the crowd as a sort of Hungarian confetti.

Busó with ratchet noisemaker in Mohács, Hungary.

A Szépbusók, or "beautiful Busók."

BUSÓ WITH RATCHET NOISEMAKER IN MOHÁCS, HUNGARY.

In the square, the racket increases as old-fashioned cannons are fired off and immense alpenhorns occasionally sounded. There are fiddlers and folk ensembles, and dancers performing the Kóló, a traditional Šokci dance after which Kóló square is named. Vendors sell steaming mulled wine and traditional Carnival snacks, and a Ferris wheel revolves in the background.

By late afternoon, there is another procession—a "funeral" for Carnival. This one includes a horse-drawn cart bearing a coffin painted with the occupant's name, "Poklade" (Carnival). It's accompanied by a figure of Death and a mock priest. At the end of the route, the coffin is loaded onto a ferry, taken to the middle of the Danube, and set adrift. The day ends with an enormous bonfire (also featuring an effigy of Carnival) in the town square. On Shrove Tuesday, much of this (including a second death of Carnival) is repeated on a smaller scale, primarily for the locals.

HOUSE CALLS

It should come as no surprise that the Busójárás of Mohács represents another transformation of good-luck visits into a municipal parade. Certain details of the costume make more sense with this in mind. The bells hung at the waist were said to drive evil from sites visited. Though the Busók of the Mohács parades today only wear a single bell,

Busójárás wagons procession through Mohács, Hungary.

Busójárás wagons procession through Mohács on Carnival Sunday.

CARNIVAL'S COFFIN ABLAZE AT MOHÁCS BUSÓJÁRÁS.

they may have worn more in the past, and the gait of the performers may also have once involved more hopping and twisting to set these ringing.

The Busó also has a traditional call, "Bao-bao!", shouted along the road and as homes are approached. Upon arrival, the mace (or walking stick) carried today was used to alert occupants of their arrival with a thump on the door. Either of these could also be used as a sort of magic wand with which all exterior corners of the house were touched, delineating boundaries evil could not cross. The same would be repeated in barns and stables. After the occupants of the home had heard enough jangling bells and shouting of "Bao-bao," the Busók would be admitted within the house, where the hearth, the heart of the home, would be touched with the mace, completing the protective spells and earning the troupe cakes or pastries.

The bag carried by the Jankele also played a role in the good-luck blessing. While today it's filled with lightweight sawdust, in the past it was messy ash, and this was sprinkled on thresholds of the home and barn to ensure protection of the structures and the health and fertility of those within. Toward that end, it was also rubbed on those visited as well as their livestock.

We also hear about additional characters taking part in Busó house-visits in an article written by József Ernyey for a 1907 edition of the *Bulletin of the Department of Ethnography of the Hungarian National Museum*. These included a Hunchback with straw-stuffed

Jankele (L) and Busó (R) visiting grandma.

hump, who chased children and cracked a whip, and a Cobbler, who grabbed the legs of girls and women and attempted to force them to try on a shoe. Characters like these belong to the "village types," we've seen in other processions, and the troupes could also include a bride and groom. A vestige of this may be found in the costumes of the Szépbusók, sometimes described as wearing wedding finery. Other old accounts even mention plowing being part of the visit, not as a magical conveyor of fertility but more as a threat in the manner of the British Plough Monday.

An interesting Shrove Tuesday tradition still preserved in the town of Moha, a bit over a hundred miles to the north, echoes something of the old Busó visits. It's called *Tikverőzés*, loosely translated as "hen tapping," in which henhouses, hens, and eggs are lightly tapped with a special walking stick to ensure health and fertility. Ash is also smeared on hens and on females and children as a blessing. The "tapper" is dressed is long ribbons of rag and accompanied by a figure in a voluminous linen suit stuffed with straw, like the hunchback mentioned in our 1907 account from the Mohács region.

BAD BUSÓ!

While the old, rural house visits were probably rowdy and even occasionally intimidating, the Busó groups, in this situation, might be restrained by the promise of handouts

Busó's naughty side.

to be given or withheld. This seems not to be the case as they began carousing in the city. According to József Ernyey's previously cited 1907 article:

> *For three days and three nights, the reveler runs all over the streets and taverns. The drinkers wander around the whorehouses, where the dissonant noise of the horns, bugles and cowbells and the wild howling of the masked men are ... mixed with the neighing of horses likewise masked, the bellowing of oxen, the sound of bagpipes and fiddles.*

Bad behavior was only encouraged by the anonymity offered by the masks, and Carnival became known as a time to act on personal vendettas. Throughout the year, "We'll meet at Busójárás!" was uttered wherever there was a score to be settled. Not only individual fights but fights between competitive gangs of Busók were not uncommon, so much so that the newspapers of the 1890s frequently began their coverage of the festivities with lines like, "This year's Busójárás also did not pass without bloodshed." Guns were occasionally brought along both as noisemakers and as protection—or used to intimidate enemies—or worse. By the early twentieth century, newspapers sought to assure the citizenry of an increased police presence during the Busójárás.

That the Busó was imagined as a fertility figure was used by masked performers as justification for improprieties with the opposite sex. A hint of this remains in the modern

Busójárás, where females receive nearly all the teasing, but in footage from the 1950s groups of Busók can be seen aggressively chasing and catching women as they tumble together to the ground.

In a 2010 video interview, Baráth Gábor, a Mohács mask carver, discusses this sort of thing with János Kalenics, regarded as one of the last old-time Busók. Presumably referring to experiences of the late 1940s, Kalenics reminisces:

> *And it was also said that the Busók were free to grope many of the wives. Because they didn't wear panties. But like that it was allowed to reach under. Because they said that the one was touched and whose hair was pulled, that person would grow tall hemp.*

After World War I, the house visits had been all but replaced by the municipal parade, but by the 1920s the activities in Mohács had come to be seen as a nuisance, and the number of performers and spectators dwindled. With the Soviet takeover, the event was further sidelined until documentary footage shot in 1955 began to attract international interest. These short films, created by the ethnographer Anna Raffay and the well-known Hungarian director István Szőts, still show groups of Busók fighting and participants wearing obtrusively large, numbered badges to help with identification of perpetrators should matters require attention from police. Apparently, this system worked, as authorities began quietly encouraging the festivities as a boost to the local economy. By the mid-1960s, the Busójárás was on a trajectory to where it is today.

EARLY HISTORY

When is the Busó first mentioned?

In 1757, the Hungarian theologian and historian Péter Bod described Carnival revelers going door to door, mentioning cross-dressed men and wooden masks, but he assigns no particular location to these customs and, if locally observed, he'd be referring to a faraway region of Transylvania considered part of Hungary at the time.

The first time Busók are referred to with any specificity is in the 1852 volume *Serbian Dictionary, Paralleled with German and Latin Words* by the Serbian philologist and anthropologist Vuk Stefanović Karadžić. He describes the Busók as:

> *those young lads who dress in all kinds of rags and put wooden masks on their faces—this is how they play all over the village (in Mohács).*

He actually uses the word *Buša,* rather than the Hungarian *Busó,* but as the Šokci are regarded as Croats, and as Serbian and Croatian are dialects of a common language, we should assume the Serbo-Croatian *Buša* is the original form later borrowed into Hungarian as Busó. It's not till 1912 that the term *Busójárás* can be found in print.

There is also a popular legend that roots the tradition in the sixteenth or seventeenth

1979 Busójárás in Mohács.

1969 Busójárás in Széchenyi Square, Mohács, Hungary.

century, during the era of Ottoman rule. In this tale, the oppressed Šokci have retreated to the marshlands across the Danube from the city proper. One night, a mysterious stranger appears with a prophecy of how Mohács might be reclaimed. The Šokci are to carve frightening masks and create noisemakers (ratchets and alphorns) and weapons (the wooden maces or pitchforks). They then must await the signal for attack, which will come in the form of a nocturnal thunderstorm. On the appointed night, a fleet of Šokci boats returns to Mohács and the masked figures charge in raising a tumult. The Turks retreat, terrified of the demons glimpsed in the flashing lightning.

Along with the masks, suits, and noisemakers, the legend explains the importance of staging the Busók's arrival by boat as well as the firing of antique cannons. While a marvelous story, there's an unfortunate issue with the timeline. As of 1687, Mohács was freed from Ottoman rule, and it would be another decade before the Šokci began settling in the city. To what extent they brought Busójárás with them from their Slavic homeland in Bosnia and Herzegovina and to what extent the Busójárás represents a Šokci adaptation of local customs is unclear, but the next chapter will offer an opportunity for comparison: a similar tradition more clearly of South Slav origin.

· CHAPTER XI ·

THE KUKERI

IN WHICH WE LEARN OF

BULGARIA'S KUKER,

A MOST FANTASTIC

CARNIVAL FIGURE

OF VARIEGATED FORMS;

THESE FORMS DELINEATED BY REGION
& THEIR MEANING DECIPHERED;
HOW THE KUKER ALSO VISITS HOMES AT THE NEW YEAR
WITH REVELERS IN THE GUISE OF

DIVERSE CHARACTERS,

ESPECIALLY A BRIDE & GROOM
AND ALSO FOUR-LEGGED BEASTS;

THE PLOW RITUAL

IN WHICH A VILLAGE SQUARE IS TREATED AS THE FARMER'S FIELD;

THE GREAT ENTHUSIASM ATTENDING SUCH ACTIVITIES;
THE KUKER AS VESTIGE OF THRACIAN RITUAL CONSIDERED;

THE HAUNTED DAYS OF CHRISTMAS
SHOWN TO HAVE BIRTHED
LUCK-BRINGING PRACTICES OF CARNIVAL
IN BULGARIA & ELSEWHERE.

A KALEIDOSCOPIC ARRAY

The *Kuker* (plural: *Kukeri*) is perhaps the strangest Carnival creature of eastern Europe, exhibited in a bewildering variety of forms in the International Festival of Masquerade Games or *Surva* or Surva Festival in the Bulgarian city of Pernik, roughly twenty miles west of Sofia. Held over the last weekend of January in a grim Soviet-era plaza, Surva draws more than ten thousand performers from over 150 Carnival troupes, primarily from Bulgaria, but also masked performers from other European countries and even Asia and Africa.

Describing a Kuker is nearly impossible, as the figure's embodied by a kaleidoscopic array of regional masks and costumes with little in common but the wearing of bells at the waist. Even the name is hardly fixed, with variations used including *Survakari*, *Babugeri, Dzhamali, Chausi, Startsi* ("old men"), *Dervishi* (dervishes), *or Mechkari* (from the word for "bear"). *Kuker* is often simply translated as "mummer," so it can also apply to a wider cast of costumed characters that accompany the bell-wearing creatures.

Some Kukeri are incredibly tall, elongated by conical caps or lofty headdresses; others wear incredibly intricate masks, headdresses, vests, and shawls densely beaded and embroidered, stitched, and glued with fringes, tufts, tassels, sequins, buttons, mirrors, and streaming ribbons. Others are more rustic constructions, formed from animal hides and horns, skulls, pelts, tails, and feathers. Some display a multiplicity of heads, piled atop and dwarfing the wearer's body—totem-pole-style constructions of cartoonishly primitive eyes, beaks, teeth, tongues, and waggling appendages. And others, perhaps the most eye-catching of all, are just towering spindles of dense flowing fur moving about on two legs.

REGIONAL COSTUMES

WESTERN BULGARIA

BLAGOEVGRAD PROVINCE

The last long-haired variant belongs to the mountainous Blagoevgrad province of southwest Bulgaria, where Kukeri are more correctly referred to as *Babugeri* (*Бабугери*). The suits are made from the hides of the local Kalofer goat raised for fur, originally spun into textiles and carpets but increasingly now employed in Babugeri costumes. Their luxuriant fur covers not only the body but a conical cap rising three feet or more over their heads, making the figure look something like a cross between Chewbacca and Cousin Itt of *The Addams Family* (or the former perched atop the latter). The Babugeri show off these costumes in dramatic dances, flailing full-bodied moves, which send the hair into billowing waves worthy of a shampoo commercial.

The costumes are created from a patchwork of hides, in black, brown, and cream tones. Aside from their variegated color schemes, the suits are rather featureless, marked only

PREVIOUS: KUKER COSTUME TYPICAL OF YAMBOL PROVINCE OF SOUTHEASTERN BULGARIA.

Babugeri on the road near small town of Simitli
in Blagoevgrad Province, Bulgaria.

Babugeri (or, less correctly, Kukeri) typical of Blagoevgrad Province in western Bulgaria.

by narrow eye-slits, and occasionally a sort of longer ponytail of differently colored hair topping the cap, sometimes replaced by red ribbon or tassel (red here being the color of fertility). Bell belts are worn, but virtually invisible beneath the cascading hair.

PERNIK PROVINCE

Not far from Blagoevgrad in the west of Bulgaria, is Pernik, host of the Surva festival and capitol of Pernik province. Here the Kukeri are more properly called *Survakari* (*Сурвакари*).

Survakari (or Kukeri) from Breznik, Bulgaria. Costumes using animal pelts and horns typical of Pernik Province in western Bulgaria.

The truck that brings the party. Yardzhilovtsi village, western Bulgaria.

Western Bulgarian style Kukeri from Kyustendil Province.

Kuker (or Survakar) with feather-mosaic headdress typical of Pernik Province.

More is more in Kuker world!

Bulgarian national colors and gnarled wood incorporated into costumes from Zemen, Pernik Province.

Kuker or Survakar of western Bulgaria.

KUKERI (LOCALLY: STARTSI) FROM STARA ZAGORA PROVINCE IN THE SOUTH ARE RECOGNIZED BY THE DOLLS AFFIXED TO THEIR HEADWEAR.

A few distinct forms are present. The most widespread version features short-furred sheepskin tunics and pants. The same hides are used in hoods attached to masks of a rather primitive style and topped by at least one or two pairs of goat or ram horns. Horns may also be used to represent noses, eyebrows, or even mustaches. Sometimes it's more than horns topping the mask. It may be a larger headdress featuring an entire goat head (or heads) or a fox pelt complete with the animal's face, or other preserved furry bits of local fauna. A variant of this includes suits substituting bundles of dried plant fiber for animal pelts.

Primarily in the towns of Dragichevo and Zemen, another variant features fringed suits, usually in red, white, and green, Bulgaria's national colors. These are worn with lofty headdresses which are the real attention-getters. They consist of geometric wooden frames (often diamond-shaped) covered with feathers.

Bells worn throughout Pernik Province are particularly large.

SOUTHERN BULGARIA

STARA ZAGORA PROVINCE

In Stara Zagora province, the figures are called *Startsi* ("old men") and don black cloth masks with facial features outlined in white embroidery. Colorful vests and leggings are worn, with the former left open to expose the chest. Their bells are equally macho, being

Southern Bulgarian Kukeri from the village of Ivan-Vazovo in Plovdiv Province.

as large as small watermelons. Of greatest interest, however, is the triangular headdress made from the hide of short-haired goats. At the peak is fixed a commercial plastic doll in bridal array—a particularly obvious nod to the fertility theme.

RED WOODEN SWORDS REPRESENT FERTILITY. KUKERI IN THE SOUTHERN BULGARIAN TOWN OF SHIROKA LAKA IN SMOLYAN PROVINCE.

PAZARDZHIK PROVINCE

Around the town of Pazardzhik, where Kukeri are called *Dervishi* (dervishes), a version of the long-haired Kalofer suit from nearby Blagoevgrad is worn, but without the tall cap. Instead, the head is covered with a low hood of goat hair and the face is hidden by a veil-like mask falling below the chin like a beard. The mask–veil combination is covered in a colorful patchwork of fringes, embroidery, and tassels. Red is always a prominent color in the masks.

HASKOVO PROVINCE

In Haskovo province, the hats are again tall and conical but made of goat hide, fixed with multiple pairs of goat horns as well as goat skulls or even the tanned or cured faces of goats stripped from their skulls. A traditional peasant costume in black, white, and red is also worn. Sometimes goat horns are also painted red to magnify their symbolic power of fertility.

PLOVDIV PROVINCE

In Karavelovo village, the *Dzhamali* or *Startsi* also wear beard-length cloth masks, these of decorated black fabric. On their heads are caps topped with multiple goat horns, artificial flowers, and entire bird wings. White pants and tops are worn with large bells and tasseled cords dangling from performers' belts.

Southeastern style Kuker from Burgas. Long Kalofer goat fur used in Blagoevgrad is combined with sequined veil-mask worn elsewhere.

Kuker wearing the sequined "veil-mask" style of Yambol Province in southeastern Bulgaria.

In Voynyagovo, the veil-masks and white shirts are also worn, but with striped kilts and pants. The headdress is particularly tall, triangular in shape, and profusely decorated, notably with mirrors.

In Karlovo, dangling tassels and bells are prominent and decorated veil-like masks are again worn, but with matching conical caps two or three feet in height and decorated with the usual array of sequins and tassels.

SMOLYAN PROVINCE

In Smolyan province, black and red are again the colors of the costume, a Balkan kilt and short jacket trimmed with sheepskin. Tall hats of long-haired goatskin shaped rather like elongated fezzes are worn along with sheepskin leggings.

SOUTHEASTERN BULGARIA

BURGAS PROVINCE

In eastern regions, certain elements are repeated in the costuming. In Burgas province, the long-haired "Chewbacca style" is again worn with decorated veil-mask, as in Pazardzhik province, the only major difference being the addition of a dangling mustache of plant fiber. A distinguishing feature throughout the southeast is the use of much smaller bells, hung from the belt in double tiers.

YAMBOL PROVINCE

In the town of Yambol, the double-rowed bell belts are hung from beaded suspender-harnesses. The mask is again of the veil style but is extended to rise over the head in the form of a sort of crested headdress decorated with ribbons or pom-poms. The entire surface is also thoroughly tiled with beads, sequins, or buttons. The face often features a beak-like nose resembling a carrot stuck in a snowman.

In the town of Boyanovo, tall headdresses are worn similar in shape to those worn in Voynyagovo, in the west. Like those, they always feature mirrors, but are otherwise covered in lace and tassels.

Veselinovo is home to the "Black Kukeri," dressed rather austerely in dark, monkish robes, conical fur hats, with faces blackened with soot.

SLIVEN PROVINCE

In Silven province, Kukeri wear distinctive sheepskin coats spot-dyed with surprising colors, including bright blue and red as well as hot pink. Their veil-masks are richly adorned and rise over the head in the shape of a bishop's mitre, or a squared off version of the same. The "snowman" nose is also common here.

KUKERI FROM SIULISTRA PROVINCE IN NORTHEASTERN BULGARIA CAN BE DISTINGUISHED BY THEIR SQUARE BANNER-LIKE HEADDRESSES.

NORTHEASTERN BULGARIA

SILISTRA PROVINCE

There are fewer examples of Kukeri in the north, but around the town of Kalipetrovo performers can be seen wearing tall squared-off headdresses completely covered in white feathers dyed in various colorful hues. A veil-mask is worn with these.

SHUMEN PROVINCE

Headdresses from this region display a totem-pole-style stacking of horns, taxidermized bits, and roughly implied facial features, as in Pernik province, but with a unique touch: a sort of encompassing "halo" constructed of plant fibers dyed in vividly colored bands.

The town of Strandzha celebrates with a single performer representing the "White Kuker," a figure dressed in white sheepskin, including a short conical cap, and with his face blackened with soot. He wears only a few small bells.

SIGNIFICANCE OF THE COSTUME

As you would guess, wherever the Kuker goes he repels evil and leaves luck and fertility. As with the German Fastnacht, the Slovenian Kurent, and Hungarian-Croat Busó, the bells he wears are his primary means of doing so, and the leaps he executes to set the

KUKERI (SURVAKARI) ON THEIR ROUNDS IN THE VILLAGE OF BOGDANOVDOL, IN PERNIK PROVINCE, WESTERN BULGARIA.

bells ringing again reflect his efficacy, as in "the higher the Kuker leaps, the higher grows the grain." Similarly, the mirrors found on a number of Kuker headdresses deflect evil (something also seen in Alpine *Perchten* costumes).

Red, white, and black dominate the color scheme of the Kuker's costume (the same preferred for traditionalist Busó and even Percht or Krampus masks). White, within the Kuker tradition, is said to represent the heavens or purity, and black the earth, but most important is red representing fecundity, vitality, and prosperity.

This color symbolism is important in another Bulgarian ritual marking the beginning of spring on Baba Marta or "Grandmother March" (March 1). Red and white thread or yarn is used to create a token exchanged on that day, the *Martenitsa,* a cord or bracelet with tassels or braided figures (a male and female as symbols of fruitful coupling). The Martenitsa is sometimes associated with Kuker events if the region celebrates closer to March 1. Baba Marta is also celebrated by Albanians, Macedonians, and Romanians, the last of whom similarly use red tassels to decorate the costumes of New Year's "bears" bringing good luck (a detail like the red tassel worn by certain Babugeri in Bulgaria's west).

The pelts and fur employed in western Bulgarian costumes do not disguise the wearer as a particular animal (as with the popular Carnival Bear) but are more vaguely zoomorphic, representing a supernatural monster, as marked by the accumulations of extra horns, heads, etc. While sometimes the Kuker is said to represent an "evil spirit," this is only understood in the sense of fighting evil with evil, à la fire with fire. The monstrosity of the Kuker is not a matter of wickedness or diabolicalness but of fearsome power or

Brass bells, fur, feather, and plenty of horns. Kukeri in the town of Breznik, Pernik Province, also hold crooked sticks used in a circle dance.

uncanny otherworldliness. Throughout Bulgaria, these qualities are evoked by the towering headdresses, which convert the mortal performer into something of supernatural dimensions.

A similar intent lies behind the intensely decorative bricolage of sequins, feathers, tassels, etc. found on masks and headdresses. This lends the figure a peculiar elevated status, and—like richly adorned liturgical robes or a knight's ornately etched plate armor—suggests a sort of sort of imposing wealth or status and thereby power.

Likewise, the rest of the costume (pants, tunics, vests, kilts) is generally distinct from day-to-day wardrobe. It is markedly archaic and traditionalist. Its folkloric quality reinforces the tradition's connection to the ancient past and is similar or identical to what might be worn to a village wedding, reinforcing that association seen with other Carnival customs.

TOOLS OF THE KUKER

The Kuker generally carries with him some sort of symbolic tool. Most frequently it's a long, wooden implement brandished like a sword. Rather than a custom-made wooden sword, it's usually a beam removed from a traditional loom, handily offering an end notch that works as a grip. These "swords" may be painted red or covered with red cloth to increase their potency as fertility symbols. A more literal symbol, a carved wooden phallus, may also be worn on the bell belt in some regions.

A mid-January bonfire marks the start of the Pernik Festival of the Masquerade Games "Surva."

Rather than a sword, the Kuker may also carry a stick crooked on the end, or of a T shape. These are often gripped on either end by performers linking themselves in a chain dance (the *horo*) performed in the town square. Occasionally, the choreography may become more elaborate, and performers may interlock sticks to form patterns as with sword dances of Britain and elsewhere.

In Pernik province, the Survakari carry staves topped with green leaves, symbolic of fertility and reminiscent of the uprooted tree carried by the Wild Man.

A final item used in some regions is a "sweeper" (*pometash),* a wet rag (or rabbit pelt) fixed on a long stick. This would be an item used in traditional households to clean the hearth or chimneys, meaning the rag is covered in wet soot. As the Kuker makes his rounds, the sweeper may be slapped on the walkways or streets, producing a startling noise. When it's slapped against the gates of homes, the sooty mark left imparts good luck. This sort of luck-bringing smudging, which has already been seen in the Egetmann Festival and Polish customs, will be a recurrent theme in later chapters. The luck-bringing aspect of the *pometash* also offers obvious comparison with superstitions associating luck with chimney sweeps, beliefs nearly universal throughout Europe.

CALENDAR CONFUSION

The historical tendency for the customs of Christmas (through Epiphany) to mingle with those of Carnival is again evident with the Kukeri tradition. In western Bulgaria, activities are more associated with the New Year (the middle of the Christmas cycle), while in the east they take place during the week before Lent.

AT THE INTERNATIONAL FESTIVAL OF MASQUERADE GAMES "SURVA" IN PERNIK.

This calendrical span may be explained by Bulgaria's late adoption of the Gregorian calendar in 1916—a change that applied only in the secular world, as the feasts of the Bulgarian Orthodox Church (and hence the calculations of Easter and Lent) were not conformed to the Gregorian calendar until 1968. This Gregorian–Julian disparity, representing a difference of thirteen days (twelve in previous centuries), accounts for the peculiar date of the International Surva Games in Pernik. Though it's lately been moved to the end of the month, it was formerly held on January 13-14, that is, thirteen days after the Old (Julian) New Year's, or Surva. It also accounts for the use in western Bulgaria of the related term *Survakari* rather than *Kukeri*. In regions where this is the date, the Survakari may make their first appearance at a bonfire gathering on the night of January 13, followed by daytime outings on the 14, the latter being the most common for Surva outings.

Because the customs are recognized as a *New Year* activity, some communities celebrate on the modern date, January 1. Sometimes this date is chosen over January 14 to stagger celebrations between nearby villages, allowing neighboring populations to visit one another's festivities or even share certain masks, props, or other resources.

Where January 1 is the official date of celebration, particularly eager Survakari may begin sneaking into the streets as early as December 26. So, while January 14 is the most common date in the west, it's possible to encounter Survakari roaming any time between December 26 and January 14.

At the other end of things, in the east, the Kuker appears in the week before Lent. Costumes most often are first donned on Shrove Sunday or, in Bulgarian, *Sirni Zagovezni*. *Sirni* is the word for "cheese," as it's the last day on which dairy products may be eaten (while meat has already been banned since the previous Sunday). While this date may be the occasion for some nocturnal forays, the following day, Shrove Monday, is considered the most traditional date for activities. As in the west, however, there may be some costumed outings during the entire preceding week.

THE EVOLVING KUKER

Bulgaria's Kuker customs are based on two previously encountered themes: the mock wedding and—in the east only—ritual plowing. In both east and west, these traditions entailed both house visits and a closing public performance in a town square, schoolyard, or other central place. Since the 1960s, Kukeri traditions have evolved in accordance with the familiar pattern, seeing house visits deemphasized over municipal events. This has been encouraged by the involvement of the Soviet-created community cultural centers (*chitalishta*) found in even the smallest towns, particularly so thanks to cash prizes they began offering for outstanding masks, costumes, and performances. Visiting Kuker troupes from neighboring towns often take part in these municipal events, and a handful of cities, including Yambol in the east and Razlog in the south, draw performers from their respective regions just as Pernik draws performers from across the nation.

Until the early twentieth century, Kuker groups were composed strictly of unmarried males in their teens and twenties (aside from a group leader who was expected to be a married man). Nowadays, particularly in larger cities, one encounters female Kukeri and even quite a few small children donning costumes. Each troupe consists of more than a dozen or even several dozen performers, though only a portion of these wear the characteristic bell-belts, masks, and headdresses.

Others are costumed according to varying roles, including bride, groom, priest, king, etc. These peripheral figures are often now sidelined or eliminated in favor of the more impressive figures in bells and headdresses, here again thanks to the enticement of prize money for elaborate costumes. This is especially the case in larger municipal events. The size too of the headdresses has vastly increased over the years, no doubt fueled by both a naturally competitive spirit and cash prizes. While old photos depict relatively modest costumes, certain headdresses today can reach heights of fifteen feet, requiring several people to transport them and place them on the performer's head, and a system of counterweights may be required to keep them stabilized.

NEW YEAR'S ACTIVITIES

In western Bulgaria, the minimal configuration of a New Year's Survakar group consists of around a dozen bell-ringers wearing some sort of animal hide, the bride and groom, a mock priest, and a troupe leader costumed as something like a cross between a nineteenth-century military officer and a marching-band musician. He serves to guide the fur-wearing bell-ringers in a relationship reminiscent of a bear-trainer and his charge. The priest wears improvised wardrobe approximating that of an Orthodox cleric and carries a pail of make-believe holy water. Occasionally he may be costumed as an imam thanks to Bulgaria's heritage of Turkish rule. Musicians are also part of the troupe: a drummer, to set rhythm for the Survakar's bell-ringing leaps, and a horn, the shrill double-reed zurna. Additionally, there may be a costumed bear and bear-trainer as well as figures with soot-blackened faces known as "Gypsies." Tasked with collecting donations from homes visited, they may also be seen pulling behind them a cart decorated like a Romani wagon.

A particularly large group expands to include additional wedding-party characters including festively dressed performers hamming it up as the bride's and groom's parents. Other tag-alongs might include obnoxiously flirty cross-dressed males or even a Santa Claus (since New Year's is part of the Christmas cycle, after all).

As the group arrives at each house, they are greeted by the occupants with hospitality befitting a wedding party. Often there is a table set in the yard with a spread of food along with drinks and *rakiya*, home-distilled fruit brandy. The priest greets the residents and performs a quick wedding ceremony, or a version of one, executed either with campy pomp or as nonsensical parody. If this is done outside, the homeowner may fire off a gun in celebration, an old Bulgarian custom once signaling the confirmation of the bride's virginity. During the bell-ringing dance, performers not only jump at an increasingly frenzied pace but may roll on the ground, something said to more directly convey fertility into the earth. After this, the trainer introduces his bear into the mix and the costumed beast wrestles with a male of the household, something else said to bring luck, even if the "wrestling" amounts only to a particularly aggressive bear hug.

Then it's time for more *rakiya*, perhaps even a quantity "to go" poured into a communal jug and shared throughout the day. Foods offered usually include *banitsa*, a flaky cheese pastry, or possibly sweets, oranges, apples, sausages, nuts, or even a portion of dried beans, grain, or other staples. A few coins are also given, either collected by the Gypsies or dropped into the holy water carried by the priest. After the group has repeated this performance at all homes on their list, they head to the village square for a sort of wedding party complete with live music, dancing, and of course more *rakiya*. In some places this is followed by a nighttime bonfire with fire leaping.

FOUR-LEGGED FRIENDS

In certain western Bulgarian villages, an entirely different routine takes place on New Year's Eve. Instead of a bride, groom, and priest, the fur-wearing bell-ringers (*dividzhii* here) are accompanied by a "camel," a framework of willow branches covered in cloth or hide and jangling bells. Beneath are two performers, one puppeteering the animal's head.

At each house visited, the camel's "owner" declares that he's traveled far and his camel can't go further as it's in need of horseshoes. Without these, he explains, the animal is of no use and must therefore be slaughtered. To emphasize the point, the camel collapses forthwith and refuses to get up until the homeowner kicks in a little money "for horseshoes." When this is received, shoeing the animal is pantomimed, but the camel still re-

In certain western Bulgarian villages, a "camel" shows up on New Year's Day. The performance involves a camel wrangler and two performers inside the costume.

fuses to arise. It needs medicine, in this case a kebob, which is rubbed over the head of the animal, to miraculous effect. The camel rises, and the bell-ringers react with a joyous dance. The camel's name, should anyone ask, is Maria.

Similarly, four-legged figures are trotted out for house-visit in pre-Lenten celebrations elsewhere in Bulgaria, a deer-headed *Dzahmal* in the central village of Popintsi and a more elaborately realized creature of the same name in the northern village of Koshov. The latter is equipped with a fearsome mouth that claps and a body festooned with ivy and (for some reason) popcorn strings. Like the camel, it also keels over during the performance but is resurrected not with a trusty kebob rub but with air blown through a tube comically inserted into its backside!

SHROVE MONDAY HOUSE VISITS

The majority of Bulgaria celebrates Kuker customs on Shrove Monday, and with that greater number comes a greater diversity of customs. But there are some common threads, which can be sketched out.

House visiting customs in the west serve more as informal preliminary to the all-important gathering in the town square where a plow ritual is enacted. The mock-wedding motif is also alluded to in the presence of bride and groom characters, but there may or

Refreshments reward Kukeri on their rounds in the village of Turia in the Stara Zagora Province of southern Bulgaria.

may not be a priest or parodied nuptials. Generally, the priest serves as a sort of troupe leader, or the groom will if a priest is lacking. Failing either of these, a *baba* (grandma) may play a central role. This cross-dressed character usually cradles a (doll) baby.

In some regions, the role of the Gypsies is filled by *Arapi*, or Arabs (from the Turkish word). They are similarly blackened with soot, may wear bits of Middle Eastern costume, and occasionally bring with them a "camel." Elsewhere, these auxiliary figures are "Old People," that is, male youths wearing rubber masks and affecting hobbling gaits and bent postures. There may also be a bear and trainer.

Performances at each stop would be a mix of mock weddings, death-and-resurrection camel pantomime, and the bell-ringing good-luck dance, this being the one consistent element throughout all regions and across all dates. There are also comedic efforts to "sweep out bad luck" from the home, accomplished literally with a broom wielded by the bride or *baba*. The clearing process also involves mischievously tossing random items from the home or porch into the yard (schtick used also by Krampus and Percht troupes).

All or none of these may occur alongside comical improvisations involving bear and trainer, Gypsies, old folk, Arapi, or cross-dressed flirts or prostitutes. Troupes may also be accompanied by folk dancers who perform the *horo* (a chain dance) en route and upon arrival at each site.

THE PLOW RITUAL

In the late afternoon, after the house visits, performers arrive at the central square where the town turns out for the plow ritual. While the troupes are gathering, some of the schtick from the house visits is repeated. In larger towns, there may be additional figures

Kukeri yoked in the plowing ritual are sometimes masked to resemble oxen.

The plowing ritual enacted at the Starchevata festival in Razlog in Blagoevgrad in southwestern Bulgaria.

circulating through the crowd teasing and entertaining them: "tax collectors" equipped with ledger books and chains to capture those with unpaid debts, "policemen" issuing tickets, "doctors" offering unsolicited examinations, and "barbers" attempting to shave victims with a wooden razor.

Two Kukeri, from the southeastern town of Burgas, yoked like oxen for the plow ritual.

One of the mock priests may serve as a sort of master of ceremonies, and one of the grooms may become the plowman. A particularly old form of the play spotlights neither groom nor priest but a Kuker king. Where he is still represented, he's outfitted in a special version of the goatskin Kuker costume, or more conventionally costumed as a king with a false white beard, crown, or turban. He arrives in the square in a cart drawn by his guardsmen, i.e., Arapi or Gypsies, who may be armed with wooden clubs, swords, or bows. These sometimes carry bags of ash with which to intimidate anyone stepping out of line. The king then seats himself at a table laid with food and will be served a few symbolic bites and sips of wine by his guardsmen, after which he proclaims good wishes to all, health, wealth, and fertility for the coming year.

After this comes the plowing itself. Two Kukeri are yoked to the plow. The other Kukeri form a circle separating spectators and performers and throughout the performance will act as a sort of Greek chorus, responding intermittently with bell-jangling leaps. Before plowing, the plowman paces out the measurements of his "field" and marks its perimeter. Three circular furrows are then symbolically plowed. The bride or grandmother walks before the plow, and behind it comes the king in his cart, sowing seed over the imaginary furrows. He is followed by the hopping Kukeri ringing their bells.

When the king has scattered all the seeds, he tosses the round seed basket to the ground, watching carefully how it rolls to a stop. If it lands right side up, a bounteous year is promised. Upside down would be bad, but that never happens, as the bride or some other performer dashes out to give it a kick in the right direction. There may also be a simulated harvest, conducted with a threshing board pulled over imaginary grain and Kukeri pantomiming cutting sheaves. The ritual is finished with more declarations from the king for a bountiful year and Kukeri joining hands to dance the *horo,* eventually accompanied by spectators.

The extremely basic play is usually enlivened with a few comedic complications. The Kukeri may obstinately resist being yoked to the plow or endure the pantomimed nailing of horseshoes to their "hooves" beforehand. Wooden swords may be put to use in battles between rival guardsmen or between Kukeri and guardsmen. The sower or king may be killed and resurrected through some comic burlesque. The baby or bride may also be abducted and recaptured, after which the abductor receives a beating.

It's said that in the old days the king Kuker and his wife pantomimed intercourse and a doll was then introduced as the offspring. While this sort of thing is not to be found in contemporary performances, it would not only provide a tidily on-the-nose parallel with the agricultural seeding pantomimed but would also explain the baby carried by the grandmother.

However, mimed sex *does* occur as part of the bride theft. This can either be planned as a staged comic interlude within the performance or might be spontaneously undertaken by rowdy spectators as it's said whoever steals the bride will be blessed with good luck.

During house visits in eastern Bulgaria, the bride is also sometimes stolen, and the cross-dressed performer may be wrestled to the ground by one of the males of the house, much as the lucky bear is but with more lewd pelvic thrusting. Interestingly, it's behavior like this that is used to justify the barring of females from roles in Kuker troupes. It's simply for their "protection," you see.

AN IDEAL CELEBRATION

As seen with the Hungarian Busójárás, it's quite possible that more overt or aggressive sexual gestures over time were cleaned up, in this case under the watchful administration of the community cultural centers. Certain elements of the tradition that reflect years of Ottoman rule as well as Romani influence also tend to be minimized or receive outright scorn as Kuker traditions are promoted as expressing a pure and cohesive Bulgarian identity. This nationalizing intent lay behind the founding of the Pernik festival in the 1960s, and its success can be seen in the proliferation of Bulgarian flags and colors frequently used in Kuker events.

While Communist oversight also downplayed the tradition's magical roots, a certain residual superstition still attaches to the customs. Kukeri visiting homes are still occasionally asked to direct their dances around certain trouble spots—ailing fruit trees or grape arbors, for instance. Rather than a matter of wholehearted belief, this may be done more in the spirit of "can't hurt, could help." Magic aside, enthusiasm for the customs can be passionate to the point of religious devotion. The website of the Surva Festival, assembled by the National Culture Fund of Bulgaria, is full of rapturous firsthand narratives about losing oneself in the clamor of Kuker bells, the countless man-hours and financial hardships happily endured to create impressive costumes, and extraordinary feats of endurance involved in bearing 150 pounds of costuming on day-long outings.

THE DEPICTED HARAPIA FIGURE FROM VOLAKAS, GREECE, IS A COUSIN TO THE BLACKED MACEDONIAN ARAPIDES AND BULGARIAN ARAPI, ALL ASSOCIATED WITH THE "PAGAN" OR "UNCHRISTENED" DAYS AROUND THE NEW YEAR.

KUKER ORIGINS AND THRACOMANIA

There is not much that can be definitively said regarding the history of Kuker customs, as the oldest explicit references date only to the late nineteenth century. These rural customs produced none of the usual traces one might discover in researching medieval or Early Modern Europe, no condemnations by local clerics or town council records of expenditures or public unruliness. Part of this surely has to do with the occupation of the country by the Ottomans from the fourteenth to late nineteenth centuries. A certain degree of historical erasure, both intentional and accidental, seems to have come with this, and, while the era of the Bulgarian national revival produced a generation of ethnographers finally studying folk customs, this arrived with a political agenda. Central here was the goal of establishing a continuity between modern Bulgaria and ancient Thrace.

Because the mythology of Dionysus arrived in Greece via the Thracians and because the god was associated with goats and frenzied dance, Kuker rites have long been interpreted as a modern expression of a millennia-old Thracian legacy. While a few modern scholars have cast doubt on all this, the association between the Kuker and Dionysus is still robustly supported, particularly in popular histories online. These have been influenced by a new wave of pseudohistorical enthusiasm, sometimes dubbed "Thracomania."

I'm not sure how one so easily ignores the vast historical gulf between pre-Christian rites and customs first documented less than 150 years ago. It seems presumptuous to ignore other, more recent possible sources. The Kukeri tradition shares more than a few obvious commonalities with Carnival customs we've examined: symbolic plowing and sowing, mock weddings, costumed bear and trainer, performers representing village archetypes, conical (or tall) headgear, and above all the wearing of jangling bells to promote fertility and repel evil.

TWELVE NIGHTS OF TERRORS, A CARNIVAL ORIGIN

Throughout this chapter and others, I've made casual and interchangeable use of terms like "promoting fertility" and "repelling evil" in describing the purpose of those bell-ringing house visits. But while one of these looks forward to the promise of the agricultural year, the other is attached to more immediate evils, the dangers and deprivations of winter.

In the case of Bulgaria, Surva is associated with winter as it represents the traditional New Year (later moved via the Julian–Gregorian shift to mid-January). New Year, in Bulgaria, is one of the Unclean Days (*Mrusnite Dni*) or Pagan Days *(Poganite Dni*), an interval bookended by Christmas and Epiphany. The belief that evil forces are loosed on these days is common throughout the Balkans.

Across the border in North Macedonia, this period is referred to as the "Pagan" or "Unchristened Days," and customs like those in Bulgaria are used to combat malevolent spirits afoot during the period. Around Epiphany, when these powers are at their apex, soot-blackened figures known as *Arapides* (analogous to Bulgarian *Arapi*) can be seen processing through towns and villages jangling bells to frighten off evil spirits. The same customs with all but identical costumed characters extend into Greek Macedonia in Thessaly, under the name *Rougatsia*. Among these celebrations are those in the vicinity of Drama, where a figure known as Babougera, comparable to the Babugeri of Bulgaria, does the bell-ringing, and elsewhere one might find ritual dances with wooden swords and mock weddings.

More widely known in Greece is the mythology of the *Kallikantzaroi* (widely translated as "Christmas Goblins"), who arise from the underworld to wreak havoc during this period. Bulgarian folklore has an analogous figure sometimes said to be the target of Kuker magic, the *Karakonjul*. Similar beings associated with this period are found also in Serbia and Albania and throughout the Balkans—not just these but witches, werewolves, vampires, and other beings for which there is no immediate equivalent are empowered at this time. In Slovenia, home of the Kurent, these are the "Wolf Days," as wolves are then supernaturally predisposed to attack. Across the border in Austria, the bell-ringing Perchten, presumptive cousins to the Kurenti, are associated particularly with Epiphany and are represented in folklore as demanding spirits placated by certain offerings and actions but prone to harm human beings. My *Krampus* book devotes an entire chapter to other terrors of the German Twelve Nights, or *Rauhnächte*, along with the customs used to protect against them.

I've spent some time piling up evidence representing the folkloric danger associated with these days because I believe it's the origin of widespread apotropaic bell-ringing customs associated with Carnival, as well as good-luck visits, which make no use of bells. That "repelling evil" is primary in forming these customs is intuitive, as "promoting fertility" or "bringing prosperity" represents a less pressing hope for prosperity and fertility in the coming months and year. This is less urgent than combatting evils besetting a home or community during a limited period of twelve perilous winter days.

In Bulgaria, therefore, we can consider the winter customs of Surva as primary, expanding later into the Carnival rites concerned with fertility. Calendrical shift would aid this process, i.e., the adoption of the Gregorian calendar, which pushed Surva celebrations forward to mid-January, moving them closer to Carnival. But a quirk of Bulgarian history increased that proximity.

While the Gregorian system was adopted by the state in 1916, the Bulgarian Church only switched in 1968. As the Church sets the date of Carnival by its Easter calculations, for a period of fifty-two years the old (earlier) dates for Easter and Carnival existed alongside the newer (later) New Year date set by the state. This closed the gap enough that Surva and Kuker customs became less distinct, and the evil-repelling bell-ringing customs of Surva became those of Carnival, taking their place alongside Kuker plowing rituals, which concern themselves instead with the coming agricultural season.

This calendrical shift, of course, is not unique to Bulgaria. The same happened all over Europe at different times—complete with the lag and overlap of old dates with the new, offering a general theory explaining the presence of luck-bringing Christmas customs within the Carnival season.

This process also supports the notion of the New Year Kalends as a source of Carnival practices. Interestingly, the Christmas customs of Slavic countries, the costumed (good-luck) house visits occurring between Christmas and Epiphany, go by a variety of names thought to be related to the Roman Kalends: *kolyada, koliadá* (Russian, Ukrainian), *koleda* (Czech, Slovak, Slovene), or the Polish *kolęda*, from the Old Polish *kolenda*, the same form used in Serbo-Croatian. The Greek *kalanda* is even more obviously similar.

Given all this, it's easier to see a form of proto-Carnival in the old Kalends accounts and worth repeating one previously offered. It comes from Peter Chrysologus, who wrote in fifth-century Ravenna. He understood the revelers as impersonating pagan gods (who knows—perhaps even Dionysus!):

> *There is not enough charcoal that can blacken the faces of such gods ... and so that their appearance may reach the level of utter and complete terror, straw, skins, rags, and dung are procured from all over the world, and anything connected with human shame is put on their face.*

Not sure about the dung, but the rest sounds quite familiar!

· CHAPTER XII ·

CARNIVAL BEARS

WHY THE BEAR APPEARS IN CARNIVALS OF MANY LANDS,
HIS AWAKENING AT CANDLEMAS MAKING HIM A SUITABLE SYMBOL,
HIS MAGICAL CONNECTION TO THE UNDERWORLD;

HOW GYPSIES TRAINED BEARS & CAUSED THEM TO
VISIT HOMES TO BESTOW HEALTH & GOOD FORTUNE;
HOW THE ANIMAL WAS PUT TO SUCH USES
IN OLD BYZANTIUM;

THE BEAR CARNIVALS OF THE EASTERN PYRENEES

IN WHICH THE BEAR IS AIDED BY HUNTERS
AND COMBATS ONLOOKERS;
HOW HE BECOMES HUMAN THROUGH SHAVING;

THE BEAR-HUMAN HYBRID
IN THE LITERATURE & LORE OF FRANCE;

CHARACTERS & VARIATIONS OF THE BEAR CARNIVAL
IN BASQUE COUNTRY, INCL.

SHOCKING SCENES OF PANDEMONIUM

CHARACTERS BESPATTERED IN BLOOD
IN NAVARRE, SPAIN.

The Carnival Bear, Hans G. Jentzsch, 1897. Illustration from the German periodical *Die Gartenlaube*.

SPRING AWAKENING

After our exotic foray into Bulgaria, let's consider for a moment a topic more familiar in America, Groundhog Day.

Our notion that the little animal forecasts six more weeks of winter should he see his shadow on February 2 comes from Germany via Pennsylvania Dutch settlers. Their forebears in German-speaking Europe looked to the badger for their magical weather predictions but, finding no badgers in the New World, swapped him for the groundhog. Similarly, larks singing on this day are understood by Britons and Czechs to forecast a longer winter. The Irish and Scottish waited to see if snakes or hedgehogs emerged from their holes (also bad). In parts of France, Italy, Hungary, Serbia, and Croatia, the question was whether the bear emerged to see his shadow. In Romania, it's a matter of whether the bear simply bothers to emerge at all on February 2, "the Bear's Day"; if so, it betokens an early spring.

PREVIOUS: A quiet moment for the "bear" of the St Laurent de Cerdans Carnival, France.

Looking for pagan elements in Carnival celebrations, you might expect to find more references like this to the awakening of nature in spring. The closest we've come thus far to any customs referring to the natural world would be the mock plowing and sowing or suggestions that bell-ringing dances help bring forth grain from the earth, though these are less about nature's seasonal changes and more about human efforts to control and shape them. The Wild Man, the Busó, the Kurent, and the Kuker all embody, in some way, nature's power and fecundity, but these are creatures of the human imagination rather than of the natural world. This isn't the case however, with bears, and we've certainly seen a lot of these popping up at Carnival.

There have been numerous straw bears in Germany and a brief cameo by an English straw bear from Whittlesea, a fur-costumed bear yoked up for the log-haul in Fiss, Austria, bears with their trainers in Czech and Polish house visits, and even Bulgarians in certain regions (as well as Macedonians) who refer to what would otherwise be Kukeri as *Mechkari* (bears). These, of course, are only those in my necessarily limited survey, but this chapter should make up for that.

The bear has been a popular figure in Carnival customs not only because of its size and power but as a particularly evocative symbol of seasonal change. The subterranean den or cave from which it rises draws easy comparison with the mythic underworld of the dead or with the fairy realms. All of this becomes more powerful thanks to a resemblance, particularly in its bipedal stance, to humans. Before apes were known in Europe, the bear offered the best analogue to man. Therefore, any not-quite-human figure of imposing size, presumed strength, and generally frightful appearance might, for lack of any better term, be referred to as a "bear," as is the case with "straw bears." Also important within Carnival traditions was the intelligence of the animal, which could appear to rise to that of a human, something exaggerated and promoted by the tradition of bear-trainers traveling throughout Europe with their educated animals.

A ROMANI CONNECTION?

The actual trained bears imitated by costumed characters in Carnivals throughout central and eastern Europe were popularized by trainers coming largely from Romania, Poland, Russia, and later the French Pyrenees. As touring performers, they would appear at fairs in the summer and spring and during Carnival. In Russia particularly, no Carnival celebration was complete without performances by a trained bear.

The Romani people have been particularly associated with the exhibition of bears. In Romania, where trainers are known as *ursari*, bears are valued not only for their gift of mimicry but for their luck-bringing and healing associations. In a close parallel to the house-visiting customs of Carnival troupes, a bear led over one's property, or made to dance in the yard, helped protect the crops and livestock from blights, infestations, or animal attacks. Their presence could also ward off human ailments. Until quite recently, in fact, Ursari were summoned for "house calls" where sick patients resided, and these customs were spread beyond Romania throughout the Balkans. The Serbian ethnographer Tatomir P. Vukanović wrote in a 1959 article "Gypsy Bear Leaders in the Balkan Peninsula" of customs then still embraced by older rural people:

> *Among the many healing techniques utilized was the ancient custom of having tame bears tread upon people who were sick, especially those suffering from arthritis. In fact, the animal was also encouraged to tread upon healthy people for the sake of their general welfare. Bear's hair is also cited as having prophylactic attributes and that it was used in "incensing." For that, it was burned on live coals and the ashes were then swallowed as a cure against "fevers."*

URSARI IN TRANSYLVANIA, ARTIST UNKNOWN, 1869.

Bear fat was also regarded as an efficacious topical treatment, and trainers would keep it on hand for sale during their rounds. The treading of bears upon the patient's back was nicknamed "Old Martin's step," as Martin was the name commonly given bears in Romania and elsewhere thanks to a legend associating St. Martin with the animal—one in which a wild bear kills the donkey ridden upon by the saint and is forced to take its place, carrying the holy man's baggage all the way to his destination in Rome.

Lucky bear visits were particularly welcomed in the week before Easter, before Christmas, and on New Year's Eve.In Romanian Moldavia, in the east of the country, this custom is mirrored during the period between Christmas and New Year's by troupes of performers costumed as bears (along with musicians, singers, and cross-dressed performers) visiting homes where the bears' dancing is said to bring good luck. Traditionally, a short play in which the bears die and are resurrected is part of those visits. Originally these costumes were made of straw or a patchwork of sheep and goat skins, but more recently real bear skins have been adopted as these house-visit customs undergo the transition into larger municipal processions.

The association between the Romani and the magical power of the bear has ancient roots in the Byzantine East. In the Canons of the Council in Trullo, held in 692 in Constantinople, in the context of listing penance to be meted out for those practicing or pretending to practice magic, figures anticipating the Ursari are mentioned, described as those

The Skomorokhs in a Russian Village, François Nicholas Riss, 1857. Troupes of traveling entertainers (skomorokhs) usually included a trained bear.

> *who carry about she-bears or animals of the kind for the diversion and injury [exploitation] of the simple; as well as those who tell fortunes and fates, and genealogy, and a multitude of words of this kind from the nonsense of deceit and imposture.*

While there's no explicit connection here between the Romani and these practices, the first references to what are believed to be the Romani people appear later, in twelfth-century Byzantium where the term *Atsinganoi* is used, one later adopted in numerous languages: *Zigeuner* (German), *Zingara* (Italian), *Tzigane* (French), etc. One of the twelfth-century writers to employ the term is Theodore Balsamon, Patriarch of Antioch, who, in his commentary on the Trullo Canons, describes the *Atsinganoi* as those "active as bear-keepers, snake charmers, and, in general, as animal trainers; also as acrobats and jugglers."

Elsewhere in the commentary, a somewhat problematic passage in the Greek refers to

> *dyed hairs on the head and on the entire body of the animal. Then they would cut these hairs and offer them along with parts of the animal's hair as amulets, and as a cure from diseases and the evil eye.*

It's easy to see here a comparison to the talismanic use of bear fur and fat encouraged by the Ursari throughout the Balkans. From there, one might imagine luck-bringing bear visits associated with the Romanian New Year (both by the Ursari's real bears and costumed troupes) and how these might be adopted into neighboring Bulgaria's Surva traditions and later into Kuker traditions of the eastern Carnival.

It's an interesting speculative thread to be traced back to twelfth-century Byzantium and perhaps (if Balsamon's commentary is accurate) even to practices of the seventh century. Is it possible that good-luck bear-visit customs of the Balkans were absorbed into New Year's and Carnival customs of Orthodox Russia and Ukraine, and in house-visits further west such as those of Poland and the Czech Republic, or even to the straw- or fur-wearing bears of Austria and Germany? Do the Ursari and their magical seasonal visits have something to do with the widespread and rather mysterious presence of costumed "Gypsies" at Carnival events from Bulgaria to Austria? I suspect at least some of this may be true, but an adequate investigation sadly lies beyond the scope of this book.

BEAR SCHOOL

Whether the presence of bears in Carnival customs is related to luck-bringing rituals or finds its place there simply as a standard entertainment belonging to fairs and festivities, the Romani bear-trainers and their charges exercised an undeniable influence on Carnival traditions. Centers of Romani bear-training eventually developed outside Romania as Russia and Hungary also earned reputations for producing trained bears. But perhaps the most famous center was in the Belarusian town of Smorgon, a bear school dubbed the Smorgon Academy, which operated throughout the seventeenth and eighteenth centuries under the patronage of the noble Radziwiłł family (and is still commemorated with a statue in the town park). At its height, several dozen bears (along with monkeys) underwent instruction with the Romani staff. By the end of the nineteenth century, the techniques of bear-training were being disseminated outside Romani circles. In southwestern France, in the Ariège Pyrenees, home to a thriving bear population, bear-training was embraced as a lucrative opportunity. Into the 1930s, the area was known for this activity, one particularly associated with the commune of Ercé, which now hosts a small museum on the subject (Exposition sur les montreurs d'ours) in the former post office used as a town hall. Thanks to the centuries-long reputation of the Ursari as masters of this craft, however, the bear trainers of the Ariège valley were known to don characteristic Romani wardrobe while performing to command greater respect from spectators.

A CORK-POPPING START

To the south in the French Pyrenees, in particular the culturally Catalan area near the Spanish border known as Northern Catalonia, the bear not only is central to Carnival traditions but was regarded as possessing curative powers like those led by the Ursari.

POSTCARD FROM LORMONT IN SOUTHWESTERN FRANCE, c. 1900.
TRANSLATION: "TRAINER-PRESENTER OF BEARS. A GROUP OF ROMANI."

The *montreur d'ours* (bear exhibitor) was traditionally called in, for instance, to aid children suffering from epilepsy or chorea, in which case the (presumably terrified) child would be made to ride the bear as treatment. Thankfully, a ride of only nine steps was required for the cure. The *montreur d'ours* would also sell bear fat, used for a variety of practical and medicinal purposes, including greasing a newborn to help it grow strong. And naturally the animal's emergence from his den on Candlemas was looked upon as a weather omen, the rules being the same as with the groundhog. An amusing, if somewhat unverified, custom associated with Candlemas prognostications describes inhabitants of the Pyrenees, eager to observe the bear's behavior on this day, visiting sites where bears hibernated to listen for the *pet de l'ours* (fart of the bear), which signaled his awakening. Apparently, bears do develop a hardened fecal plug during the months of hibernation, something which could indeed produce a buildup of gas and a literal pop-corking start to the festive Carnival season there.

BEARS IN VALLESPIR

While formerly there were more, there remain three Carnival celebrations thematically resembling bear hunts in the Vallespir region of the eastern Pyrenees. Originally, these were all held on Candlemas, but the neighboring towns more recently divvied up festivities to more conveniently fall on three consecutive Sundays in February. The three municipalities in question are (in order of celebration) Prats de Molló, Sant Llorenç de

A GRANDSTANDING "BEAR" AT THE PRATS-DE-MOLLO CARNIVAL IN SOUTHERN FRANCE.

Cerdans, and Arles sur Tech. Festivities in each are initiated in a ceremony involving the mayors handing off a taxidermized bear paw, which circulates among the towns.

THE HUNT IN PRATS-DE-MOLLO

The event in Prats-de-Mollo, perhaps because it benefits from its position as the first, is known to be the wildest of the three. It may also be the most traditional, as the costume worn by the three bears who are hunted is particularly primitive. It consists of two sheepskins sewn together to cover the trunk down to the knees, with a third formed into a tall, roughly conical hat. The performer also always carries a wooden staff or walking stick, and his face is blackened with a mixture of ash and oil. Applying this in public, he lets out a mighty roar to alert the public that he has now become a beast.

The bears also occasionally attempt to smear ash on the faces of spectators, a gesture taken as a token of good luck. Though we've seen this custom in other Carnival traditions, Prats-de-Mollo is the only one of the three municipalities where the practice prevails, another hint that the town's version of the hunt is the most traditional. The bears are pursued by a team of hunters carrying fake guns, wardrobed as modern hunters. Surprisingly, however, the hunters are actually on the side of the bears in this festival. It is topsy-turvy Carnival season, after all.

THE "BEAR" OF THE PRATS-DE-MOLLO CARNIVAL IN SOUTHERN FRANCE.

THE SHAVING OF THE BEAR AT THE PRATS-DE-MOLLO CARNIVAL IN SOUTHERN FRANCE.

TO SHAVE A BEAR

Rather than the hunters, it's the spectators pitched against the ursines. As the bears charge through the streets, giddy onlookers scream, cheer, and taunt the beasts, trying to provoke an attack during which the "victim" will be smeared with soot. This is where the bear's staff comes in. When he decides upon a victim, he tosses his stick onto the pavement as a sort of invitation to rumble. His prey is expected to pick it up and toss it back to indicate readiness. The invitation is rarely declined as it's considered an honor and good luck to receive this attention. After a few of these exchanges, the victim is seized, struggles playfully, is probably wrestled to the ground, and receives the mark. A slug of congratulatory wine is usually shared, and the hunters fire their guns skyward in celebration. Potential victims seeming particularly worthy of the treatment are also sometimes wrangled up by the hunters for the bear's mauling.

These games continue through the day until, one by one, the bears arrive at the village square to encounter their true nemesis, the barbers, performers outfitted in white smocks and caps and with faces painted white. The facepaint creates a rather ghoulish effect given that the barbers are played by the old men of the community. The goal of the white team is to capture the black bear, shave him, and thereby convert him into a human. Their age presumably signifies greater integration into the civilized world into which the wild young bears are to be initiated.

The barbers carry chains with which to capture the bear. One is equipped with an axe, which he menacingly sharpens on a stone. After much roaring and staff-shaking, the bear

THE "BEAR" IN THE PRATS-DE-MOLLO CARNIVAL EMPLOYS A LONG STAFF, WHICH MAY HAVE BEEN BORROWED FROM THE FOLKLORE OF JEAN DE L'OURS (JOHN OF THE BEAR).

is caught, breaks loose, and is caught again, eventually ending up wrapped in chains and on the ground with the axe-wielding barber sitting astride him ready to do the deed. At this point another barber steps in, wielding something that's treated as if it were a shaving brush but hardly produces lather. In fact, the prop is a blood sausage soaked in red wine in order to spread around a bit of simulated gore, as the bear is not so much to be shaved as skinned. After the mess is made, the sooty, wine-soaked skins are tossed into the crowd, and the bear stands up, now revealed as human. A band strikes up a traditional folk tune and spectators jump in, forming rings to dance the *sardana,* the traditional Catalan dance of the region. After much whirling in the square, crowds drift into the cafes to drink, laugh, and show off sooty traces left by their bear encounters.

All three Vallespir celebrations include the shaving of the bear. The initiation endured by the young bears at the hands of the older performers represents individual sacrifice made to the communal good. A similar lesson is imposed on young people bucking ex-

The "bear" of St Laurent de Cerdans shows himself.

pectations of marriage through the humiliation of the plow or log rituals. Both dramatize the need to set aside youthful and individual concerns as the cost of joining a community built on stable matrimonial pairings and the production of offspring.

Grand themes aside, it's also worth noting that mock barbers giving spectators shaves is also a bit of comedic business included in other Carnival traditions; the Bulgarian example cited earlier (see Chapter XI) is one of many. The gag doesn't usually include simulated blood, however. Prats-de-Mollo gets points for that.

THE BEARS NEXT DOOR

Next door, in Saint-Laurent-de-Cerdans, an extra bit of drama is added to the shaving, namely a beheading. The effect is facilitated by an extra head—a taxidermized bear's head—worn atop the performer's head, with the rest of the animal's hide as his costume. This handsomely realistic suit was an innovation of the 1940s, before which the costume was made of sheepskins.

The Saint-Laurent-de-Cerdans Festival includes a greater variety of characters. There is, of course, the bear named Marti (in honor of the saint); Menaire, the presumptive leader of the hunt who actually aids the bear; the Gamarús, a silent observer of the drama outfitted in a feathered costume resembling an owl; two characters bearing the names Blood Sausage and Figs, who are dedicated to smearing spectators with those respective items; La Monaca, a two-man costume resembling Siamese twins; La Brueta (the Brute), a man

The "bear" of the St. Laurent de Cerdans Carnival in southern France.

Jean de l'Ours (John of the Bear) defeats a serpent. Illustration by Édouard François Zier for *Les Légendes de France*, E. Henry Carnoy, (1885).

dressed as a baby transported in a wheelbarrow; and the Old Man and Old Woman, who wear creepy rubber masks and old-fashioned clothing and carry an antique bed-warmer. The business with the bed-warmer is unpleasant, as the pan is used to burn handfuls of hair and the noxious smoke wafting forth is used to cense passersby. Females are especially targeted and especially those wearing skirts, under which the pan is slipped. The vile smoke rising between their legs is said to enhance fertility. Surprisingly, most victims are happy to play along.

The third town hosting a bear festival, Arles sur Tech, uses a peculiarly modern bear costume featuring an enormous Muppet-like head with toothy mouth. The event begins with the Muppet-bear hiding in the woods outside town, where he is rousted by a group of hunters, who drive him back into one of the seven town squares where the action is staged.

Unlike the first two Vallespir festivals, the Arles event is largely a folk play interrupted by carnivalesque chases from square to square. The main characters are the hunter Menaire and his wife Rosetta, a comic drag character used as bait to lure the bear to his fate (and occasionally to be caught and humped by the lusty bear along the way).

There are some other very strange characters, who would seem more appropriate to a Mummenschanz performance than a folk play. "Barrels" are just that, animate barrels whose role it is to occasionally offer Rosetta an opportunity to hide. The barrel costume consists of flexible hoops and white cloth, worn by performers in white makeup. "Turtles" also come to her aid and are likewise abstractly realized as cloth-covered frames.

Menaire provides most of the dialogue with boastful declarations regarding his bear-hunting skills as well as warnings to women about the bear's lustful ways. There is also an interlude in which Menaire demonstrates how he has taught the bear to dance.

IN ANDORRA

To the west of Vallespir, there is another region in the eastern Pyrenees where bear-oriented festivities are celebrated, in the principality of Andorra, an independent microstate sandwiched between Spain and France. Even more so than in Arles, celebrations in Andorra have taken the form of an annual play, without the wild chases and spectator interactions. Though once widespread, only two examples now survive, in the towns of Encamp and Ordino. While some presentations occurred on Candlemas, as in Vallespir, others might be staged around Christmas or New Year's. Like the Arles play, these included the bear pursuing the maiden, the bear's death and resurrection, and a dance in which the bear participated.

LITERARY CONNECTIONS

The plays of Andorra appear to be adapted from a theatrical piece known to have been popular throughout the region in the nineteenth century, *Le Bal de la Rosaura de l'Os* (French Catalan for *The Dance of Rosaura of the Bear*). The name of the "woman" pursued by the bear in Arles, Rosetta, likely also comes from this play in which a bear not only abducts a noblewoman but leaves her pregnant with a hybrid bear-human son. The story also has parallels with an 1891 short story, "Montalba," by Carles Bosch de la Trinxeria, a native of Prats-de-Mollo. It also presents a bear (a form assumed by the devil) abducting a young woman and stealing her virginity. His story may well borrow elements from a local folk tale told in the 1890s in Prats-de-Mollo, as it offers a calendrical connection to the festival, describing woodcutters freeing the maiden from the bear's lair on Candlemas.

Going a bit deeper into the past, one finds this idea of a bear-human hybrid embodied in a figure of French folklore, Jean de l'Ours (John of the Bear, or John the Bear). Not only throughout France but also in nearby Spanish Catalonia, this enormously powerful Wild Man is the hero of countless popular tales. Also noteworthy in this context would be the iron staff always carried by Jean de l'Ours, which in the Prats-de-Mollo festivities is transformed into the staff with which the bear challenges spectators.

The tales of Jean de l'Ours themselves appear to be folk adaptations of a Carolingian romance of the fifteenth century, *Valentine and Orson*. In this story, twin brothers are abandoned in the woods in infancy. Valentine is discovered and raised in the court of Pepin, while Orson is found by a she-bear and raised in her den. Later the Wild Man, Orson, arrives, in the court of Valentine, where he is tamed and becomes a trusted servant and friend to Valentine. Later, discovering their kinship and the act of treachery by which their mother was forced to abandon them, they set out to right these wrongs. While there is no impregnation by bear in these tales, Orson still functions as an influential French symbol of a peculiar kinship between bear and man.

CULT OF THE CAVE BEAR?

The connections traced above—from a Carolingian romance to folk tales of Jean de l'Ours to nineteenth-century plays adapted into modern Carnival games—are examples of high culture trickling into "lower" forms. However, because the contemporary Carnival rites involve figures wearing animal hides and acting rather wild, more romantically inclined writers regard the Vallespir games as a reflection of something more primitive, namely, a putative paleolithic bear cult, a sort of "Cult of the Cave Bear." This anthropological trope, based upon some discoveries in the 1920s of extinct bear bones in caves used by Neanderthals, was already debunked in the 1970s but lingers online and is sometimes called in to interpret bear masking customs.

As we've seen elsewhere, the vast gap in chronology and historical records argues against this. There are no attestations to Vallespir bear customs before the late nineteenth century. One could, however, say with certainty that the customs are a local variant of widespread mock bear-leading (as with straw bears) traditions associated with Christmas, Carnival, or other public celebrations. While most of these only appear in the nineteenth century, there is a smattering of earlier examples, including one from Catalonia. *The Book of Solemnities of Barcelona* (*El Libre de les solemnitats de Barcelona*) mentions a Corpus Christi celebration of 1424 featuring one such performer, "an excellently represented bear, composed of black lambskin." Corpus Christi is a moveable feast 100 days after the start of Lent, so hardly a calendrical match, and, even if it were, this single regional reference is not much upon which to build a theory.

GROUP OF TRANGAS ON THE STREETS OF BIELSA, SPAIN.

URSINE IMPROPRIETIES

Older records of the bear festivals make clear that in earlier times the bear exclusively chased females, sometimes grabbing them in highly improper ways. The sooty prints left by his pawing could be regarded as a sort of symbolic defilement echoing the ravishing bear found in sensationalist plays, stories, and folk tales. Expectations shaped by these stories gave leeway to young male performers to act on all their grabbiest tendencies. That it was all for "good luck" provided a further rationale for acting out.

Until the appearance of documentary crews at the events in the 1980s, the bear festivals had been in a state of decline, considered fit only for the lower classes, in no small part due to a reputation for sexual liberties. Interest from outside the community, spurred by visiting journalists and documentarians, caused authorities to clean up the event, making it a safer, more pleasant experiences for females and children.

IN BIELSA

Traveling northwest along the Pyrenees, one finds more Carnival bears. While the ursine element does not dominate festivities in the same way, the Carnivals in which they appear are nonetheless worth mention thanks to their unique and rustic customs.

On the Spanish side of the border, in the municipality of Bielsa, the performer simulates the animal in an interesting way. To suggest the stance of a quadruped, he leans over slightly, extending his arms to the pavement with two crutch-like sticks. A hump, created from a straw-stuffed burlap bag, rounds out his back, and this is draped with a sheepskin to add the requisite shagginess. His face is blackened, which provides a nice contrast to

Bear flanked by Joaldunak in their festive headgear,
Ituren-Zubieta Carnival, Spain.

his monstrously jutting teeth. The last are simulated by a carved raw potato placed like a set of dentures in the performer's mouth. As if holding a potato in your mouth endlessly weren't bad enough, the performer must also endure being led about on a chain by his "trainer," who administers blows with his club each time the bear lunges at spectators (targeting the straw cushion on his back, of course).

Another bestial (or half-bestial) figure found in Bielsa is the *tranga*. This performer wears a set of goat horns with draping pelts attached, a long black skirt, a clattering bell-belt, grotesque potato-dentures, and black facepaint. The name *tranga* comes from the Catalan *tronca* (trunk), designating eight-foot fir trunks stripped of bark and carried like enormous walking sticks. These are intermittently hurled to the pavement with alarming effect. Formerly, the trunks were used in scaling buildings so that the *trangas* could appear on balconies, tap on bedroom windows, and flash those potato-dentures.

THE ITUREN-ZUBIETA CARNIVAL

A few hours north through the Pyrenees in the Basque region of Navarre, we find more vcostumed bears in the neighboring towns of Ituren and Zubieta, where a joint two-day Carnival is held. The bears here are particularly fearsome, spending most of their time lunging at spectators while their trainers attempt to pull them back. Their appearance is made more monstrous by a pair of goat horns fixed to their masks. This detail is sometimes said to be symbolic of the devil, possibly echoing the French legends in which Satan

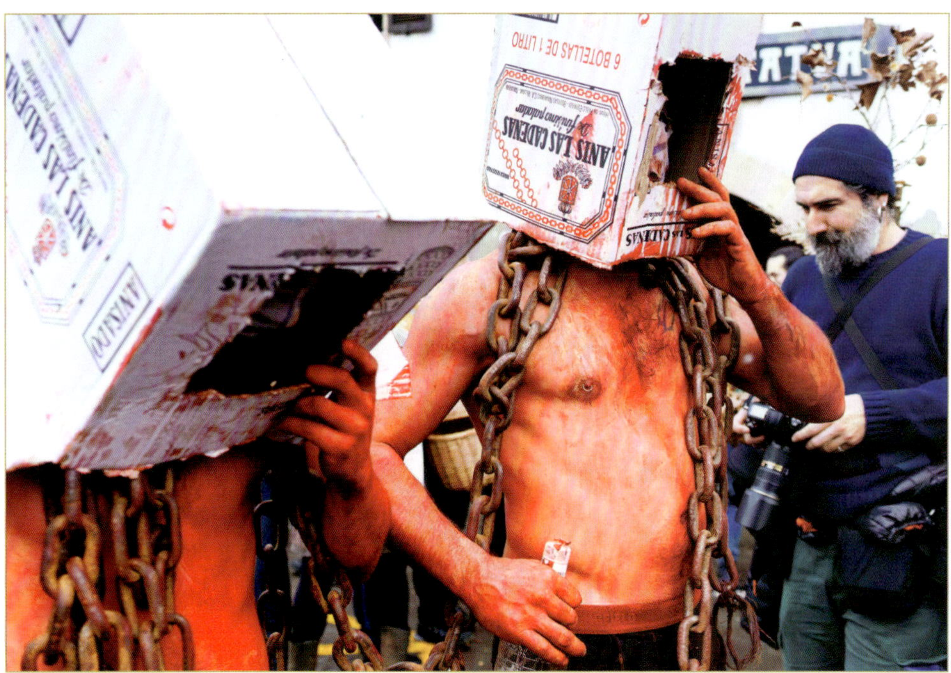

Organized chaos is part of the Ituren-Zubieta Carnival in Basque Spain. The Mozorroak, evil spirits of local folklore, are embodied by participants donning outrageous costumes and sometimes engaging in wild stunts.

More Basque anarchy at the Ituren-Zubieta Carnival.

assumes ursine form. But more likely the horns are simply there to make the figure more frightful. We've seen the word *bear,* used in this way, applied as a catchall describing other hard-to-identify monsters with few ursine qualities, e.g., straw bears, men with blackened faces, sheepskin tunics and caps, or Bulgarian Kukeri locally designated as *Mechkari* (bears).

The star of the Ituren-Zubieta Carnival, however, is the *Joaldun* (plural: *Joaldunak*), a figure also found in a few other nearby towns. These wear massive sheepskin vests over women's petticoats, tall beribboned hats, and massive copper cowbells roped to their waists. The function of the latter, as you would expect, is to bring luck, prosperity, and fertility wherever they go, qualities also conveyed by a flick of the horse-tail whips they carry.

While the Joaldun is the most-photographed character in the region's Carnival, his similarity to other tall-capped, fur-and-bell-wearing figures makes him less interesting than his symbolic nemesis, the *Mozorroak* (a term simply meaning "masked" or "costumed"). Theoretically, these are embodiments of the evil the Joaldunak are sent to dispel, but if there was once a traditional costume or action prescribed for the Mozorroak, it is lost, and the figures today are largely free-ranging agents of carnivalesque mischief.

Among the Mozorroak, cross-dressing is common, as are caricatures of various rural professions, represented in ragged costumes thrown together from burlap, old clothes, and animal pelts. Just as common, however, are looks completely devoid of anything traditional—rubber gorilla masks, army surplus, balaclavas, motorcycle helmets, heads bandaged with gauze, and as much exposed (male) flesh as the weather allows. Underpants

The Momotxorro enjoying a primeval fireside moment at the Carnival of Alsasua, Spain.

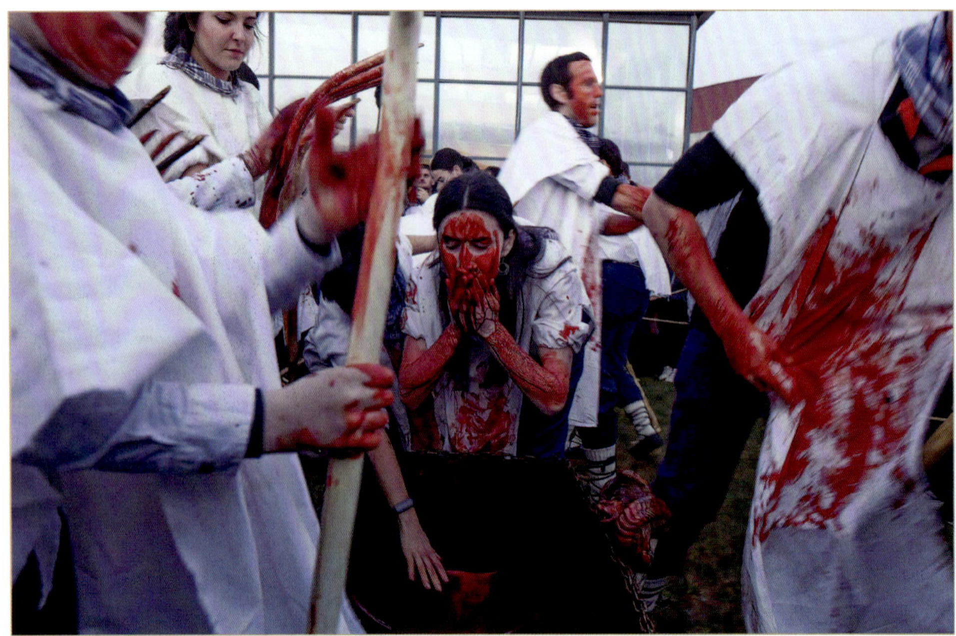

ADDING THAT SPECIAL INGREDIENT! PERFORMERS PREPARE TO EMBODY THE MOMOTXORRO, A CARNIVAL FIGURE OF ALSASUA, SPAIN.

worn with nothing but combat boots is an increasingly common look. Pitchforks, axes, and chainsaws are often carried. Wheelbarrows filled with manure or garbage are trotted out and smoke bombs set off. Mozorroak stage independent processions featuring tractor-pulled flatbeds on which provocative scenes are enacted. Spectators are smeared with soot and mud or pelted with flour and sawdust, and here and there the parade breaks down into a sort of demolition derby. Performers might leap atop junkyard cars to smash out the glass or gather forces to overturn an old camper van, abuse it with sledgehammers, and then see its pieces dragged off by tractors. In theory, these Mad Max antics are terminated by the arrival of bell-ringing Joaldunak, but the anarchic momentum of the evil Mozorroak increasingly seems free of their influence. Beware!

BLOODY MONSTERS

An hour to the southwest, the Navarrese town of Altsasu offers no bears but is worth mention for its own idiosyncratic contribution to the weird world of Basque Carnival.

Shrove Tuesday brings out the figure known as the *Momotxorro* (plural: *Momotxorrak*). He carries a wooden hayfork and wears a few cowbells and an oversize sheepskin headpiece topped with horns, and, though his face is not blackened, it's covered by a veil-like fringe of black horsehair. What really sets him apart, however, is his white smock generously splattered in animal blood. The performer's face, though not visible, is also painted in blood before the headdress is donned. Hordes of these devilish creatures stampede

The bloody Momotxorro, traditional Carnival monster of Alsasua, Spain.

through the streets of Altsasu with nary a bell-ringing Joaldun in sight to ward off the evil they embody.

Momotxorro's historical reputation lends an even darker quality to the character. Older residents talk of Carnivals past when unwelcome groups of Momotxorrak would burst into homes to loot what they could and sexually manhandle female occupants. Whether these stories are entirely true or not, Altsasu has not exactly helped matters, celebrating Carnival by night with bonfires around which Momotxorrak dance alongside *Sorginak* (Basque witches). An *Akerra* (the black goat said to have been worshipped at witches' sabbaths) also puts in an appearance dressed in black goatskins and hooded headpiece topped with a goat skull. His goatish sexuality is emphasized by two inflated bladder balloons serving as prominent testicles.

· CHAPTER XIII ·

SARDINIA

WHEREIN THE MYSTERIOUS NATURE OF SARDINIA IS DISCUSSED & THE BARBAROUS REGION OF NUORO IS SHOWN TO HOST MOST FANTASTIC CELEBRATIONS;

THE TRAGIC MAMUTHONES

MASTERED BY THE ISSOHADORES;

WILD ANTICS OF URSINE CHARACTERS;

THE HIDEOUS COLONGANOS DRESSED IN BONES;

MEN HERDED LIKE CATTLE IN OTTANA;

FILONZAN WHO THREATENS TO CUT THE THREAD OF LIFE;

THE BLIND ONES OF OROTELLI

WHO DRAW THE PLOW LIKE BEASTS;

A SPANISH ORIGIN

OF THESE CUSTOMS PROPOSED;

PRAYERS FOR RAIN MADE TO

MAIMONE,

AN EFFIGY CONTRIVED OF STICKS & GREENERY AND LATER DROWNED.

"ORCUS," HELL MOUTH STYLE ENTRANCE FROM THE 16TH-CENTURY PARCO DEI MOSTRI (PARK OF THE MONSTERS) IN BOMARZO, ITALY.

MYSTERIOUS ISLAND

When is a bear not a bear? Or Carnival not Carnival? In Sardinia, common words and definitions may not fit local realities, as in the case of Carnival. Though ostensibly part of Italy, most Sardinians would only grudgingly admit the possibility. Incorporation into the nation of Italy was a late-breaking eighteenth-century development after centuries of rule or occupation by Phoenicians, Vandals, Goths, Byzantines, Aragonese, and Spanish. And behind all this lies the Bronze Age mystery of the Nuragic civilization, named for the *nuraghi*, curious conical towers built of immense stones. More than seven thousand of these dot the island's rocky landscape, along with dolmens, menhirs, underground temples, "giant's" tombs, and holy wells, all surrounded by legends spun strictly out of oral tradition, as the Nuragic culture had no known system of writing.

Sardinia also had no bears. And though this is the English translation offered to describe particular Carnival figures, we might well wonder what it means. *Urthu* and *Urtzu* are both names said to be related to the standard Sardinian *ursu* (bear), but the figures thus designated don't seem particularly bear-like. They may wear ram or goat horns or in one case the skin of a boar with the preserved head serving as a sort of mask. Some have

PREVIOUS: THE MAMUTHONE, A MOURNFUL FIGURE OF THE CARNIVAL OF MAMOIADA, SARDINIA.

suggested an etymological link with *orcu,* the Sardinian word for ogre, a figure associated with megaliths such as the *domu 'e s'orcu* (ogre's home). Here, ogres are understood as a folkloric evolution of the Roman Orcus, the god of the underworld—possibly itself a connection to the mythic bear and its habit of spending winters in the underworld. While *Urtzu* and *Orcus* may not seem terribly similar, the Carnival figures under discussion seems less bear than ogre. Perhaps "demon-bear" is the best description.

Some of this confusion lies in the fact that the Sardinian language, though spoken for centuries, has never been standardized and exists in three major dialectal forms and several subdialects. Though Italian now serves as the island's official language, this lack of a standardized language in previous centuries can also be related to discontinuities in the historical record, adding to the island's aura of mystery.

Also highly idiosyncratic is the Sardinian word for Carnival, *Carresegare,* literally "meat-sawing" or "meat-cutting/tearing." The mood of the celebrations, in certain rural regions, can also be quite remote from those of festivities elsewhere. Visitors are often surprised by their somber, even gloomy quality, enlivened here or there by chaotic activity enacting scenes which could be described as barbaric or cruel. Comparisons are drawn to the island's harsh and mysterious landscapes, a legacy of shepherds and goatherds, and a subsistence life lived close to animals, and few come away without feeling they've witnessed something ancient and pre-Christian.

CELEBRATIONS IN NUORO

While there are more conventional festivities elsewhere in Sardinia, the celebrations I'm referring to take place in the sparsely populated central regions of the island, mostly in the province of Nuoro, which lies in an area the Romans dubbed Barbagia, "land of the barbarians." Cicero referred to the natives of this mountainous region as "*latrones mastrucati*" (thieves in rough woolen garments), and centuries later the area was famous for its bandits and outlaws. The Byzantines found them impossible to convert and pagan Barbagians raided adjacent Christian settlements until their leader Ospitone finally submitted to Pope Gregory I around 594.

MAMUTHONES AND ISSOHADORES

As in many places in Italy, Nuorese Carnival begins on January 17, the feast of St. Anthony (St. Anthony the Abbot, not St. Anthony of Padua). More correctly, it begins on the eve of that day, with nocturnal bonfires where costumed figures make their initial appearance. They return, of course, on Shrove Tuesday, Carnival Sunday, or both.

The town most famous for its traditions is Mamoiada, where the *Mamuthones* are known for their black wooden masks carved into striking expressionistic grimaces and worn with dark headscarves. The word *Mamuthones* (or more widely, *Mamuttones*) can be applied to any masked folk performer, but to some extent these figures have usurped the term as the island's best-known example.

The mask of the Mamuthones, classic Carnival figure of Mamoiada, Sardinia.

The Mamuthones carry thirty pounds of oversized cowbells—the bulk of these on their shoulders with a few dangling in front—and wear long, shaggy vests of dark sheepskin. Dark shirts, pants, and boots complete their somber look. The piles of bells atop their backs give them a forlorn, hunched appearance, and their movements seem slow and pained.

The Mamuthones are accompanied by minders known as *Issohadores,* who wear expressionless white masks, berets, short red jackets, breeches, a strap of sleighbells, and riding boots. They carry ropes from which their name (meaning "lariat") is derived and occasionally use them to lasso spectators, usually women—something bestowing good luck or enhanced fertility naturally.

There are eight Issohadores, one of whom barks orders to the Mamuthones, who progress slowly through the streets in two columns of six. The Chief Issohadore sets the rhythm for their movements, which consist of a series of twisting hops and pauses, a hitched gait that culminates every so often in a shockingly synchronized crash of bells. The Issohadores match this cadence with their own nimble leaps, their graceful figures and jocular interactions offering an almost bitter contrast to the halting progress of the slave-like Mamuthones.

The scene is hardly that of a Carnival frolic. At best, it is darkly comic (at least intermittently), but the overwhelming feeling is of some portentous tragedy or of something penitential and religious.

THE RED-JACKETED ISSOHADORES COMMAND THE MAMUTHONES IN THE CARNIVAL OF MAMOIADA, SARDINIA.

IN FONNI

In the town of Fonni, we have some of the "bears" already discussed, known here as *Urthu* (plural: *Urthos*). They wear long grey or black sheepskin vests and shaggy hoods of the same and have their faces and arms blackened with burnt cork (cork being particularly plentiful throughout this island known for its worldwide export of wine corks).

These beasts are restrained via chains held by figures known as *Buttùdos*, at least one per Urthu, but often two. Like the bears, their faces are darkened with burnt cork and they wear black hooded tunics with straps of smaller cowbells slung around the shoulders.

The mood here is extremely antic compared to that in Mamoiada. The Urthu is the star, with a reputation for not only attacking spectators, in as far as the restraining chains allow, but also brawling with other bears. These attacks often end with bear and victim wrestling on the pavement. The Urthos are also known for scaling light posts and trees and climbing up to balconies to terrorize spectators. The Buttùdos are not always agents of control and will occasionally point out individuals in the crowd (usually female) worthy of the Urthos' attention or sometimes participate in the chase themselves.

Joining the Urthos and Buttùdos are other figures known as *Mascheras bruttas* (dirty masks), as well as more benign female characters known as *Mascheras limpias* (clean masks). The latter are played by both male and female performers in folkloric female costumes, including bonnets and lace veils. They are accompanied by accordionists and often stop to perform traditional dances en route.

Portrait of an Urthu Figure of the Carnival of Fonni, Sardinia.

The Urthu's antics include scrambling on balconies at the Carnival of Fonni, Sardinia.

The Urtzu, in the guise of a wild boar, is the sacrificial victim of the Nuorese Carnival in Orani, Sardinia.

CARNIVAL OF MACOMER IN NUORO PROVINCE.

IN AUSTIS AND VICINITY

In the town of Austis, another ritual takes place involving *Urtzu*. He plays the victim in a weird and brutal bit of folk theater that feels almost prehistoric, like something dreamed up for *One Million Years B.C.* (but with black tunics). I'm really not sure how else to describe a performance enacting the slaughter of a wild boar with figures costumed in clattering animal bones.

The ones wearing the bones, *Colonganos,* are dressed in sleeveless tunics of dark, shaggy sheepskin (including the animal's head), and any visible skin blackened with cork. Their heads are hooded by fox or marten pelts and their faces veiled with dangling greenery from the strawberry tree (a small tree, bearing a fruit like its namesake). The bones clatter as they move, synchronized into a rhythmic percussion by the stylized hop-and-stop movement adopted by the Colonganos.

Another set of characters, *Bardianos,* interact directly with the *Urthu* as cruel masters. A Bardiano wears a black robe and black cork and carries in one hand a gnarled walking stick. With the other, he grips a chain securing the Urtzu, usually wrangling the beasts in pairs.

The Urtzu is outfitted in the skin of a boar. It's worn as a cape with the intact head serving as the Urtzu's face, while the performer's own face beneath the boar head is blackened. A rough patchwork of boar hides fills in the rest of the costume, and a single cowbell is worn around the performer's neck.

One of the Colonganos decorated with strawberry-tree greenery and bones at the Carnival in Orani, Sardinia.

The animal bones hung from the back of the Colonganos clatter rhythmically as they progress through the streets of Orani, Sardinia.

PROCESSING CARNIVAL FIGURES IN ORISTANO PROVINCE, WITH GOAT HORNS MOUNTED ON FUR-COVERED BLOCKS OF CORK.

The Bardianos taunt the beast as they goad him forward, stopping at intervals to drag the Urtzu to the ground and beat him with their sticks. Thankfully, there is a mass (of cork naturally) beneath the boar hide to buffer the blows. As the creature howls and the Bardianos cackle, the Colonganos form a ring around the action, tightening the circle as the pantomimed death nears. The Urtzu eventually stops his flailing, and the Bardianos blow a mournful blast on cow horns announcing the death. The Colonganos execute several rattling leaps and the weird and wordless spectacle ends.

A nearly identical rite is performed outside Nuoro in the towns of Ula Tirso and Samugheo, in the adjacent Oristano province. In Samugheo,

> *the Urtzu is horned and represented as a sort of monstrous goat rather than boar. Its horns are fixed atop a large headpiece, a block of hide-covered cork which increases the performer's height imposingly. Also distinctive are the smaller bells of this region, arrayed on tiered rows of straps crossing the torso.*

In Ula Tirso, the brutality of the scene is dramatically underscored with an element of gore. Each Urtzu carries with him a concealed wineskin, used to emit a spray of simulated blood as the beating takes place. In the same town, there is also a figure called *Maskinganna*, impersonated by a performer in goatskins and burnt cork crowned by a horned goat skull strapped atop his head. Although the name *Maskinganna* belongs to a forest trickster and shapeshifter of Sardinian lore, the character here is widely understood to be the devil (as if the spurting gore didn't make the ritual dark enough).

The demonic Ainu Orriadore (braying donkey) is a Carnival figure represented in Scano di Montiferro with masks made of donkey pelvises.

IN SCANO DI MONTIFERRO

The final town in the province of Oristano worth a mention is Scano di Montiferro. Its remarkable mask (seen on the cover of this book) is made from the pelvis of a donkey or cow and represents the *Ainu Orriadore,* a sort of demon of local legend which, like the banshee, heralds an impending death in the community with cries. In this case, these noises are said to resemble the braying of a donkey, and the figure is usually imagined in that form but can also appear as a white dog with donkey legs and hooves or as a donkey sporting chicken legs. Sometimes the Ainu Orriadore is also made responsible for dragging doomed souls to hell and for this reason the performers also drag chains with them. These costumed figures only showed up in Scano di Montiferro in the 1990s, though the performing troupe regards what they do as a "rediscovery" of a lost tradition.

BOES, MERDULES, FILONZANA

In the town of Ottana, the beasts to be subdued are not bear-like monsters, boars, or goat-men but something reflecting the island's agricultural realities—oxen. Called *Boes,* from the Sardinian word for bulls (*bulos*), these characters wear bovine masks with peculiarly long, spindly horns. The wooden masks are faced with tooled and dyed leather and worn with massive vests of white sheepskin, leggings of the same, and a shoulder strap of cowbells, some as large as small watermelons. They never speak but may grunt like animals.

A Merdule grabs an unruly Boe straying from the herd at the Carnival of Ottana, Sardinia.

Herding the beasts are the *Merdules*. They are dressed in the same sheepskin vest and leggings but without the bells. The character's mask, which is worn with a headscarf, resembles the Mamuthones of Mamoiada, though a bit less expressionistic and tragic. The Merdule is a caricature of the old cattleman of Sardinia, and as a figure of the hardscrabble past he adopts a hunched posture. He's given a stick and whip with which to control the Boes. Each Merdule is usually responsible for a few "oxen."

The Boes may, for a while, march neatly along in synchronized bell-ringing step, but at intervals they rebel, charge spectators, square off and butt heads with each other, or simply petulantly lie down and kick their legs—all of which earns a thrashing from the Merdule. Occasionally, there are more dramatic conflicts ending with the creature's pantomimed death and resurrection.

As well as being beaten to death, the Boes may simply die on command, that is, when cursed by a third character, *Filonzan*. Played by a male dressed in an old-fashioned black dress and sinisterly grinning black mask, Filonzan represents a sort of witchy version of one of the Fates and is equipped with the requisite attributes: a spindle of wool, distaff, and pair of scissors suspended from a chord around her neck.

From time to time, Filonzan will approach onlookers, lifting her scissors as if to cut the thread of life, a fate forestalled only by offering to buy Filonzan a drink. The performer usually moves through the crowd with a hunched or bowlegged gait appropriate to a crone.

A Boe, an ox-like figure of the Carnival of Ottana, Sardinia.

THE *MAIMUL* (MASQUERADE) OF GAIRO BEGINS WITH A MAD FLURRY OF ACTIVITY AROUND A BONFIRE ON ST. ANTHONY'S NIGHT (JANUARY 17).

THE MAIMUL OF GAIRO

An identical figure appears in the Carnival of Gairo, at the far southern end of Nuoro. Called the *Filadora*, meaning the spinner, it is one of an extensive retinue of figures performing the *Maimul* (masquerade). The Filadora appears alongside the Ingrastula, another cross-dressed man wrapped in a long black shawl and tasked with cursing spectators, a clownish figure known as the *Martinque* (monkey woman), and the *Cuadderi* (knight), whose connection with the equestrian arts is symbolized not only by the horse skull topping his walking stick but also by a sort of helmet made of the preserved and stiffened skin of a horse's head. The Cuadderi serves as a sort of master of ceremonies, inaugurating the Maimul by calling out, "*Accodei ca dd'oceus*," meaning, "Come, we kill him!"

The victim again is a sort of "bear" wrapped in dark hides—the Urtzu or, more fully, *Urtzu ballabeni,* coming from the phrase shouted at the bear by his wranglers, meaning "Urtzu, dance well!" The music to which he must dance is the rhythm of cowbells worn by his wranglers, the *Peddinciones,* who move forward in synchronized hopping steps. The Urtzu naturally defies these orders, charges at spectators, is beaten by his attendants, intermittently "dies," and then leaps up again. At each "death," another character, the *Poddinaiu,* scatters a handful of milled seed on the body, some of which routinely lands on spectators, bringing good luck. Particularly memorable in Gairo is the startling headwear of the wranglers, a sort of mummified animal head, crafted like that of the Cuadderi, from the facial skins of cows, sheep, goats, or other animals.

THE *CUADDERI* (KNIGHT) SERVES AS MASTER OF CEREMONIES FOR THE CARNIVAL OF GAIRO.

PERFORMERS IN THE CARNIVAL OF GAIRO HAVE A STYLE ALL THEIR OWN.

THE THURPOS OF OROTELLI

In the town of Orotelli, a similar motif is played out by characters known as *Thurpos,* a name meaning either "blind ones" or "crippled ones." Outfitted in black, hooded robes, bandoliers with small bells, and blackened faces, there is nothing in their contemporary appearance or behavior which would justify that name, but it seems likely they once adopted a hunched posture, like the Merdule. Infirmities like this generally would signify age and thereby a connection to tradition and to a generation more tied to the old agricultural ways, the beast–master relationship pantomimed in the Nuorese rites.

The Thurpos play the roles of both man and beast and are organized in groups of three: two as beasts, one human master. The beasts wear around their waists ropes with which the human character controls them. In some cases, they may pull an old plow, as seen elsewhere. Thurpos also mimic other agricultural tasks, including scattering seed or capturing and shoeing oxen. At intervals, a spectator may be (literally) roped into playing one of the oxen, a fate escaped for the price of a drink, as with Filonzan. The Thurpos tradition, more than other Nuorese customs, still exists in the form of house visits, during which performers are treated to sweets, sausage, or wine.

YOU'RE NEVER TOO YOUNG TO PERFORM IN THE ORANI CARNIVAL.

ANCIENT ORIGINS?

The aura of mystery hanging over Sardinia thanks to its Nuragic landmarks seems to color interpretations of Nuorese Carnival rites. While it's often admitted that the origins of these are shrouded in mystery, it's just as often claimed that they represent an ancient, vestigial form of Dionysus worship (as with the Kuker customs). The evidence offered is primarily linguistic, beginning with the Sardinian word for Carnival itself. The frenzied Dionysian rites, during which cult devotees were said to have torn apart and eaten living animals or even humans, is here related to the word *Carresegare* (Carnival), the form *segare,* meaning, in Sardinian, "tearing" rather than "sawing," as it would in Italian). Another appellation for these ecstatic followers of Dionysus, *Maenoles* (mad or raging ones), is likewise taken as the source for the Sardinian word used for figures of the Nuorese Carnival, *Maimones*.

Other ancient sources suggested for the rites include the Phoenicians or Carthaginians who occupied Sardinia between the ninth and third centuries B.C.E. or even a few millennia earlier, during the Nuragic culture. A problem with any of this is the same noted with the Kuker customs, namely the vast chronological gulf between these ancient cultures and the first written references to anything resembling the current traditions.

In Sardinia, that earliest account was one written in 1895 by the historian and journalist Pietro Nurra. Very briefly referring to customs in Fonni, in his travel diary *In Northern Barbagia: Travel Impressions*, he mentions figures

> *called "buttudos," they are grotesquely dressed in rags, dyed with soot on their faces, and enjoy the widest freedom in chasing the girls and embracing them.*

Before this, there appears to be no reliable reference to the customs, though I did for a time find myself drawn down a rabbit hole involving eighteenth-century poems supposedly describing the customs in detail. Ostensibly written in Latin by the Jesuit priest Bonaventura Licheri, these texts were supposed to have been transcribed from originals later "eaten by rats," but the text in question has been discredited by scholars as a literary hoax.

While the suggestion that these traditions are rooted in pre-Christian rites may be wildly speculative, Spain presents itself as a much better candidate. From the early thirteenth to the early eighteenth century, Sardinia was under the control of Aragon, a Spanish kingdom, and Castilian and Catalan were spoken. That Aragon and Catalonia lie in northeastern Spain, sharing a border with France, suggests a link with the Carnival bears of the Pyrenees, the Basque customs in Navarre, or the bears of Bielsa in Aragonese Spain. The presence of bears, which are not indigenous to Sardinia, in Sardinian customs might be explained in this way, and there are certainly curious parallels between the customs discussed in this chapter and the previous.

A RAIN EFFIGY DROWNED

Returning to nineteenth-century Sardinia for a final attestation, we find an interesting use of the name *Maimone*, though here it is not related to Carnival but to a condition of drought. An 1892 edition of the journal *Archive for the Study of Popular Traditions Quarterly* mentions that in the town of Ghilarza,

> *when the crops begin to feel the drought, the boys make a stretcher of branches, slats of wood, or large reeds, cover it with leaves of squilla, (chibudda marina) or other herbs and carry it in triumph from house to house, shouting:*
>
> *Maimone! Maimone!*
> *The sown land needs water.*
> *The dry land needs water.*

Ever since the publication of this account, Maimone here has been identified as a water spirit or, less plausibly, as a Phoenician divinity. But even the author is unwilling to attach an identity to the name, remarking only that the word *Maimone* was then used as an expression for a big but slow-witted fellow. If regarded as the Sardinian equivalent of the English word *dummy,* it can carry both that meaning of "empty headed" as well as that of an effigy or scarecrow, the latter being a decent match for the personified construction of greenery in the account.

The custom, including the quoted chant, was noted by various observers up into the 1950s. Other accounts comment that, as part of the ritual, the jumble of reeds, wood, and greenery representing Maimone would be sprinkled with water by those visited. Those bearing the litter would be rewarded with sweets or wine and, after circumambulating the town, the green figure would be dumped into a stream, a river, or even a well.

This brings us no closer to a well-articulated identity for *Maimone,* but it does bring us to our next chapter, in which surprisingly similar customs appear in very different contexts.

Busójárás 2020

· CHAPTER XIV ·

KILLING CARNIVAL

HOW CARNIVAL'S END IS SHOWN AS
AN EFFIGY TRIED & FOUND GUILTY
ON FANCIFUL CHARGES;
CARNIVAL CONSIGNED TO FLAMES OR
MOURNED AS IN A FUNERAL;
INSTANCES OF THE SAME IN ITALY & SARDINIA, INCL.
A FIGURE WHO IS GIVEN WINE
THEN DISEMBOWELED;
A MUSICAL INSTRUMENT BURIED IN CARNIVAL'S STEAD;
STRAW BEARS BURNED;
THE BATTLE OF SUMMER & WINTER IN GERMANY;
WINTER FIXED TO A
FLAMING WHEEL
& ROLLED DOWN A HILL;
THE EXPULSION OF DEATH ON THE SUNDAY OF THE DEAD;
THE POLISH DEATH CALLED MARZANNA, WHO IS BOTH
DROWNED & BURNED;
THE RUSSIAN CARNIVAL IN WHICH
MASLENITSA
IS BURNED;
LIKENED TO THE MYTH OF KOSTROMA;
FINAL OBSERVATIONS ON THE ORIGIN OF SUCH CUSTOMS
& THESE RELATED TO CARNIVAL GENERALLY.

MEMBERS OF "THE CHEERFUL BROTHERHOOD OF THE BURIAL OF THE SARDINE" PRESIDE OVER THE CARNIVAL FUNERAL IN MADRID.

DEATHS IN ITALY

Everything dies.

Carnival is no exception, but its death is always festive, usually involving a giant bonfire on the season's final day. Spain's "Burial" (incineration) of the Sardine was mentioned at the beginning of this book (see Chapter II), but the Spanish embodiment of Carnival as a Lenten fasting food is quite contrary to the usual image of the doomed effigy. Going by King Carnival or some localized name, the figure would usually represent instead the requisite seasonal excesses, might wear a necklace of sausage links or sport a giant over-indulged belly or even an obscenely prominent phallus.

More often than not, the effigy is subjected to a mock trial before its execution. It's an occasion for community wits to come forward with improvised accusations describing outrageous acts of lust or villainy, ideally related in some sly way to real-life local scandals. The comic venting of communal anxieties here is like the reading of the fool's books in the German Fastnacht. Satiric funeral songs and theatrical lamentations as the effigy is delivered to its doom are another typical occasion for hammily improvised comedy.

PREVIOUS: CARNIVAL IS DISPATCHED TO ITS WATERY GRAVE IN THE DANUBE IN MOHÁCS, HUNGARY.

This tradition of killing Carnival has been documented in Italy as early as the fourteenth century. Outside of Rome, in the town of Frascati, they burn an enormous papier-mâché figure of the trickster-clown Punchinello. The recumbent effigy is marched to the central piazza in a funeral cortège complete with candle-bearing choristers and mournful lamentations. The mock solemnity is offset by an enormous phallus attached to the figure, which in recent years has been mechanized to flip to an erect position. Pressed to explain why the Neapolitan clown was embraced as a symbol for a town in Lazio, residents offer a curious explanation involving a local heretic burned at some unknown point in history, one whose attire just happened to resemble the Neapolitan figure. Whether anyone actually believes the story is questionable, but perhaps it helped dispel hostile feelings down in Naples.

In that city, no single giant effigy is burned, but the custom survives on a smaller scale in several outlying areas, in Marcianise and Torre del Greco, where death notices are published for Vincenzo Carnevale or Giuseppe Carnevale and figures are presented laid out in coffins with strategically placed salamis. In Amalfi, the nattily attired figure of Tatillo, with bowler hat and cane, is tucked into his casket, sent off with a bedpan full of pork meatballs and bucatini on his chest and a flask at his side.

MARDI GRAS JOHN AND HIS GUTS

Sardinia offers some remarkable examples of this tradition. The custom of Juvanne Martis Sero ("Mardi Gras Giovanni" or "Mardi Gras John") in Mamoiada is particularly weird. The straw-stuffed effigy bearing this name is taken door to door on the last day of Carnival ensconced in a bower of greenery constructed upon a donkey cart. His wooden head is carved with a scowling expression and implanted with a funnel. The reason for his unhappy mien and the funnel is that Juvanne is suffering, *dying* in fact, from a lack of wine, which must be begged from each home visited and then deposited in the funnel running through the head and into a wine barrel around which his straw body is formed. Those collecting these vital transfusions are his many "aunts," men dressed in black shawls and mourning dresses, who loudly lament Juvanne's impending death. As with any Carnival outing in Sardinia, their faces are also blackened with cork. At each house the "aunts" sing parodies of funeral songs, with improvised bits mentioning the hosts visited. After collecting what wine they can (and repeatedly tapping the keg en route), they drunkenly make their way to the town square. Come evening, there is a final attempt to save Juvanne through emergency surgery. Performers dressed as doctors remove Juvanne's "guts," a variety of raw pork products (especially intestines) placed there in advance. While the operation never seems to save the patient from death, the shrieking aunts are rewarded for their services with the viscera removed, and the corpse of Juvanne Martis Sero is delivered to the bonfire for cremation.

THE BABY NEEDS MILK!

What's done in Mamoiada appears to have evolved into a rather different custom in the town of Bosa. Rather than a large effigy in a donkey cart, it's plastic dolls in need of a drink. These are carried about by revelers who harass passersby for "a drop of milk for the baby." Both women and men in drag participate in this, clownishly wailing as they hug their dolls or cart them about in strollers or wheelbarrows. The babies are said to be in a state near death, "abandoned by its mother"—and worse. As detailed in satiric funeral songs and various comedic improvisations, the child is said to have been corrupted by the spirit of Carnival so that it's given itself over to lewd behavior. "How, oh, how, could this happen to even an innocent babe!" performers wail. And as if to illustrate the point, they lift the dolly's clothing to expose grotesquely prominent genitals added for the occasion. No joke is too rude on this day, and the collective lamentations (called *attittid*u) reach the frenzy of a citywide primal scream session, with performers collapsing and rolling on the ground for a period of several hours. It's likely the plastic dolls used in *s'attittidu* at some point replaced a larger effigy used both as the focus of daytime begging and as kindling for evening bonfires. Today, these two activities are distinct.

The bonfire effigy is a life-size figure known as Giolzi (George), who's made of white cloth and stuffed with straw. Many of these are burned throughout the city by small groups dressed to match, that is, also all in white, employing cloaks made from bedsheets and hoods from pillowcases and swapping their black cork makeup for white greasepaint. Though wardrobe has been reversed from funereal black, the lewdness remains, and white-robed residents also carry lanterns through the streets "looking for Giolzi." Approaching strangers, they bring their lights close to illuminate the crotches of those they encounter, shouting, "*Giolzi! Giolzi! Ciappadu! Ciappadu!*" (I found it!). After a day of obscene jokes and drunken screaming, burning the effigy must bring a sense of quiet relief.

ANARCHY IN OVODDA

Also in Nuoro, the town of Ovodda hosts what is surely the most surreal spectacle of all, not on Shrove Tuesday as might be expected but on Ash Wednesday, a reflection of the rule-breaking spirit of the thing. Carnival here is embodied in an effigy known as Don Conte Forru, a grotesque papier-mâché giant paraded about the town in a donkey cart. Crudely sculpted in every sense of the term, his physiognomy changes every year, but he is never without a giant, erect phallus, sometimes held firmly in hand (which may or may not be mechanized to simulate stroking action).

Vying with the Basque Mozorroak and their car-smashing antics for the title of the most anarchic Carnival celebration in Europe, Ovodda's streets on this day become a scene of collective madness with little distinction between performers and spectators, whose attendance is a de facto agreement to submit to a burnt-cork makeover.

Along with blackened faces, costumes are improvised from ragged old clothes, military surplus, animal hides, tarps, cardboard, and water bottles, accessorized with assorted

Dada frippery, jangling junk, cowbells, and bones. Shaggy sheepskin vests are worn with pink wigs. Wine is shared with one and all. Anything to create further chaos is encouraged: percussion on pots, pans, and scrap metal or dragging out into the streets broken furniture, old washing machines, televisions, and toilets. Live animals—donkeys, goats, and pigs—are led about on leashes or tenderly cradled. Rattling wheelbarrows pass by stacked with squawking poultry in cages or brimming with freshly skinned goats' heads.

All of this transpires under the hideous yet watchful eye of Don Conte Forru, who in the end is set afire. Trailing smoke and flame, he's carted through narrow streets to the edge of town and finally sent over an embankment to crash down in a blazing pile.

FUNERAL FOR A DOUBLE BASS

Italy is hardly the only home to this tradition. It's also common in regions near the Spanish-French border, an area offering curious parallels with Sardinian customs, as noted. Effigies are burned in the previously mentioned Spanish towns of Ituren, Zubieta, and Bielsa, and in Zalduondo the Basques burn a character dubbed Markitos, who is paraded around on a donkey accompanied by a variety of village types seen elsewhere, and—of course—more bears. Markitos also wears a necklace of dyed eggs, curiously reminiscent of the necklace of raw potatoes seen on Juvanne Martis Sero in Mamoiada, Sardinia.

In the Busójárás of Mohács, we've seen not one but two coffins given a "Carnival Funeral," one dumped into the Danube and another destroyed in a bonfire. In Romania, in the Hungarian Catholic enclave of Harghita County in eastern Transylvania, a more funeral-like funeral is staged, including performers costumed as priests and cardinals, along with shepherds, witches, goats, and other creatures disguised in animal hides. As you might expect, the coffin is carted house to house, with the price of a viewing being sweets or a round of drinks. The crotch of the straw-stuffed effigy named Elijah is equipped with a carrot and two potatoes for the requisite Carnival lewdness, and he is theatrically lamented in ribald verse.

Another curious Hungarian custom, first documented in the 1880s and also found in Poland, Slovakia, and the Czech Republic, was a funeral for Carnival in the form of a double bass or contrabass, a symbol of the season's merrymaking. Often this would take place on the evening of Shrove Tuesday, perhaps near the stroke of midnight signifying the start of Lent. The venue would often be an inn or hall where music would be provided, and the contrabass, sometimes dressed in a woman's dress, would be laid upon a table or across a pair of chairs and surrounded by candles. Participants costumed as priests provided satiric funeral rites, and farcical eulogies were provided by others, after which a cortège bearing the deceased instrument would march through the neighborhood or even to a cemetery. In Poland, the bass was occasionally actually buried, temporarily. If there were door-to-door visits, money was collected for "funeral expenses" and delivered to musicians, who suffered financially for the banning of weddings (and their gigs) during Lent. The custom was enthusiastically promoted by the Romani in regions where they served as prized musicians. The Poles of Masovian voivodeship in eastern Poland once embraced a more elaborate version of the tradition in which the figure of the musician himself, or a straw representation, was burned as a representation of Carnival. The musician was wrapped in straw and taken door to door on begging rounds, after which the straw jacket was removed and burned in his stead.

A thematically related custom involves saying goodbye not to the music enjoyed during Carnival but to the liquor. In Germany's Harz Mountains, a mock funeral was formerly staged, during which a man was borne to the cemetery on a stretcher. In his stead, a glass of brandy was buried, remaining there until the subsequent Carnival, when it was disinterred and passed around. With that first sip of the revenant brandy, the Carnival season began anew.

STRAW BEARS MUST DIE

Killing Carnival by burning a recently worn straw costume is a custom more widely observed as part of straw-bear traditions. In southwestern Poland, the straw bear is particularly prominent in house-visiting customs of the Opole and Silesia voivodeships, beginning sometimes with the start of Carnival but most often falling on Shrove Tuesday. The bear's costume is traditionally constructed by wrapping the performer in ropes braided from straw. A large retinue of village types, all with their characteristic schticks, accompany the bear, whose role it is to dance with the hosts. In a curious parallel to certain Bulgarian Kuker practices, the dance with the bear is an essential element of these visits, bringing good luck when the custom is observed or bad luck if neglected.

The bear meets his end as part of a final party funded and catered by collections from the day's rounds. In the evening, a trial is held featuring comic accusations scapegoating the creature with a variety of community ills, and a sentence is passed. While he may be executed by a costumed hunter firing his gun, in most towns the suit is burned. An interesting twist involves the shedding of "bear's blood" during the execution (a pre-filled pan into which the bear "bleeds" during his pantomimed death). The blood (red wine) is then drunk throughout the evening.

Bears are also symbolically dispatched at Carnival's end in Austria, Slovakia, the Czech Republic, and Germany. In his classic folklore survey *The Golden Bough*, James Frazer mentions a similar blood effect as part of a straw-bear custom current at the time of the book's publication (1890). On Shrove Tuesday, in Tübingen, Germany, he says, the bear was subject to a mock trial, and

> *a fresh black-pudding or two squirts filled with blood are inserted in his neck. After a formal condemnation he is beheaded, laid in a coffin, and on Ash Wednesday is buried in the churchyard. This is called "Burying the Carnival."*

The "Shrovetide Bear" Frazer describes as "dressed in a pair of old trousers," which doesn't match the look of any surviving straw bears but is reminiscent of other figures of the Swabian-Alemannic Fastnacht. The Wuescht of Villingen's Carnival, for instance,

Carrying Out Death and Bringing in Summer, Adolf Liebscher, 1894. Illustration for *The Austro-Hungarian Monarchy in Word and Image*, Volume 14, *Bohemia*.

wears a sort of old-timey fat-suit made of burlap stuffed with straw. The stuffed suit (sans performer!) is burned just before midnight on Shrove Tuesday.

Though the Wuescht does not suffer the scapegoating of a mock trial, he does, in another way, function as a sort of community whipping boy. Tied to his back is a wooden board intended as a target for pinecones thrown by kids (or adults if so moved). In less gentle times, rocks were used, but pinecones are now collected and made available for this purpose.

DRIVING OUT WINTER

It's now a commonplace of popular histories to describe Carnival as originating in rituals intended to drive out winter. While it's hardly the whole story, it's definitely part of it.

Some of those evils dispelled from homes and farms in the house-visiting customs examined could be understood in practical terms, as physical hardships imposed by winter weather, small seasonal annoyances, cabin fever, monotonous food and company—all things actually alleviated by visits from neighbors performing in crazy costumes. In no region or era examined in this book was it truly believed that the coming of spring depended on the clanking of cowbells. Small variations in the inevitable cycle, a few lucky days of rain or sun when needed—these might be playfully attributed to those costumed visitors, but it's important to realize that these traditions lived on because of the pleasant diversions offered, not purportedly magical results. The "driving out winter" explanation can be a bit disdainful in its treatment of our ancestors as primitive and gullible, so all this seems worth a mention.

SUMMER'S FLAMING VICTORY

The destruction of straw effigies representing not Carnival but winter is also noted in German-speaking lands. Frazer records these in his *Golden Bough*:

At Goepfritz in Lower Austria, two men personating Summer and Winter used to go from house to house on Shrove Tuesday, and were everywhere welcomed by the children with great delight. The representative of Summer was clad in white and bore a sickle; his comrade, who played the part of Winter, had a fur cap on his head, his arms and legs were swathed in straw, and he carried a flail. In every house they sang verses alternately.

Again, in the region of the middle Rhine, a representative of Summer clad in ivy combats a representative of Winter clad in straw or moss and finally gains a victory over him. The vanquished foe is thrown to the ground and stripped of his casing of straw, which is torn to pieces and scattered about, while the youthful comrades of the two champions sing a song to commemorate the defeat of Winter by Summer. Afterwards they carry about a Summer garland or branch and collect gifts of eggs and bacon from house to house.

You may be wondering, "What about Spring?" The omission reflects the old Germanic custom of dividing the year into only two seasons: summer and winter. This was the case for the Icelandic calendar, used from the tenth to eighteenth centuries, and the English monk and scholar Bede in his *De temporum ratione* (*The Reckoning of Time*), written in 725, remarks that the Anglo-Saxons of his day thus divided their year. It was only under Roman influence that the four-season system would eventually take hold, and until the sixteenth century Early Modern English lacked a standard word for spring. As in other Germanic languages, a version of the word *Lent* would be used to pinpoint weeks between winter and summer.

Frazer also notes that these German customs pantomiming a battle between Summer and Winter were staged during Lent, i.e, after Carnival:

> *In the Palatinate this mimic conflict takes place on the fourth Sunday in Lent. All over Bavaria the same drama used to be acted on the same day, and it was still kept up in some places down to the middle of the nineteenth century or later.*

Sommergewinn procession in *Eisenach*, 1899. After drawing by Wilhelm Rögge the Younger.

The German town of Eisenach, in Thuringia, to this day hosts a large, traditional celebration also on this same fourth Sunday. It's called the *Sommergewinn* (summer's victory). In 1892, a procession was added to the festival, presumably featuring performers embodying Summer and Winter. Today, this parade ends in the town square with Lady Summer and Lord Winter arguing (in self-consciously antiquated dialogue scripted in the twentieth century) over who should rule. Naturally, Winter fares poorly and is consequently burned in effigy.

The *Sommergewinn* was inspired by a passage in the Eisenach Chronicle written by a local rector, Johann Michael Koch, in 1704. While the *Sommergewinn* of his day was little more than a fair at which decorated greenery (known as "summers") were sold, in its earlier form, Koch explains, it involved setting fire to a large wooden wheel to which a straw effigy was attached and sending this rolling down the nearby Mädelstein mountain. His source on this custom was a handwritten document from 1650. In 2010, the fire wheel was recreated for the *Sommergewinn* and continues to be part of celebrations to this day.

LENTEN FIRES

Flaming wheels rolling down hillsides were once common in German-speaking lands as part of midsummer celebrations and to a lesser extent Easter. An example of the latter can still be witnessed in the North Rhine–Westphalian town of Lügde.

1880 ILLUSTRATION OF BAVARIAN *SCHEIBENSCHLAGEN* (DISK FLINGING), ONE OF SEVERAL FIERY GAMES MARKING *FUNKENSONNTAG* (SPARKS SUNDAY) IN GERMANY.

Farther south, in Swabian-Alemannic regions, the first Sunday of Lent, *Funkensonntag* (Sparks Sunday) is the preferred occasion for fire customs. Among these are the building and burning of towers of stacked wood, called *Hüttenbrennen* (hut burning) or *Burgbrennen* (castle burning), and the flinging of flaming wooden squares, known as *Scheibenschlagen*. The last, primarily a custom of Austria, was first noted in the eleventh century, in the records of the monastery of Lorsch, which mention an outbuilding accidently set ablaze by one of the flaming projectiles. Because Lent was synonymous with spring in ancient times, these customs could be regarded as welcoming in that season.

SUNDAY OF THE DEAD

Funkensonntag fire customs along with those of the Eisenach *Sommergewinn* both tend to be interpreted under the "driving off winter" rubric. But this does not conform to the earliest description of the event in Eisenach. It was not an embodiment of Winter set afire and rolled to its doom, Koch says. Instead, the figure tied to the wheel was a "straw man whom they call Death."

While the nineteenth-century adoption of this custom as "Summer's Victory" puts a much cheerier spin on things, Eisenach's flaming wheel belonged to the forgotten traditions of *Totensonntag* (Death Sunday).

The date is fixed to the fourth Sunday in Lent, or Laetare Sunday, named for the introit of the day's Mass, "Laetare Jerusalem." But the customs of Death Sunday had nothing to do with the Church. Frazer again provides a trove of information on these now extinct German traditions, referencing a sixteenth century source:

> *At Mid-Lent, the season when the church bids us rejoice, the young people of my native country make a straw image of Death, and fastening it to a pole carry it with shouts to the neighbouring villages. By some they are kindly received, and after being refreshed with milk, peas, and dried pears, the usual food of that season, are sent home again. Others, however, treat them with anything but hospitality; for, looking on them as harbingers of misfortune ...*

In the villages near Erlangen, when the fourth Sunday in Lent came around, the peasant girls used to dress themselves in all their finery with flowers in their hair. Thus attired they repaired to the neighbouring town, carrying puppets which were adorned with leaves and covered with white cloths. These they took from house to house in pairs, stopping at every door where they expected to receive something, and singing a few lines in which they announced that it was Mid-Lent and that they were about to throw Death into the water. When they had collected some trifling gratuities they went to the river Regnitz and flung the puppets representing Death into the stream. This was done to ensure a fruitful and prosperous year; further, it was considered a safeguard against pestilence and sudden death. At Nuremberg girls of seven to eighteen years of age go through the streets bearing a little open coffin. Others carry a beech branch, with an apple fastened to it for a head, in an open box. They sing, "We carry Death into the water, it is well," or "We carry Death into the water, carry him in and out again." In some parts of Bavaria down to 1780 it was believed that a fatal epidemic would ensue if the custom of "Carrying Out Death" were not observed.

Frazer's extensive cataloging moves geographically from western Franconia east toward Thuringia, home to Eisenach's *Sommergewinn*. He notes of this area that "the population was originally Slavonic" (which is significant as the custom was more long-lived in Slavic regions). His description of Thuringian customs is amusing, noting how the Death effigy is:

> *borne in procession, the young people holding sticks in their hands and singing that they were driving out Death. When they came to water they threw the effigy into it and ran hastily back, fearing that it might jump on their shoulders and wring their necks.*

In the eastern German regions of Lusatia and Silesia, the terror associated with this effigy, he says, offers a certain financial incentive, as:

Carrying Out Death in Mähren, W. Grögler," 1887.
Illustration from the German periodical *Die Gartenlaube*.

> *the puppet is sometimes made to look in at the window of a house, and it is believed that some one in the house will die within the year unless his life is redeemed by the payment of money.*

Throughout the early eighteenth century, efforts were made in Germany to discourage or even ban these customs as a superstitious vestige of paganism. However, as the century drew toward a close and a newfound respect for folk culture developed under the influence of Romanticism, it was rediscovered here and there. In cities like Eisenach, it was purged of its unsavory association with historical plagues and the existential terror of death. Winter was substituted for Death, and the event thrived under a prettified heroine, Lady Summer.

CARRYING OUT DEATH

In nearby lands settled by the West Slavs (what are now the Czech Republic, Slovakia, and Poland), the custom of Carrying Out Death was not erased, as in Germany. Though it generally waned after World War II, the custom has been intermittently revived and is most widely perpetuated as a seasonal entertainment for children. With few exceptions, the date of celebration here is shared by the *Sommergewinn,* the fourth Sunday in Lent.

At the beginning of the twentieth century, the custom was widespread enough, in Czech and Slovak lands, to be the subject of a 1910 monograph by the ethnographer

POLISH CHILDREN WITH PUPPET OF MARZANNA HEAD TO THE RIVER, C. 1970-1980.

Čenek Zíbrt: *Smrt nesem ze vsi* (*I Bring Death from the Village*). Today it most famously survives in the Czech municipality of Josefov, in South Moravia.

The effigy, usually called Smrt (Czech for "death"), was made of old wood, straw, and rags and carried aloft on a pole. Frequently it also wore a garland of hollow eggshells (sometimes snail shells). Those carrying the figure were usually young and more frequently girls. Formerly, these were children of poorer families collecting humble rewards from homes visited, including eggs, flour, and salt. Eggs are still considered a traditional payment for the visits.

As the custom came to be more exclusively practiced by females, the figure might also be dressed in female wardrobe, usually cast-offs but in some cases an old wedding dress (removed before the figure's destruction). The effigy in some regions became smaller, more like a child's doll, and might be dressed in children's clothes or swaddled like a baby.

Zíbrt notes that the doll could also be present only in the form of a small figure attached to a bit of greenery, the top of a spruce or fir decorated with painted eggs, ribbons, and bows and crowned with the doll, like an angel atop a Christmas tree. In other cases,

Children throwing Marzanna into the Dunajec River, southern Poland, c. 1970–1980.

Children with puppets of Marzanna and Marzaniok (a male version of Marzanna), Paprocany, Poland, 1934.

decorated branches were all that was carried, and Death was present only as a reference in songs describing how Death is driven out and Summer arriving. This pairing of Death with Summer (instead of Winter) is transitional, moving the customs closer to the German *Sommergewinn*. The greenery carried by the carolers is like the "summers," decorated branches, sold at the Eisenach festival. Oddly, Zíbrt also mentions a few towns in Hanakia, in central Moravia, where a hollowed pumpkin, carved and lit like a jack-o'-lantern, is used to represent Death.

While in rare instances the figure was burned, destruction of the effigy usually involved throwing it in water. Even a puddle, Zíbrt says, would do. The Smrt would sometimes be torn apart before it was tossed into the stream, river, or pond.

Czech Girl with arrangement of decorated greenery (the *gaik*), representing Summer. Illustration by Pelr Maixne from *I Bring Death from the Village*, Čenek Zíbrt, 1906.

DROWNING MARŽANNA

In Poland, the custom is more robustly preserved, again largely as a heritage experience for children. Schools in certain areas may even organize field trips, during which kindergartners and elementary students can hurl the effigy they have created together into a body of water. Here also, the custom is associated more with girls than with boys.

The practice is most common in Silesia and adjacent areas of Sieradz and Krakow, as well as the Greater Poland voivodeship. The traditional date for this was, as elsewhere, the fourth (or, in a few places, the fifth) Sunday in Lent. However, in the twentieth century, under Communist rule, the date was moved to March 20-21, to coincide with the vernal equinox and to detach the tradition from the calendar of the Church.

The effigy here is larger, exclusively female, and always constructed atop a pole with a crosspiece forming outstretched arms. It is not simply referred to as Death but is given the name Maržanna. The related *Mařena* or *Morena* is also used in parts of the Czech Republic (Moravia) and Slovakia, where it is considered a more "ancient" appellation.

Similar songs are sung by participants, calling on Winter to leave and welcoming Spring. Carols are addressed to Maržanna rather than Death, though certain older ones included references to driving out the pest, or plague.

Just as the "burial" of Carnival can actually designate a bonfire, the Polish use *Topienie Maržanny* (drowning Maržanna) to refer to her destruction, whether by water or by fire.

The effigy is most frequently tossed in water, though burning is often part of the ritual, with the figure set on fire just before it's thrown into water. Rarely is it simply burned, an option traditionally pursued only if no body of water is to be found. Even when it's destroyed in a bonfire, old accounts mention "drowning" the figure beforehand, meaning dipping it into puddles or other water en route to the fire.

In Poland, too, there was a fear associated with fleeing the discarded effigy (suggesting its identity with Death). Drowned or not, Maržanna might still rise to catch those slow in running home. The last to reach his door brings doom upon himself or a family member, now fated to die within the year. A superstition also attaches to touching any effigy found in the water. Doing so will "dry out" or wither your hand.

The sort of "summer" or spring greenery tangential to rites in Germany or Czech and Slovak lands is more important in Poland, though not universally present. The *gaik*, as it's called, is either a decorated bouquet of evergreen branches, a sapling, or the top of an older tree, decorated with ribbons, paper ornaments, hollow eggs, and the like. In current practice, it's necessarily prepared in advance, but the lyrics of traditional Maržanna songs represent it as greenery freshly gathered from the woods after the effigy is drowned, i.e., a token of spring born from winter's expulsion. Where the *gaik* custom is present, it's considered the necessary completion of the drowning ritual. Visiting homes, singing, and collecting donations (usually eggs or money) is more commonly done with the *gaik* in those regions than with the effigy of Maržanna.

A MEDIEVAL CUSTOM

Unlike other customs laying claim to centuries-old origins impossible to verify, Maržanna is well attested in history. A description from 1597, for instance, from Joachim Bielski's *Chronicle of Poland*, is quite recognizable as the modern custom:

> *They drowned an idol after first having put human clothes on a hemp or hay bundle. And the whole village led this idol away to a nearby lake or puddle and there, having taken the clothes off, they tossed it into the water singing mournfully. Thereafter, they ran away from this place as fast as they could back home, whosoever should, however, fall so they got an augury that this one should die this year.*

From 1582, we have the matter described in further detail in Maciej Stryjkowski's *Kronika Polska* (*Polish Chronicle*):

> *when mid-Lent Sunday comes, children having made an idol in the shape of the woman Ziewona or Marzanna that is Diana, the Goddess of the Hunt (which idol they used to venerate), they place it on a stick and carry it around singing sadly and one and the other praising or carrying it in a wagon. Then, in a puddle or into a river from a bridge they throw it and run away to their houses. They called this idol Marzana.*

Effigy of Morana. National Museum, Prague.

The equation of Maržanna with Diana is puzzling, as the fearful sprinting from the site of the drowning suggests the effigy represents Death, something asserted in a series of statutes issued by Andrew, the Bishop of Poznan, in 1420:

> *XXXV. Of [the carrying of] straw imagines during fasting: Also prohibit on the Laetare Sunday, the superstitious custom of carrying around a kind of a puppet that they call "death" (i.e., Marzanna), which they then throw into the mud as they are not free from these kinds of superstitions.*

The very oldest account equating such an effigy with Death is Czech, not Polish. In 1366, the *Statutes of the Prague Synod* included:

> *On the image of Death (regarding those who bring death to the outskirts of town in the middle of Lent). It is known that in some cities, towns and villages the pernicious habit has taken root, on the part of clergy and laymen, of bringing images in the form of Death around town to the river in the middle of Lent, accompanied by chants and superstitious representations and that there they submerge said images vehemently arguing to their own shame that in this way death will not do them more harm because it has been destroyed and wiped out from the town's boundaries.*

It's worth noting that none of these early attestations mentions fire, suggesting that submerging the figure in water is critical to the ritual. This might explain why the phrase "Drowning of Maržanna" is used to this day, even when the effigy is actually burned.

BUT WHO IS MARŽANNA?

So, what to make of this confusion regarding Maržanna's identity as either Death or Diana? The former certainly seems more likely, especially when Death is understood to include nature's seasonal death in Winter. Not only is this the understanding presented in our earliest fourteenth-century account from Prague, but the etymology of the name tentatively points this direction. A Proto-Indo-European root *mor/mar* has been suggested as the source of the name Maržanna, as well as other Slavic figures, including Morana (Czech) or Morena (Slovak). The Latin *mors* (death) or even the Russian *мор/mor*, meaning "plague," have also been called in to explain the name. However, all these connections are somewhat tenuous. Identifying Maržanna with Diana is likewise so.

Medieval attempts to equate local pagan figures with deities from the Classical pantheon are notoriously clumsy, but, as the only available evidence, the references are worth examining. As it turns out, Diana is not the sole suggestion.

Maciej Miechow's 1519 *Chronica Polonorum* mentions "Cerera [Ceres] the Earth goddess, the inventor of all grains, whom they called Marzana" and Joachim Bielski's 1597 *Kronika Polska* says that among the pagan Poles Cerera was called Marzana. Alessandro

Guagnini, in his 1578 volume *Sarmatiae Europeae descriptio* (*A Description of Sarmatian Europe*) says that it was Venera (Venus) whom they called Marzana. That tallies as two votes for Ceres, one for Diana, and one for Venus. I can imagine no rationale for the last, but Ceres and Diana seem worth discussing.

The doubling of sources identifying her as Ceres may just represent one scholar replicating an older source. But it would not be surprising to find a goddess of agriculture associated with the passing of winter into spring. Ceres was also associated with the boundary between the living and the dead and generally associated with the underworld, thanks to the well-known myth of her search for her daughter Proserpina, abducted by Pluto (as in the Greek original, with Hades abducting Persephone). The submersion of the Maržanna effigy may represent a passage into the land of the dead, an association strengthened by the frequent mention in medieval accounts of funereal songs accompanying the rite.

While there's only a single instance equating Maržanna with Diana, these medieval accounts seem rather preoccupied with Diana's pagan analogue, repeatedly specifying her name as Ziewona, Dzeviana, Ziewonia, Dziewanna, or Ziwonia. Because of Diana's association with the moon, the forest, and its creatures, medieval conceptions of her often transformed her into a witch. Polish female spirits haunting the wilds, *dziewonie*, are related and may be a degraded form of the pagan goddess.

Though this Polish Diana may not be identical with Maržanna, the two are frequently paired together. Jan Długosz provides one of the earliest instances in his 1455 volume *Annales seu cronici incliti regni Poloniae* (*Annals or Chronicles of the Famous Kingdom of Poland*). He describes the land of the Poles consisting of:

> *vast forests and groves, which were believed by the ancients to be inhabited by Diana and claimed by Diana as her dominion over them, and Cerera was regarded as the mother and goddess of harvests, which the country needed in abundance, [therefore] these two goddesses: Diana in their language called Dziewanna and Cerera called Maržanna enjoyed a special cult and a special devotion.*

According to the Silesian poet, journalist, and pioneering folklorist Józef Lompa, this pairing lingered into the nineteenth century. In his 1863 book *Märchen, Sagen, Sitten und Gebräuche des schlesisch-slavischen Volkes* (*Fairy Tales, Legends, Manners, and Customs of the Silesian-Slavic People*), he remarks, "I heard in Bobrowniki and Rudne Piekary, villages beyond Tarnowskie Góry, they still bring out Marzanna and Dziewanna."

Perhaps the most satisfying answer suggests Marzanna and Dziewanna may represent two aspects of a single entity, Maržanna being the face she wears in winter, Dziewanna in the spring. The effigy that disappears into the river returns as Dziewanna or the green *gaik* carried from Diana's woodlands.

GIANT MASLENITSA FIGURE OUTSIDE THE VOROBYOVY GORY STATION IN MOSCOW, 1995.

AT LAST, PAGAN ROOTS!

By now you may be wondering why I've spent so long examining this single ritual, especially as it lies outside the calendrical window of Carnival.

Six and a half centuries, I answer. Research into folk customs rarely offers walks along such long, continuous, and well-marked paths. The rite of Drowning Maržanna is remarkable for its consistent attestation back to 1366. It also offers that special kind of intrigue only found in "uncovering pagan roots." It's not the sort of ho-hum "paganism" one might discover in hanging a horseshoe over a door but a full-blown religious rite, possibly dedicated to a Death Goddess, no less! The fact that the ritual is today acted out by innocent kindergartners under the watchful eye of their teachers only makes the topic more amusing.

THE BUTTER LADY, MASLENITSA

As for the connection to Carnival, the alleged topic of this book, Russia, Ukraine, and Belarus provide my rationale. There is nothing more central to Carnival in these countries than *Maslenitsa* (*Масленица*), an effigy constructed on the first day of the season and burned on its final, seventh, day. There is no Carnival without that bonfire. She's made of straw and old clothes, formed atop a pole with a cross-piece providing a base for outstretched arms, as with Maržanna. She may be life-size but is usually larger and in some cities can be represented by figures several stories high. Maslenitsa is just as symbolic of the holiday as our Christmas tree is to Christmas. Or more so, as *Maslenitsa* is also the name given Carnival in these countries.

You may point out that my favorite ritual involves drowning, rather than burning an effigy, to which I would invite you to Russia to locate some water not frozen over in

MASLENITSA GROUP AT THE BELGOROD STATE CENTER OF FOLK ART, RUSSIA.

February. Even if you do, wouldn't a bonfire feel much nicer in that weather? Allowances are made even in Poland, where Maržanna is permitted to die by fire when no water is convenient.

The name *Maslenitsa,* despite a passing resemblance, is not related to the Polish and Czech names for effigies. Rather it is derived from the Russian word for butter, *maslo* (*масло*), and alternate Russian names for Carnival are "Butter Week" or "Cheese Week." Unlike the Roman Church, the Orthodox practice a phased fast ramping into Lent, meaning meat has already been abandoned by the time Cheese Week rolls round. The sacrifice of meat after Meatfare Week leaves Russians all the more voracious for foods rich in dairy fats, namely *blini* (crêpes) in Russia and *varenyky* (dumplings) in Ukraine. Of course, there are sweets too, and there's even a day dedicated to them as all the days of Maslenitsa are given thematic names suggesting their activities.

Day 1 – Welcome Maslenitsa.
Day 2 – Be young again and play.
Day 3 – Indulge your sweet tooth.
Day 4 – Revelry Thursday.
Day 5 – Mother-in-law day.
Day 6 – Dash through the snow.
Day 7 – Say hello to spring.

Funeral of Kostroma. Illustration for *Bulletin of Archeology and History*, vol. 20, 1911. Published by the Imperial St. Petersburg Archaeological Institute.

Hello to spring, of course means goodbye to the effigy, which is burned in the evening. After which, her ashes are traditionally scattered over the fields to aid their fertility. Leftover foods, which may not be eaten the next day, likewise are thrown into the fire.

In some cases, Maslenitsa's trip to the pyre was organized as a mock funeral. The effigy might be placed in a coffin-like box, and locals might don fake beards and makeshift chasubles to play priests. A farcical sort of censer was also sometimes provided in the form of a pot filled with coals burning old shoes. The sleigh in which the effigy rode sometimes was pulled not by horses but by costumed men and would be followed by a cortège of comically howling mourners. Before the fiery send-off, a nonsensical sermon, often laced with lewd jokes, would be delivered.

THE MYTH OF KOSTROMA

A final interesting detail regarding Maslenitsa involves her earlier incarnation under a different name, *Kostroma* (*кострома*).

Whereas *Maslenitsa* is derived from "butter" and thus bound to the Church's fasting protocols, *Kostroma* comes from *koster* (*костер*) (straw, chaff, or bonfire) and thus would make sense as an older, pre-Christian name. Although it is forgotten in all but a few towns in the Novgorod region, a ritual held in June centers upon a straw effigy called Kostroma who is ritually mourned, then buried, or destroyed in water or fire. This figure comes with an elaborate mythic backstory.

Kostroma was one of two twins born to the fire god Simargl and Kupalnitsa, goddess of night. Her brother is Kupalo, who is kidnapped to the underworld. When he returns to earth, an accident of circumstance sees him marry his sister, and results in (oh so Russian!) despair and suicides. Kupalo leaps to his death in a fire and Kostroma into a lake, but she does not die, or at least not properly. She remains earthbound, haunting the lake as a ghostly siren, a *rusalka*.

It's believed that at some point in history the older, nearly forgotten Kostroma rite, which marks the transition from spring to summer, was transferred to Maslenitsa's ritual celebrating the passage from winter to spring. There are also intriguing parallels between the Kostroma and the Polish and Czech effigies, associated with death and likewise mourned and buried in water.

CARNIVAL BEGINS EVERYWHERE

I dearly wish I could claim at the end of this book that I have solved the "problem" of Carnival and it all comes down to a Russian water ghost. Sadly, not so. But there's still something instructive in observing the fluidity of these traditions, their tendencies to flow together and overlap.

It seems likely that Kostroma's spring–summer rite flowed into Maslenitsa's spring–winter celebration, in the same way we've seen eastern Bulgaria's New Year's customs drifting into the west's Kuker Carnival. All over western Europe, we've seen Christmas customs mixed with those of Epiphany, expanding past Candlemas and swallowed into Carnival. Did the same happen with the Roman New Year? Were the hide-and-horn-decked beasts of Kalends likewise absorbed into the Carnival creatures accompanying revelers on their rounds today? Clearly, some traditions migrate through the calendar from holiday to holiday just as they do from generation to generation.

And the geographic flow of traditions? Rome built the roads, and the Church with its calendar of feasts and fasts connected early Europe—not only the West but also the Byzantine East. But these were not one-way thoroughfares exporting customs from Rome or Constantinople. The traditions we've examined were not creations of the Imperium or Magisterium but largely arose in the hinterlands, folk customs traveling this way and that, at different times, from countless points of origin.

Poor Britain has largely been left out of the fun, but we've seen Brits drag out the plow on the Monday after Candlemas and in Whittlesea there's a straw bear shambling alongside it. Is it the same plow we've seen dragged all over the continent in Slovenia, Hungary, Italy, Austria, Germany, and Poland? What does the British straw bear have to do with the countless Carnival bears in Macedonia, Bulgaria, Romania, Germany, Poland, Italy, France, and Spain? Wouldn't the pantomimed death and resurrection of these ursines have something to do with other mummers' animals likewise killed and risen? We've observed mares, goats, Turoń, Kukeri, and camels dying all over the place, but then quickly back on their feet—or hooves, as the case may be. Carnival and winter too are perpetually dying, sometimes by fire, sometimes by water, but always to return twelve months out.

Why won't the snow thaw, the seeds wake, the crops grow, the animals reproduce, the couples marry, the babies be born, and sickness and death once and forever flee our homes and bodies without logs being hauled, faces blackened, bears hunted, and all these dancing Kurenti, Busós, and Kukeri? And every year, more cowbell!

All of these are fool's questions, as they'd say in the German Fastnacht. Trying to trace the origins and travel routes of particular customs, as they change and blend along the way, would be like standing in a river attempting to scoop out water representing a specific tributary. This book represents an impossibly large accumulation of questions that would require countless tediously tight-focused studies dependent upon specialized linguistic and anthropological tools not at my disposal—something impossibly complicated.

Or it's all very simple, if we let it be.

If we imagine how we ourselves might respond under the old agricultural way of life, we can easily envision scenarios that could arise in different towns and countries spontaneously and simultaneously, not as a discrete cultural good that passed along a sort of trade route.

It would be this:

The ground is still frozen. Christmas feasting has ended, and you're dreading the sacrifices of Lent. You're stir-crazy but it's too early to plow or take the livestock out. You want one final fling before the season of dawn-to-dusk labor. The larder is nearly empty. Perhaps you could send the children to collect flour and eggs from the neighbors, but they shouldn't be taking without giving. A song doesn't cost anything, nor does a recitation of seasonal rhymes your grandparents always quoted. The animals won't need all that winter forage much longer, so the straw should be braided into rope and the rope into hats, a doll, a coat, or something to make the kids' presentation more amusing, more worth a few eggs. The animals won't need their bells till they're released to pasture, so the boys could wear those and the sound of them coming down the road might bring a bit of cheer, or at least have people opening their doors in curiosity. They'll want a visit too.

And so it would go, neighboring families under the same strains might jump in and try to outdo each other. A group of holiday beggars blacken their faces to be unrecognizable or turn their sheepskin coats fur-side out and say they are bears. Perhaps someone asks the deacon to borrow masks used in the Christmas play. Other villages improve on the custom. They make taller masks, and you study these, bring home the idea, and add horns. The neighbor adds more horns and makes his taller to put you to shame. Everyone is still nervous about the plowing and sowing and work to come, but this somehow helps. Everyone hopes for a better harvest and wishes for a portent of good luck. If none is forthcoming, perhaps one could be manufactured. Let's say the bells make the grain grow high.

The origin of Carnival is in many places—wherever these problems and answers might have arisen. Becoming a rampaging bear, going a little mad, if only for a season, can't help but lighten life's grim load. It doesn't take a fool to see it, but it helps.

BIBLIOGRAPHY

GENERAL

Eisenbichler, Konrad, and Wim N.M. Hüsken. *Carnival and the Carnivalesque: The Fool, the Reformer, the Wildman, and Others in Early Modern Theatre*. Amsterdam: Rodopi, 1999.

Fréger, Charles. *Wilder Mann: The Image of the Savage*. Heidelberg: Kehrer, 2012.

Museo degli Usi e Costumi della Gente Trentina. "Carnival King of Europe," 2017, carnivalkingofeurope.it. Accessed 2023.

Testa, Alessandro. *Rituality and Social (Dis)Order.* Abingdon, Oxfordshire: Routledge, 2020.

Wright, Thomas. *A History of Caricature and Grotesque in Literature and Art*. Hildesheim, New York: Olms, 1976.

II • SARDINE VS. SAUSAGE

Butler, Alban. *The Moveable Feasts, Fasts and Other Annual Observances of the Catholic Church*. Dublin: J. Morris, 1754.

Ziolkowski, Jan. *Obscenity: Social Control and Artistic Creation in the European Middle Ages*. Leiden: Brill, 1998.

III • ANCIENT ROOTS

Cameron, Alan. *The Last Pagans of Rome*. Oxford: Oxford University Press, 2010.

Filotas, Bernadette. *Pagan Survivals, Superstitions and Popular Cultures in Early Medieval Pastoral Literature*. Vatican City: Pontifical Institute of Mediaeval Studies, 2005.

Fowler, William Warde. *The Roman Festivals of the Period of the Republic*. London: MacMillan & Company, 1899.

Graf, Fritz. "Fights about Festivals: Libanius and John Chrysostom on the Kalendae Ianuariae in Antioch." *Archiv für Religionsgeschichte*, vol. 13, no. 1, 2012.

Green, William M. "The Lupercalia in the Fifth Century." *Classical Philology*, vol. 26, no. 1, 1931, pp. 60–69.

Harris, Max. "Claiming Pagan Origins for Carnival: Bacchanalia, Saturnalia, and Kalends." *European Medieval Drama*, vol. 10, 2006, pp. 57–107.

Latham, Jacob A. "The Re-invention of the Kalends of January in Late Antiquity: A Public Festival between 'Pagans' and Christians." *Journal of Late Antiquity*, vol. 15, no. 1, 2022, pp. 69–110.

Mackenzie, Neil. *The Medieval Boy Bishops*. Leicester: Troubador Publishing, 2011.

IV• ROME

Grig, Lucy. *Popular Culture in the Ancient World*. Cambridge: Cambridge University Press, 2017.

Harris, Max. *Sacred Folly: A New History of the Feast of Fools*. Ithaca: Cornell University Press, 2017.

Pollett, Andrea. "Curious and Unusual—Rome's Carnival," roma.andreapollett.com/S1/roma-c16. Accessed 2023.

V • CARNIVAL IN VENICE

Association for Renaissance Martial Arts. "Venetian Bridge Wars." 2022, thearma.org/essays/BridgeWars.htm. Accessed 2023.

Betrand, Giles. "Venice Carnival from the Middle Ages to the Twenty-First Century: A Political Ritual Turned Consumer Rite?" *Journal of Festive Studies*, vol. 2, no. 1, 2020, pp. 77–104.

Delpiano, Roberto. "Venice Carnival History... Carnival Masks." 2023. italiancarnival.com. Accessed 2023.

Devaney, Thomas. "Competing Spectacles in the Venetian Feste delle Marie." *Viator*, vol. 39, no. 1, 2008, pp. 107–125.

O'Rourke, Peter John. *Carnevale di Venezia Performance and Spectatorship at the Venice Carnival.* October 2015.

Snyder, Jon R. "Venice Incognito: Masks in the Serene Republic." *Social History*, vol. 38, no. 1, 2013, pp. 92–93.

VI • GERMAN FOOLS

Clouzot, Martine, and Marie-José Gasse-Grandjean. *The Dancing Fool and the Mundus Inversus*. Living Books about History, 2017. www.livingbooksabouthistory.ch/uploads/media/pdf/en/the-dancing-fool-and-the-mundus-inversus.pdf?v=3. Accessed 2024.

Fischer, Karl-Heinz. "Einführung in die Geschichte der schwäbisch-alemannischen Fasnet." *Villingen im Wandel der Zeit*, vol. 29, 2006, pp.82-91.

Mezger, Werner, and Wilfried Dold. *Das neue kleine Buch der rottweiler Fastnacht*. Schwarzwald-Baar: Dold Verlag, 2013.

Narrenzunft Rottweil. "Narrenzunft Rottweil." 2024. narrenzunft-rottweil.de. Accessed 2023.

Säger, Anselm. "Historische Narronzunft Villingen E.V." 2023. narrozunft.de. Accessed 2023.

University of Missouri Special Collections and Archives. "Masks, Hells, and Books: The Nuremberg Schembart-lauf (1449-1539)." 2022. library.missouri.edu/specialcollections/exhibits/show/schembart. Accessed 2023.

Vereinigung Schwäbisch-Alemannischer Narrenzünfte. "Vereinigung Schwäbisch-Alemannischer Narrenzünfte (VSAN)." 2023. vsan.de. Accessed 2023.

Virtuelles Fastnachtmuseum. "Virtuelles Fastnachtsmuseum." 2022. virtuelles-fastnachtsmuseum.de. Accessed 2023.

Wager, Wulf. "Narri-Narro." 2024. narren-spiegel.de/geschichte/geschichte.html. Accessed 2023.

VII • GOOD-LUCK VISITS

Gryzek, Agnieszka. "The Polish Town Where They Beheaded Death." *Polish-American Journal*, March 2016, p. 13.

Tufnell, Blanche O. "Czecho-Slovak Folklore." *Folklore*, vol. 35, no. 1, 1924, pp. 26–56.

VIII • FERTILITY RITES

Egetmannverein Tramin. "Egetmann Tramin/Termeno—Official Website." www.egetmann.com/en. Accessed 2023.

Fisser Blochziehen. "Fasnacht im Oberland—Blochziehen—Fasnachtsbrauch—Fiss in Tirol." 2024. blochziehen.at/de. Accessed 2023.

Ravnik, Mojca. *Borovo gostüvanje v Predanovcih*. Založba ZRC, 2008.

University of Innsbruck. "Blochziehen—Universität Innsbruck." 2021. uibk.ac.at/geschichte-ethnologie/datenbanken/feste-und-braeuche/infoservice/blochziehen. Accessed 2023.

IX • THE KURENT AND THE PLOW

Koranti Lancova vas. "Koranti Lancova vas." 2024. koranti-lancova.si/en/809-2. Accessed 2023.

Kurentovanje. "Kurentovanje." 2023. kurentovanje.net/eng. Accessed 2023.

Marčič, Petra. *Kurent Danes-v Šegah, Slovstveni Folklori in Umetnosti*. 2010.

Zveza Kurentov. "Člani Zveze | Zveza Društev Kurentov." 2015. zveza-kurentov.si/sl-SI/46515/clani-zveze.

X • THE BUSÓ

Mándoki, László. *Busójárás Mohácson*. Pécs, Hungary: Janus Pannonius Múzeum, 1963.

Mohácsi Busójárás. "Mohácsi Busójárás." 2023. mohacsibusojaras.hu. Accessed 2023.

XI • THE KUKERI

Bakalova, Kalina. *Kukeri: Ritual Performances in Bulgaria*. Doctoral dissertation, University of Texas, Austin, 2009.

Survakari, "*Сурвакари–Сурвакари*. 2017. survakari.com. Accessed 2023.

Zlatkovskaia, T. D. "On the Origin of Certain Elements of the Kuker Ritual among the Bulgarians." *Soviet Anthropology and Archeology*, vol. 7, no. 2, 1968, pp. 33–46.

XII • CARNIVAL BEARS

Bosch, Robert. *Fêtes de l'Ours en Vallespir*. Perpignan, France: Trabucaire Editions, 2013.

Frank, Roslyn M. *Concerning Germanic Straw Bears, St. Nicholas and the Last Sheaf*. Unpublished paper, University of Iowa, Iowa City, 2021.

Museo etnológico de Navarra. "Carnaval de Ituren-Zubieta." 2024. navarra.es/es/web/museo-etnologico-de-navarra/carnaval-de-ituren-zubieta. Accessed 2024.

Pyrenées orientales Tourisme. "Fêtes de l'Ours." 2018. tourisme-pyreneesorientales.com/fetes-de-lours. Accessed 2024.

Tunaydin, Pelin. "Pawing through the History of Bear Dancing." *Frühneuzeit-Info*, vol. 24, 2013, pp. 51–60.

Voisenat, Claudie. "Les Festes de l'Os a l'Alt Vallespir." *Revista d'Etnologia de Catalunya*, no. 43, 2018, pp. 154–169.

XIII • SARDINIA

Associazione culturale Boes e Merdules. "Cultural Association Boes and Merdules Ottana—Italy." merdules.it/en. Accessed 2024.

Concu, Giulio. *Museo delle Maschere Mediterranee*, 2021. museodellemaschere.it/ebook/MyMamoiada_Ita_2021.pdf. Accessed 2024.

Mamoiada. "Bibliografie, Libri e Scrittori Mamoiadini." 2011. mamoiada.org/paese/mamoiada/bibliografie. Accessed 2024.

Mamoiada. "Mamoiada.org." *Mamoiada.org*, 2024, www.mamoiada.org. Accessed 2024.

Mannia, Sebastiano. "Masks and Carnivals in Contemporary Sardinia." *Вестник антропологии* (*Herald of Anthropology*), vol. 52, no. 4, 2020, pp. 29–44.

Mannia, Sebastiano. "Oltre Carnevale: Maschere, Travestimenti, Inversioni." *Acta Diurna*, vol. 10, no. 10, 2017.

Sandalyon. "Carnival in Sardinia—Sandalyon." 2016. sandalyon.eu/eng/categorie/archive/carnival-in-sardinia__38. Accessed 2024.

XIV • KILLING CARNIVAL

Frazer, James George. *The Golden Bough: A Study in Magic and Religion*, vols. 7, 8. Oxford: Macmillan, 1912.

Jassa. "Nos Poloni Tres Deos Habuimus." 2023. www.jassa.org. Accessed 2024.

Piesta, Jakub. "Remains of Slavic Pre-Christian Beliefs in Modern Polish Folk Traditions." *Zeszyty Cyrylo-Metodiańskie*, vol. 2, 2013, pp. 151–155.

Sommergewinn Eiseinach. "Startseite—Sommergewinn." 2024. sommergewinn-eisenach.de. Accessed 2024.

Zíbrt, Čeněk. *Nesem Ze Vsi, Pomlázka Se Čepejří*. František Šimáče, 1910.

IMAGE CREDITS

COVER IMAGE: MARIANO ARESU PHOTOGRAPHY.

I • THE UNKNOWN CARNIVAL

TITLE PAGE: PHOTO BY DJUMANDJI, COURTESY OF ADOBE STOCK PHOTO. **6:** COURTESY OF THE BULGARIAN ARCHIVES STATE AGENCY UNDER CREATIVE COMMONS LICENSE. **8:** COURTESY OF THE RIJKSMUSEUM, AMSTERDAM, UNDER CREATIVE COMMONS LICENSE.

II • SARDINE VS. SAUSAGE

10: COURTESY OF THE INDIANAPOLIS MUSEUM OF ART AT NEWFIELDS. **12-13:** PHOTO BY DOSSEMAN UNDER CREATIVE COMMONS LICENSE. **14-15:** PHOTO BY SAILKO UNDER CREATIVE COMMONS LICENSE. **18:** COURTESY OF THE REAL ACADEMIA DE BELLAS ARTES DE SAN FERNANDO, MADRID.

III • ANCIENT ROOTS

20: COURTESY OF THE GETTY CENTER. **23:** COURTESY OF THE MUSEO DEL PRADO, MADRID. **26:** COURTESY OF GALLICA DIGITAL LIBRARY. **30:** COURTESY OF THE RIJKSMUSEUM, AMSTERDAM, UNDER CREATIVE COMMON LICENSE. **31:** COURTESY OF THE METROPOLITAN MUSEUM OF ART.

IV• ROME

34: COURTESY OF THE KUNSTHISTORISCHES MUSEUM, VIENNA. **36:** COURTESY OF THE METROPOLITAN MUSEUM OF ART UNDER CREATIVE COMMONS LICENSE. **38:** COURTESY ICP/ALAMY STOCK PHOTO. **39:** COURTESY OF THE YALE CENTER FOR BRITISH ART **40:** COURTESY OF THE DOROTHEUM, VIENNA, UNDER CREATIVE COMMONS LICENSE. **41:** COURTESY OF THE MUSEO CARMEN THYSSEN, MALAGA. **42:** COURTESY OF GALLICA (BNF) UNDER CREATIVE COMMONS LICENSE.

V • CARNIVAL IN VENICE

46: COURTESY OF THE DOROTHEUM, VIENNA. **47:** COURTESY OF THE DOROTHEUM, VIENNA. **48:** PHOTO BY DIDIER DESCOUENS UNDER CREATIVE COMMONS LICENSE. **50:** COURTESY OF THE NEW YORK PUBLIC LIBRARY. **51:** COURTESY OF THE RIJKSMUSEUM, AMSTERDAM, UNDER CREATIVE COMMONS LICENSE. **52:** COURTESY OF THE METROPOLITAN MUSEUM OF ART UNDER CREATIVE COMMONS LICENSE. **53:** COURTESY OF THE NATIONAL GALLERY, LONDON. PHOTO BY SAILKO UNDER CREATIVE COMMONS LICENSE. **54:** PHOTO BY DIDIER DESCOUENS UNDER CREATIVE COMMONS LICENSE. NICO, VENICE. **55:** COURTESY OF ROBERTO GOBBO UNDER CREATIVE COMMONS LICENSE. **56:** COURTESY OF THE VIENNA THEATER MUSEUM UNDER CREATIVE COMMONS LICENSE. **57:** COURTESY OF THE METROPOLITAN MUSEUM OF ART. **58:** PHOTO BY SAILKO UNDER CREATIVE COMMONS LICENSE. **59:** PHOTO BY SAILKO UNDER CREATIVE COMMONS LICENSE. **60:** PUBLIC DOMAIN COURTESY OF SOTHEBY'S AUCTIONS VIA WIKIMEDIA COMMONS. **61:** COURTESY OF THE GERMANISCHES NATIONALMUSEUM, NUREMBERG **PAGES 64-65:** COURTESY OF THE SMITHSONIAN AMERICAN ART MUSEUM.

VI • GERMAN FOOLS

71: COURTESY OF THE MUSEUM OF FLANDERS, CASSEL, FRANCE. **72:** PHOTO BY FILMFOTO, COURTESY OF DEPOSITPHOTOS.COM. **73:** PHOTO BY ARNULF HETTRICH COURTESY OF ALAMY STOCK PHOTO **75:** IMAGE REPRODUCTION FROM VOM SCHEMBARTLAUFEN, FRITZ BRÜGGEMANN, 1936, UNDER PUBLIC DOMAIN. **76:** COURTESY OF THE BAVARIAN STATE LIBRARY. **77 (UPPER):** COURTESY OF THE UNIVERSITY OF CALIFORNIA LIBRARIES. **77 (LOWER RIGHT):** COURTESY OF THE LIBRARY OF CONGRESS. **78:** COURTESY OF THE LIBRARY OF UNIVERSITY OF CALIFORNIA, LOS ANGELES. **79:** COURTESY OF THE METROPOLITAN MUSEUM OF ART UNDER CREATIVE COMMONS LICENSE. **80:** COURTESY OF THE BODLEIAN LIBRARY, OXFORD. **81:** COURTESY OF THE BODLEIAN LIBRARY, OXFORD. **82:** COURTESY OF THE BODLEIAN LIBRARY, OXFORD. **84:** COURTESY OF THE UNIVERSITY OF EDINBURGH UNDER CREATIVE COMMONS LICENSE. **85:** COURTESY OF THE LOUVRE MUSEUM. **86:** PHOTO BY ZOONAR/ARTO COURTESY OF ALAMY STOCK PHOTO. **87:** COURTESY OF THE WELLCOME LIBRARY, LONDON. **88:** COURTESY OF THE AMBRAS CASTLE CHAMBER OF ART AND WONDERS, INNSBRUCK. **89:** COURTESY OF THE WALTERS ART MUSEUM, BALTIMORE. **90:** PHOTO BY ANDREAS PRAEFCKE. **91:** PHOTO BY ANDREAS PRAEFCKE. **92:** COURTESY OF WELLESLEY COLLEGE. **93:** PHOTO BY ANDREAS PRAEFCKE. **95 (UPPER):** PHOTO BY NLEMAND UNDER CREATIVE COMMONS LICENSE. **95 (LOWER):** PHOTO BY EARWIG UNDER CREATIVE COMMONS LICENSE. **97:** PHOTO BY ANDREAS PRAEFCKE UNDER CREATIVE COMMONS LICENSE. **98:** PUBLIC DOMAIN, IMAGE FROM *SCHWÄBISCH-ALEMANNISCHE FASNET IN ALTEN BILDERN*, WULF WAGER, 2003, VIA WIKIMEDIA COMMONS. **99:** PHOTO BY ANDREAS PRAEFCKE UNDER CREATIVE COMMONS LICENSE. **100:** PHOTO BY JAMES STEAKLEY UNDER CREATIVE COMMONS LICENSE. **101:** PHOTO BY ANDREAS PRAEFCKE UNDER CREATIVE COMMONS LICENSE. **102:** PHOTO BY ANDREAS PRAEFCKE UNDER CREATIVE COMMONS LICENSE. **103:** PHOTO by Andreas Praefcke under Creative Commons license. **105 (both):** Photo by Andreas Praefcke under Creative Commons license. **106:** Photo by Walter Bibikow - Mauritius Images GmbH courtesy of Alamy Stock Photo **108 (upper):** Photo by Penphoto, courtesy of Adobe Stock Photo. **108 (lower):** Photo by Andreas Praefcke under Creative Commons license. **109 (upper):** Photo by Ian Holton under Creative Commons license. **109 (lower):** Photo by Andreas Praefcke under Creative Commons license. **110:** Photo courtesy of Bildagentur Geduldig/Alamy Stock Photo.

VII • GOOD-LUCK VISITS

112: Photo by Svajcr under Creative Commons license. **116:** Photo by Svajcr under Creative Commons license. **117:** Photo by Svajcr under Creative Commons license. **118:** Photo by Svajcr under Creative Commons license. **119:** Photo courtesy of Robert Garstka (Regional Cultural Institute in Katowice) under Creative Commons license. **120:** Courtesy of the National Digital Archives of Poland. **121:** 1978 Photo courtesy of the National Digital Archives of Poland. **122:** Photo courtesy of the National Digital Archives of Poland. **123:** Photo courtesy of the Seweryn Udziela Ethnographic Museum, Kraków, under Creative Commons license. **124:** Courtesy of the State Ethnographic Museum, Warsaw. Photo by Edward Koprowski under Creative Commons license.

VIII • FERTILITY RITES

126: Photo by Andreas Kirschner, courtesy of Serfaus Fiss-Ladis Marketing. **128:** Scan by Rawpixel under Creative Commons license. **129:** Photo by Douglas Lander, courtesy of Alamy Stock Photo. **130:** Photo by SiGarb. **131:** Courtesy of the Albertina Graphics Collection, Vienna. **133:** Photo by Andreas Kirschner, courtesy of Serfaus of Fiss-Ladis Marketing. **134 (upper):** Photo by Manuel Pale. **134 (lower):** Photo by Fabian Schirgi, courtesy of Fisser Blochziehen, **135 (upper):** Photo by Albin Hammerle, courtesy of Fisser Blochziehen, **135 (lower):** Photo by Andreas Kirschner, courtesy of Serfaus Fiss-Ladis Marketing. **136:** Photo by Manuel Pale, courtesy of Serfaus Fiss-Ladis Marketing. **137:** Photo by Fabian Schirgi, courtesy of Fisser Blochziehen, **138:** Photo by Antie, courtesy of Egetmann Association. **139:** Photo by Antie, courtesy of Egetmann Association. **140:** Photo by Antie, courtesy of Egetmann Association. **141:** Photo by Dietmar, courtesy of Egetmann Association. **142 (both):** Photo by Antie, courtesy of Egetmann Association. **143:** Photo by Antie, courtesy of Egetmann Association. **144:** Photo by Antie, courtesy of Egetmann Association. **145:** Photo by Antie, courtesy of Egetmann Association. **146:** Photo by Dietmar, courtesy of Egetmann Association. **148:** Photo by Wolfgang Sauber under Creative Commons license. **149:** Photo by Danilo Škofič, courtesy of the Večer newspaper archives, Maribor, Slovenia, via Wikimedia Commons. **150 (both):** Photo by Danilo Škofič, courtesy of the Večer newspaper archives, Maribor, Slovenia, via Wikimedia Commons. **151:** Photo taken by I. Grossmann before 1940 and made available courtesy of the Institute of Ethnology of the Slovak Academy of Sciences, Bratislava.

IX • THE KURENT AND THE PLOW

154: Photo by Jessamine, courtesy of Dreamstime.com. **155:** Photo by Aleš Kravos under Creative Commons license. **156:** Photo by UrosPoteko, courtesy of iStock.com. **158 (upper):** Photo by Erik Zunec, courtesy of Dreamstime.com. **158 (lower):** Photo by Katja Kodba, courtesy of Dreamstime.com. **160 (both):** Photo by Rado Skrjanec. **161:** Photo by Rado Skrjanec. **162:** Image courtesy of the Austrian National Library. **163:** Public domain, image courtesy of the Večer newspaper archives, reference number 137303, Maribor, Slovenia, via Wikimedia Commons. **164:** Photo by Danilo Škofič, courtesy of the Večer newspaper archives, reference number 245183, Maribor, Slovenia, via Wikimedia Commons.

X • THE BUSÓ

166: Photo by Csák István, courtesy of Adobe Stock. **169:** Photo by Simanlaci, courtesy of Adobe Stock. **170:** Photo by Laraclarence, courtesy of Dreamstime.com. **171:** Photo by joruba75, courtesy of Depositphotos.com. **Pages 172-173:** Photo by Szabolcs Pásztor under Creative Commons license. **174 (upper):** Photo by István Csák, courtesy of Dreamstime.com. **174 (lower):** Photo by Zsolt Repasy, courtesy of Adobe Stock. **175:** Photo by István Csák, courtesy of Dreamstime.com. **176 (upper):** Photo by Sziban, courtesy of Depositphotos.com. **176 (lower):** Photo by Laraclarence, courtesy Dreamstime.com. **177:** Photo by Joruba, courtesy of Dreamstime.com. **178:** Photo by Zsolt Repasy, courtesy of Alamy Stock Photo. **179:** Photo by Paul Williams, courtesy of Alamy Stock Photo. **181 (both):** Photos by Erdei Katalin/FORTEPAN under Creative Commons license. **182:** Photo by Székely Balázs/FORTEPAN under Creative Commons license.

XI • THE KUKERI

184: Photo by Kikagogo, courtesy of iStock.com. **187:** Photo by Klearchos Kapoutsis under Creative Commons license. **188 (both):** Photo by georgidimitrov70, courtesy of iStock.com. **189 (upper):** Photo by georgidimitrov70, courtesy of Adobe

Stock Photo. **189(lower):** Photo by Lavchieva, courtesy of iStock.com. **190 (upper):** Photo by djumandji, courtesy of Depositphotos.com. **190 (lower):** Photo by georgidimitrov70, courtesy of iStock.com. **191:** Photo by TKalinova under Creative Commons license. **192 (upper):** Photo by djumandji, courtesy of Adobe Stock Photo. **192 (lower):** Photo by georgidimitrov70, courtesy of iStock.com. **193:** Photo by georgidimitrov70 courtesy, of iStock.com. **194:** Photo by Kolio Delev under Creative Commons license. **195:** Photo by nikolay100 courtesy, of iStock.com. **196:** Photo by Okotuki under Creative Commons license. **197:** Photo by Chavdar Lungov under Creative Commons license. **199:** Photo by georgidimitrov70, courtesy of iStock.com. **200:** Photo by Dimitrina Lavchieva, courtesy of Alamy Stock Photo. **201:** Photo by georgidimitrov70, courtesy of iStock.com. **202:** Photo by GeorgiD, courtesy of Alamy Stock Photo. **203:** Photo by Damian Hadjiyvanov, courtesy of Alamy Stock Photo. **206:** Photo by djumandji, courtesy of iStock.com. **207:** Photo by Tihov Studio, courtesy of Alamy Stock Photo, **208 (upper):** Photo by georgidimitrov70, courtesy of iStock.com. **208 (lower):** Photo by Kisa Markiza, courtesy of iStock.com. **209:** Photo by georgidimitrov70, courtesy of iStock.com. **211:** Photo by vverve, courtesy of Depositphotos.com.

XII • CARNIVAL BEARS

214: Photo by mvelascos under Creative Commons license. **216:** Image courtesy of CLU/iStock.com. **218:** Public domain, image courtesy of zigane.pp.ru, via Wikimedia Commons. **219:** Courtesy of the Tropinin-Museum, Moscow. **221:** Public domain, image courtesy of private postcard collection, via Wikimedia Commons. **222:** Photo by SPANI Arnaud/hemis.fr, courtesy Alamy Stock Photo. **223:** Photo by SPANI Arnaud/hemis.fr, courtesy Alamy Stock Photo. **224:** Photo by Gerard SIOEN/Onlyfranc, courtesy of Alamy Stock Photo. **225:** Photo by SPANI Arnaud/hemis.fr, courtesy of Alamy Stock Photo. **226:** Photo by JJc Milhet Photographe. **227:** Photo courtesy the Bureau d'Information Touristique (BIT) de St Laurent de Cerdans. **228:** Public domain, image via Wikimedia Commons. **231:** Photo by Jorge Fernandez, courtesy of Alamy Stock Photo. **232:** Photo by Theklan under Creative Commons license. **233 (both):** Photo by Polina Kobycheva, courtesy of Alamy Stock Photo. **234:** Photo by Polina Kobycheva, courtesy of Alamy Stock Photo. **235:** Photo by Theklan under Creative Commons license. **236:** Photo by Nacho Boullosa, courtesy of Sipa USA/Alamy Live News. **237:** Photo by Elsa A Bravo/SOPA courtesy, of Alamy Stock Photo

XIII • SARDINIA

238: Photo by Mariano Aresu Photography. **240:** Photo by Ben Skála/Benfoto under Creative Commons license. **242:** Photo by Famedo1, courtesy of Dreamstime.com. **243:** Photo by Mariano Aresu Photography. **244:** Photo by Mariano Aresu Photography. **245:** Photo by Mariano Aresu Photography. **246:** Photo by Francesco Mou, courtesy of Depositphotos.com. **247:** Photo by Elio Villa, courtesy of Alamy Stock Photo. **248:** Photo by Denise Serra, courtesy of Adobe Stock Photo. **249:** Photo by Denise Serra, courtesy of Adobe Stock Photo. **250:** Photo by Mirko Maier, courtesy of Dreamstime.com. **251:** Photo by Tamara Sini Photography. **252:** Photo by Gianni Careddu under Creative Commons license. **253:** Photo by Mariano Aresu Photography. **254:** Photo by Pier Carlo Murru under Creative Commons license. **255:** Photo by Maurone83 under Creative Commons license. **256:** Photo by Mariano Aresu Photography. **257:** Photo by francescomoufotografo, courtesy of Depositphotos.com

XIV • KILLING CARNIVAL

260: Photo by Arkinessa under Creative Commons license. **262:** Photo by Valentin Sama-Rojo, courtesy of Alamy Live News. **267:** Public domain, image via Wikimedia Commons. **268:** Image by INTERFOTO, courtesy of Alamy Stock Photo. **270:** Image by Sunny Celeste, courtesy of Alamy Stock Photo. **272:** Public domain, image via Wikimedia Commons. **273:** Photo courtesy of the National Digital Archives of Poland. **274 (both):** Photo courtesy of the National Digital Archives of Poland. **275:** Public domain, image courtesy of National Institute of Folk Culture (nulk.cz/), via Wikimedia Commons. **277:** Photo by Matěj Baťha under Creative Commons license. **280:** Photo by V. Marinho/Mos.ru under Creative Commons license. **281:** Photo by Lobachev Vladimir under Creative Commons license. **282:** Public domain, image courtesy of booksite.ru, via Wikimedia Commons.